Doing
Sex
Education

Critical Social Thought

Series editor: Michael W. Apple
John Bascom Professor of Curriculum and Instruction and
Educational Policy Studies, University of Wisconsin at Madison

Already Published

Critical Social Psychology Philip Wexler
Reading, Writing and Resistance Robert B. Everhart
Arguing for Socialism Andrew Levine
Between Two Worlds Lois Weis
Power and the Promise of School Reform William J. Reese
Becoming Clerical Workers Linda Valli
Racial Formation in the United States Michael Omi and Howard
  Winant
The Politics of Hope Bernard P. Dauenhauer
The Common Good Marcus G. Raskin
Contradictions of Control Linda M. McNeil
Social Analysis of Education Philip Wexler
Keeping Them Out of the Hands of Satan Susan D. Rose
Primary Understanding Kieran Egan
Capitalist Schools Daniel P. Liston
The New Literacy John Willinsky
Becoming a Woman Through Romance Linda Christian-Smith
Growing Up Modern Bruce Fuller
Getting Smart Patti Lather
Teacher Education and the Social Conditions of Schooling Daniel P.
  Liston and Kenneth M. Zeichner
Teachers and Crisis Dennis Carlson
Views Beyond the Border Country Dennis L. Dworkin and Leslie
  G. Roman (eds.)
I Answer With My Life Kathleen Casey
Japan and the Pursuit of a New American Identity Walter Feinberg
Race, Identity and Representation in Education Cameron McCarthy
  and Warren Crichlow (eds.)

Doing
Sex
Education

Gender Politics and Schooling

BONNIE NELSON TRUDELL

Routledge

New York • London

Published in 1993 by

Routledge
29 West 35th Street
New York, NY 10001

Published in Great Britain by

Routledge
11 New Fetter Lane
London EC4P 4EE

Copyright © 1993 by Routledge

Printed in the United States of America on acid-free paper.

Library of Congress Cataloging-in-Publication Data

Trudell, Bonnie Nelson.
    Doing sex education : gender politics and schooling / Bonnie
Nelson Trudell.
        p.   cm.—(Critical social thought)
    Includes bibliographical references and index.
    ISBN 0-415-90502-8
    1. Sex instruction for teenagers—United States. 2. Sex
educators—United States. 3. Sex discrimination in education—
United States. I. Title. II. Series.
HQ57.5.A3T78 1993
306.7'07—dc20   93-5502
                                                         CIP

Contents

Acknowledgments   vii

Series Editor's Introduction   ix

1. The Politics of School Sex Education: Whose Interests
    are Served?   1

2. The Informal Sexuality Curriculum: "A Lot of Eyes and
    Ears Out There"   32

3. Mrs. Warren's Working Conditions: "Runnin' on Empty"   54

4. Mrs. Warren: Nurturing Mom, Cheerleader, and
    One-of-the-Girls   75

5. The Classroom as Social Arena: "Good Kids," "Dirts,"
    and Black Students   89

6. School Knowledge about Sexuality: "Just Stuff You
    Had to Know"   103

7. Students Actively Weighing Their Own Interests: "I Can
    Put On All Kinds of Faces"   132

8. Situation-Specific Constraints and Possibilities: "Much
    Has Been Said. Now Much Must be Done"   171

Contents

Methodological Appendix   191

Notes   209

References   219

Index   230

Acknowledgments

From its moment of conception to its birth as a book, *Doing Sex Education* has required focused and patient labor in the context of ongoing cooperation and support from others. I want to thank Mrs. Warren (a fictitious name) and her students for allowing me into their sex education classroom and lives; Michael Apple for simultaneously valuing/expanding my ways of thinking about schooling and for maintaining confidence in my ability to put this thinking into words; Joann Foss for her steadfast encouragement and skillful preparation of the manuscript; my colleagues Elizabeth Ellsworth and Mariamne Whatley for their advice and personal support.

The process of bringing this book into the world has involved profound personal and professional growth, and I am grateful for help and sustaining love from my family/friends—Dennis, Jack, Devin, Woody, Maria, Wendy, Mace, Rhoda, Jen, Hannah, Dawna, Andy, Linda, Katie, and others whose lives have enriched mine.

I dedicate *Doing Sex Education* to a younger Bonnie, to all children—especially those whose nightmares also come in the daytime—and to all adults willing to help.

Series Editor's Introduction

There is a story told by a teacher about a discussion that arose in her elementary school classroom. A number of her students were excitedly talking about some "dirty words" that had been scribbled on the side of a building during Halloween. Even after the teacher asked the children to get ready for their language arts lesson, most of them continued to talk about "those words." As often happens, the teacher sensed that this couldn't be totally ignored. She asked her students what *made* words "dirty." This provoked a long and productive discussion among these second graders about how certain words were used to hurt people and how "this wasn't very nice."

Throughout it all, one child had not said a thing, but was clearly deeply involved in listening. Finally, he raised his hand and said that he knew "the dirtiest word in the world." He was too embarrassed to say the word out loud (and also knew that it might be inappropriate to even utter it in school). The teacher asked him to come up later and whisper the word in her ear. During recess, he came over to the teacher, put his head close to hers and quietly, secretly, said "the word." The teacher almost broke up with laughter. That dirty word, that word that could never be uttered, was "statistics." One of the boy's parents worked for a local radio station and everytime the ratings came out, the parent would angrily state, "those damn statistics!" What could be dirtier?

For large numbers of parents and conservative activists, other things are a lot "dirtier." Discussions of the body, of sexuality, and of the social issues surrounding these topics, are a danger zone. To deal with them in any way in school is not wise. But if they are going to be dealt with, these conservative activists claim that they must be handled in the context of traditional gender relations, the nuclear family, and according to sacred texts like the Bible.

For conservatives, sex education is one of the ultimate forms of "secular humanism" in the schools. It is attacked by the New Right as a major threat to parental control of schools and because of its teaching of "nontraditional" values. For the coalition of forces that make up the New Right, sex education can destroy the family and religious morality "by encouraging masturbation, pre-marital sex, lots of sex, sex without guilt, sex for fun, homosexual sex, sex." These groups view it "as education for, not about sex, which will create an obsession which can override Christian morality" and threaten God-given gender roles (Hunter, 1988, p. 63). These were important elements in the controversy over the Rainbow Curriculum in New York City and certainly contributed to the successful moves to oust the city's school superintendent from his position.

The vision of gender roles that stands behind these attacks is striking. Allen Hunter, one of the wisest commentators on the conservative agenda, argues that the New Right sees the family as an organic and divine unity that "resolves male egoism and female selflessness" (Hunter, 1988, p. 15). As he goes on to say:

> Since gender is divine and natural . . . there is [no] room for legitimate political conflict. . . . Within the family women and men—stability and dynamism—are harmoniously fused when undisturbed by modernism, liberalism, feminism, [and] humanism which not only threaten masculinity and femininity directly, but also through their effects on children and youth. . . . "Real men" do not need protection by a regulatory state which destroys individual freedom, productivity, and incentive. . . . "Real women," i.e. women who know themselves to be wives *and* mothers, will not threaten the sanctity of the home by striving for self. When men or women challenge these gender roles they break with God and nature; when liberals, feminists, and secular humanists prevent them from fulfilling these roles they undermine the divine and natural supports upon which society rests. (Hunter, 1988, p. 15)

This is connected to their view that public schooling *itself* is a site of immense danger (Apple, 1993). "Modern public education is the most dangerous single force in a child's life: religiously, sexually, economically, patriotically, and physically" (Tim La Haye, quoted in Hunter, 1988, p. 50). As Hunter puts it:

> Until recently, as the New Right sees it, schools were extensions of home and traditional morality. Parents could entrust their children to public schools because they were locally controlled and reflected Biblical and parental values. However, taken over by alien, elitist forces schools now interpose themselves between parents and children. Many people experience fragmentation of the unity between parents and children. Many people experience fragmentation of the unity between family, church, and school as a loss of control of daily life, one's children, and America. Indeed, [the New Right] argues that parental control of education is Biblical, for "in God's plan, the primary responsibility for educating the young lies in the home and directly in the father." (Hunter, 1988, p. 57)

It is possible to see here why sexuality education has become such a major issue for conservative parents. Its very existence, and especially its more progressive and honest moments, threatens the crucial elements of the entire world view of these parents and activists.

Of course, issues of sexuality and the body are not the only focus of attention of conservatives. These concerns are linked to a much larger array of questions about what counts as "legitimate" content in schools, as I show in *Official Knowledge: Democratic Education in a Conservative Age* (Apple, 1993). In the larger arena of concerns about sex education and the entire range of curriculum content, conservative activists have had no small measure of success in pressuring textbook publishers and in altering aspects of state educational policy as well.

For example, the power of these groups can be seen in the "self-censorship" that publishers engage in. Thus, for instance, a number of publishers of high school literature anthologies have chosen to include Martin Luther King's "I Have a Dream" speech, but *only* after all references to the intense racism of the United States have been removed (Delfattore, 1992, p. 123).

Another example is provided by the textbook law in Texas which stresses patriotism, authority, and the discouragement of "deviance." Quoting from the legislation, the author of a recent study on textbook censorship puts it this way:

Series Editor's Introduction

"Textbook content shall promote citizenship and understanding of the essentials and benefits of the free enterprise system, emphasizing patriotism and respect for recognized authority, and promote respect for individual rights." Textbooks shall not "include selections or works which encourage or condone civil disorder, social strife, or disregard of the law," nor shall they "contain material which serves to undermine authority" or "which would cause embarrassing situations or interference in the learning atmosphere of the classroom." Finally, textbooks approved for use in Texas "shall not encourage lifestyles deviating from generally accepted standards of society." The Texas law's endorsement of free enterprise and traditional lifestyles and its prohibition of lawlessness and rebellion are regularly cited by textbook activists to support their efforts to remove material which, in their view, promotes socialism, immorality or disobedience. (Delfattore, 1992, p. 139)

I mention all of this because it is essential that we place the issue of sexuality education in its larger social context, something Bonnie Trudell does here. But even placing it in its larger social ideological context is not sufficient. We must go further. It is also essential that we get inside schools, that we understand what now *counts* as sex education in the daily life of institutions such as schools. There is no one better at doing this than Bonnie Trudell.

The debate over sexuality education—the attacks by conservatives, the defense by many educators—all too often is carried on in a vacuum. *What* is actually taught in schools? How do teachers structure their lessons? How do they cope with the contradictory ideological demands on what they teach? What do students do with what is taught? Do they accept it? Reinterpret it based on their own knowledge and experiences? Simply reject it?

We can best understand this by placing it into the context of the daily lives of teachers as they go about their jobs of doing the best that they can in educating their students, in dealing with school bureaucracy, in coping with the intensified nature of teachers' work loads, and in facing the pressures brought to bear on them about sex education from all sides (Apple, 1988).

Bonnie Trudell gives us the first detailed picture of sex education in practice. She situates it in the context of teachers' and students' lives inside and outside of schools. She presents the tensions and difficulties of trying to teach responsibility in schools where social pressures are intensifying, where so much else has to be done by teachers, where

students themselves have their own experiences and interpretations—
some of them quite telling—of sexuality, and where gender, race, and
class relations provide a backdrop for everything that is done. Trudell
rightly understands that all of this is about cultural politics. It is about
different visions of "sacred knowledge" and authority (Apple & Christian-Smith, 1991). Yet she also so clearly understands that it is also,
and profoundly, about the lives of real teachers and students, lives
that are deeply affected by the ways sex is dealt with in all of the
institutions in our society. *Doing Sex Education* brings all this close
to home. It will be essential reading for all who care about sexuality,
about the politics of education and gender relations, and above all
about the present and future educational conditions of our youth.

Michael W. Apple
University of Wisconsin, Madison

1

The Politics of School Sex Education: Whose Interests are Served?

"Bringing in many of the comprehensive sex educators and family planning specialists to help teenagers deal with their sexuality makes as much sense as calling in an arsonist to put out a fire."—Josh McDowell (*The Myths of Sex Education*, 1992, p. 34)

"It's homosexual indoctrination and don't let anyone tell you it isn't."—Mary Cummins, President of Community School Board 24, regarding New York City Public Schools' *Children of the Rainbow* curriculum (Chicago *Tribune*, Dec. 22, 1992)

"These kids are hurting and they want information. They come into my drama group and ask me where they can get AIDS testing and contraceptive information. They're scared, but they're so much smarter than their parents."—Joan Gifford, Florida parent volunteer who organized opposition to *Teen-Aid* (Gainesville *Sun*, March 30, 1992)

"I don't think the lady who wrote this is in touch with real society."—South Carolina high school student council president involved in successful opposition to *Sex Respect* (quoted in E. Flax, "Sex education plan sparks controversy in South Carolina," *Education Week*, March 14, 1990)

1

The Politics of School Sex Education

Sex education[1] is currently one of the most controversial and politi-cized aspects of school curriculum. It engages adults with distinct cultural, political, and economic agendas in heated and acrimonious debates in which student voices are largely unheard. In the context of a conservative resurgence over the past two decades that has shifted the terms of educational, economic, political and cultural debates (Apple, 1993), Far Right and religious fundamentalist coalitions have had considerable success in creating a climate in which even moderate approaches to school sex education can appear radical (Phillips & Fine, 1992; Trudell & Whatley, 1992). Concerned more with ideologi-cal purity than democratic educational decision making, local religious and conservative groups backed by a network of national organiza-tions[2] are increasing their attempts to impose sectarian and traditional points of view about sexuality and gender relations on public school students (Kantor, 1993; Kerr, 1992a, 1992b; Sedway, 1992).

As described in a parent's handbook widely distributed by Focus on the Family (Newman & Richard, 1990), they advocate a narrow version of "healthy" school sex education that teaches young people:

- moral absolutes "consistent with Judeo-Christian values" (p. 20);
- premarital abstinence ("restraint from all sexual activity") as the absolute standard (p. 21), with "secondary virginity" (choosing to stop) the standard for those who have already been sexually active (p. 22);
- premarital abstinence and marital fidelity as the only forms of "safe" or "responsible" sex (p. 23);
- heterosexual intercourse as the norm, with other forms of sexual activity as "deviant" (p. 24);
- contraception only in terms of risk/failure rates and "in the context of marriage and family" (p. 24), the latter defined as "blood or legal relationship" (p. 26);
- traditional family roles (p. 27);
- "abortion as taking the life of an unborn child" (p. 25);
- "the joy of having children" without "limiting family size" (p. 28).

The most recent tactic of this well-funded New Right national net-work has been developing and marketing prepackaged curricular mate-rials that rely on scare tactics to exclusively promote chastity and avoidance of all sexual activity (including necking and petting, espe-cially for young women) until marriage (Sedway, 1992). These "fear-based" curricula (Kantor, 1993), typified by titles like *Sex Respect: The Option of True Sexual Freedom* (Mast, 1986, 1990) and *Teen-Aid: Me, My World, My Future* for junior high (Roach & Benn, 1987) and *Sexuality, Commitment and Family* for senior high (Potter & Roach, 1990), heavily emphasize the dangers of sexual arousal, beginning with a "prolonged kiss" (Mast, 1986, p. 4; 1990, p. 7), negative consequences of premarital intercourse, and risks of contraception and abortion. They offer limited information about anatomy and physiology; biased and inaccurate information about sexually transmitted diseases, abortion, and sexual response; and virtually no information about contraception (beyond inflated risks), safer sex, or homosexuality (Kantor, 1993; Trudell & Whatley, 1991; Whatley & Trudell, in press).

The essence of this New Right "abstinence-only" approach is captured in the words of Phyllis Schlafly, founder and President of the Eagle Forum:

> Schools ought to teach that the consequences of sex fall twice as heavily on girls as on boys . . . little girls ought to be taught about the terrible price that girls pay in terms of the side effects of contraceptives, of abortion and its trauma, venereal diseases, the poverty, the cervical cancer, the emotional and psychological trauma. (Phyllis Schlafly Report, Oct., 1989, cited in *SIECUS Report*, 1992, p. 18).

As this quote also suggests, these "just say 'no' " sexuality curricula are permeated with gender bias and stereotypes. Young men are portrayed as easily aroused and thus more likely to be sexual aggressors, while young women—perceived as having little sexual desire—are innocent protectors of their virginity, responsible for saying "no" to this aggressive male sex drive and for preventing sexual assault (Kantor, 1993; Trudell & Whatley, 1991; Whatley & Trudell, in press).

These curricula also ignore the realities of a pluralistic society, validating only traditional heterosexual family structures and making disparaging comments about divorced an single-parent families as well as gays and lesbians. They reflect a white middle-class bias in their underrepresentation and distorted images of low-income groups and people of color (Kantor, 1993; Trudell & Whatley, 1991; Whatley & Trudell, in press). In the case of *Sex Respect*, this bias is especially reprehensible, since targeted schools in the first phase of the grant its developers received from the U.S. Office of Adolescent Pregnancy Prevention were made up mostly of inner-city, low-income and minority students (Trudell & Whatley, 1992). Dominant interests and racial stereotypes embedded in the curriculum are made overt in the following comment by Kathleen Sullivan, Eagle Forum member and Executive Director of the Illinois Committee on the Status of Women, a group that has received $1.7 million in federal and state funds since 1985 for the development and implementation of such curricula (Whetstone, 1992):

> We can't raise kids saying, "you're hopeless, you won't amount to anything anyway." That's what we're trying to get rid of, especially for the black community. They're not going to learn to punch the time clock and to be there on time and produce a day's work if they can't even control their own emotions in the important area of sexuality. (quoted in Whetstone, 1992, p. 5)

This rightist resurgence has gained strength partly because it offers a simple "solution" to a "problem" of widespread concern. Most adults agree that youthful sexual activity is in some ways problematic, although they disagree vehemently about the nature of this "problem." For many, it is the percentage of teens who engage in premarital heterosexual coital activity at an increasingly young age. By age 20, 75 percent of females and 86 percent of males have had intercourse (Centers for Disease Control, 1991a; Sonenstein, et al., 1989).[3] About one-fourth of 15-year-old females and one-third of 15-year-old males have had sexual intercourse (Baldwin, 1990; Sonenstein, et al., 1989); between 1982 and 1988, the percentage of 15- to 19-year-old young women who had ever had premarital sexual intercourse went from 43 percent to 51 percent (National Center for Health Statistics, 1982 and 1988).

For others, the "problem" is unprotected heterosexual coitus and the possibility of negative consequences associated with teenage pregnancy. Forty-one percent of 15- to 19-year-old females and 38 percent of males of the same age report using no contraception or an ineffective method at first intercourse; 29 percent of females and 23 percent of males report failure to do so at last intercourse (Sonenstein, et al., 1989; Baldwin, 1990). Over 1 million teens become pregnant in the United States each year (Henshaw and Van Vort, 1989), with an estimated 43 percent of all teenage women becoming pregnant by age 20 (Hayes, 1987). Forty-two percent of these pregnancies to both white and nonwhite 15- to 19-year-olds result in abortion, as do 46 percent of pregnancies to those 14 and younger (Henshaw & Van Vort, 1989). Overall, the United States has the highest rates of teenage pregnancy, childbirth, and abortion rates in the industrialized world (Jones, et al., 1985).

For others, the "problem" is the potential for contracting sexually transmitted diseases, a concern that has become more urgent over the last decade as HIV makes death one possible outcome. One in four sexually active teens is infected with an STD (Centers for Disease Control, 1989), and reported AIDS cases among 13- to 19-year-olds increased by 29 percent between July, 1990 and July, 1991 (Centers for Disease Control, 1990, 1991). Even more disturbing, over one-fifth of all people with AIDS are in their twenties and, because of the average ten-year period between initial HIV infection and onset of symptoms, the majority were likely infected as teenagers (Centers for Disease Control, 1991b).

For still others, the "problem" is coercive sexual behavior. The number of reported cases of child sexual abuse has increased dramatically—4,327 cases in 1977 to 22,918 in 1982 (Finkelhor, 1984) to 404,100 in 1991 (Daro & McCurdy, 1992).[4] Estimates of actual prevalence range widely, depending on how sexual abuse is defined and the methods used to collect data. In seven major studies reviewed by a leading researcher in the field (Russell, 1986), the rate varied from as low as 5 percent of women (Sapp & Carter, 1978) to 62 percent (Wyatt, 1985). It is estimated that one in three women and one in seven men are likely to experience some form of sexual abuse by age 18 (Bass & Davis, 1988). Research also suggests that about one in ten high school students has experienced physical violence in dating relationships, with females more likely to experience severe forms (Levy, 1991). One-quarter of over six thousand female students surveyed at thirty-two colleges and universities said they had been victims of rape or attempted rape, 84 percent of them by acquaintances (Koss, et al., 1987).

In the context of these concerns, most adults in the United States agree that some type of school sexuality education is a necessary and/or acceptable aspect of the "solution." National public opinion polls consistently suggest that an overwhelming majority of adults (75 to 90 percent) support the general concept (National Opinion Research Center, 1982; Gallup & Clark, 1987; Harris, 1985; Kahn, 1990). Nearly fifty professional and other organizations concerned with children and youth have formed a National Coalition to Support Sexuality Education (Haffner & de Mauro, 1991, p. 49).[5] Furthermore, an increasing number of states have mandated some version of school sex education—seventeen in 1992, compared to three plus the District of Columbia in 1982 (Haffner & de Mauro, 1991). Forty-seven states either mandate or recommend such programs (Haffner, 1992). Although there is widespread support for the broad concept of school sex education, there is considerable and vehement disagreement over content, method, and timing of curricular offerings.

Michelle Fine (1988) has described four major discourses that characterize national debates over school sex education. First, a small number view "sexuality as violence" and presume that a decrease in adolescent sexual behavior will result if families—not schools—are entrusted with sexuality education. Second, those involved in the discourse of "sexuality as victimization" depict "males as potential predators and females as victims" (p. 32) and support school sex education that emphasizes "saying 'no' " as well as the risks and negative consequences of sexual intercourse. Participants in the third discourse perceive "sexuality as individual morality" and urge schools to teach restraint, with sexual activity permissible only within the context of marriage. The fourth discourse, which Fine describes as a mere "whisper" in U.S. schools, recognizes "sexuality as desire" and invites adolescents to explore sexual pleasure on the basis of their own "experiences, needs, and limits" (p. 33).

In its broadest terms, the current debate centers around two approaches to classroom instruction about sexuality. The first, which I have already described, is *abstinence-only*. The second is *abstinence-based*; it incorporates a focus on abstinence along with information to enable teenagers who may already be having or will have sexual intercourse to minimize risks of pregnancy and sexually transmitted diseases. As I will document, reviews of state mandated topics and reported curricular content suggest that most school sexuality education takes this approach. Virtually all sex educators teach abstinence, with nearly nine out of ten stressing it as the best method for preventing pregnancy and sexually transmitted diseases (Donovan, 1989; Forrest & Silverman, 1989). Most abstinence-based programs offer information on sexual and reproductive anatomy and physiology, more limited information about contraception, and generally avoid more controversial issues such as sexual pleasure, masturbation, homosexuality, and abortion.

James Sears (1992b) points out that, in spite of the differences in these competing approaches, they share a common belief in reducing the heterosexual coital activity of adolescents, emphasizing individual self-control and postponement of sexual gratification, and view this reduction as a "benchmark" for evaluating the success of school sex education (p. 16). Thus, most official school sexuality curricula define a narrow range of legitimate options (heterosexual, coital) and portray sexuality as an activity for adults that has serious negative consequences for adolescents.[6]

Debates about school sex education have largely focused on this official curriculum—what educators, elected officials, community advisory groups, and parents believe should be taught at each grade level. Although the planned curriculum can take a variety of forms (state mandates or guidelines, an official K–12 local district curriculum, or prepackaged materials prepared by "experts" and purchased by the district), it is basically a statement of intent to teach: these versions of the official curriculum are not necessarily an accurate reflection of what is *actually* taught or learned in a specific classroom. Existing research on school sexuality education provides little insight into these day-to-day realities of classroom life—what happens in a particular school context as the official sexuality curriculum works its way through teacher and students (the curriculum-in-use). Relatively little has been reported about what is actually presented in the classroom, dynamics of classroom interaction, lived student responses, and what factors affect the teacher's selection and organization of school sexual knowledge.

While the planned curriculum appears to represent rational technical consensus, it can actually obscure both the political and ethical nature of the decisions and the ambiguity, uncertainty, and conflict inherent in its development. In addition, this widely used technical and behavioristic approach to curricular planning treats sexual knowledge as primarily cognitive and reducible to defined content-based modules for teacher presentation and student consumption. This conventional model conceptualizes students as more or less homogeneous "raw materials" (measured, tested, and otherwise classified) who enter the classroom to be processed through the official curriculum, as rationally planned by curricular experts, into "finished products" (measured by comparison of prespecified goals with student outcomes, usually test scores). The greater the acquisition of classroom knowledge or congruity of student attitudes with those of the curriculum makers, the greater the effectiveness of the curriculum. Thus, debating and describing the official curriculum (the knowledge about sexuality that adult educators and other decision makers at the state and local district level can agree they want to impart to young people), measuring its outcomes, and searching for the most effective methods to impart it have been of major importance in the sex education literature.

In contrast, *Doing Sex Education* takes readers into one ninth-grade sexuality education classroom to explore what actually happens between "raw materials" and "finished products." My ethnographic

narrative draws on daily classroom and school observation of a required full-semester health class that included a unit on sexuality and
on interviews of teacher, students, and other school personnel; this
in-depth study of a particular setting captures the multilayered complexity and tension of lived classroom culture that technical and statistical techniques miss. It illuminates the dynamic, complex, and sometimes contradictory process by which traditional versions of
appropriate gender relations and sexual behavior are legitimated as
well as contested. *Doing Sex Education* describes in detail how classroom knowledge about sexuality is produced by interactions among
teacher and students, the planned curriculum, and social organization
of the school and community. It explores factors, particularly those
related to working conditions within the school, that affect teacher
selection, organization, and presentation of material. Finally, it pays
attention to student voices, investigating how teacher-presented classroom knowledge is accepted and contested, mediated and interpreted
by students and addressing such questions as: Do students "receive" the
same messages the teacher "transmits"? Are these messages passively
accepted, resisted or rejected by students? How are student interpretations and reactions similar or different across gender, race, and class
lines? To what degree are these messages congruent or contradictory
to students' lived experience outside the classroom?

Overall, *Doing Sex Education* reveals that organizational constraints
and working conditions within the school and district (lengthy district
syllabus, course requirement for graduation, administrative value on
efficiency and discipline, and so forth) significantly affect the teacher's
curricular decisions. Students' reinterpreted classroom points of view,
and their active responses, helped create an informal bantering atmosphere; marginalized students, particularly the three African-Ameri-
cans and two female "dirts" in the class, more prominently challenged
dominant norms. In an active attempt to negotiate both structural
dilemmas inherent in her working conditions and student classroom
responses, the teacher covered mostly noncontroversial topics, presented fragments of technical information geared toward passing exams, and limited substantive student discussion. Thus, *Doing Sex Education* details the complex and contradictory day-to-day process by
which the rich, relevant subject matter of sexuality was reduced to
details for meeting grade requirements.

The technical model of curriculum planning that characterizes education (including sexuality education) has been widely criticized by
curriculum theorists over the last two decades (Bowles & Gintis, 1976;
Bernstein, 1977; Bourdieu & Passeron, 1977; Apple, 1982, 1988;

Sears & Marshall, 1990). They have argued persuasively that the educational system is structurally related to power and control in the wider society and plays a role in the continued dominance of particular social and economic groups. Because there has been little communication between such curriculum scholars and sexuality educators (Sears, 1992a), I am concerned with expanding possibilities for classroom practice by applying the fundamental curricular questions raised by these critiques to sexuality education. I am involved in this process intimately, having been a sexuality educator for more than two decades in a variety of school and community settings. For the last five years I have been a faculty member in the Department of Curriculum and Instruction at the University of Wisconsin-Madison, where I teach preservice and inservice courses in health and sexuality education. I acknowledge the political dimension of my work both as a sexuality educator and as a curriculum scholar.

Thus, the research questions upon which *Doing Sex Education* is based emerge from my own practice, a particular theoretical perspective that explores the school's role in perpetuating dominant points of view and interests, and my concern with challenging the stereotypical gender, race, and class relations, traditional antisex norms, and heterosexual assumptions that underpin most school-based sex education. These questions include: What are the assumptions underlying school sex education as a "solution" to the complex social "problems" of teenage pregnancy and HIV/AIDS? What are the obvious and latent effects of this particular solution? Which groups stand to gain and which to lose as a result? Which social group's version of sexual knowledge is represented as objective fact in the content and organization of the curriculum? Which is excluded? What ideological assumptions underpin the way this knowledge is presented?

The rest of this introductory chapter provides a backdrop for the particular classroom I studied. It offers a brief overview of the political context of sex education in the United States, including its conservative historical roots and the emergence of the New Right during the last twenty years; a description of its current status; and an elaboration of the conceptual framework upon which *Doing Sex Education* is based.

Political Context of U.S. School Sex Education

It is not my intent here to offer a thoroughgoing analysis of the history and politics of school sex education but to illuminate the assumptions and economic/social interests of groups who have had a major impact on school sexuality curriculum. I pay particular attention to two periods of American history (1890–1920 and 1960 to the present) during which the structure of the family was undergoing major change and popular movements around issues of family life and sexual morality emerged most visibly. The earlier period was related to industrialization and separation from the home of productive work for wages. The present period is linked to the youth culture and women's movement of the mid 1960s, which called into question both middle-class sexual morality and the traditional division of labor within families (Epstein, 1983). Leming (1992) asserts that curricular initiatives to ameliorate pressing social problems, which he labels "contemporary issues curricula," typically follow historical periods like these during which a particular issue galvanizes the public and the educational establishment. Precisely how the problem is defined and what represents the optimal solution are political issues and, like other aspects of the curriculum, sex education has taken shape largely as a result of struggle between interest groups (Kliebard, 1987). Thus, as family life and sexual morality became major topics of public debate during these periods, sex education in the school curriculum emerged as an ameliorative strategy—one, I will maintain, that privileged the perspectives of dominant groups.

Because this critical historical perspective has been, for the most part, absent from the professional journals and literature likely to be read by practitioners in school sex education, I offer it here as a backdrop for the classroom I studied. Thus, I will briefly describe the version of the "problem" of teenage sexual behavior and nature of the "solution" put forth by leaders of the first organized campaign for school sex education; by professionals who initially defined teenage pregnancy as an "epidemic" beginning in the late 1970s, and by the New Right, which has been instrumental in the current conservative trend.

Historical Roots

The first organized, although largely unsuccessful, campaign for the inclusion of sex education in the public school curriculum emerged in the context of the scientific social hygiene, eugenics, and purity movements of the early 1900s, which were primarily concerned with combatting venereal disease and prostitution through education. Because the assumptions of early school sex education proponents were fairly explicit, a critical historical perspective (largely missing from the literature read by current sexuality educators) will help illuminate assumptions underlying more recent efforts.[7] Early efforts to include such programs in schools were led mainly by white male physicians and university professors and culminated with the organization of the American Social Hygiene Association (ASHA) in 1913 and publication of *The Journal of Social Hygiene* in 1914. Dr. Charles Eliot, President Emeritus of Harvard University, served as ASHA's first president (Imber, 1982). He, along with other influential proponents of school sex education, was also connected to the scientific curriculum, child study, mental measurement, and eugenics movements of the period. These attempted to check what their spokespersons—also mostly white male professionals—saw as societal "deterioration" (Eliot, 1913, p. 15) brought about as immigrants crowded into industrial urban centers. That economic interests of dominant groups were partially behind ASHA's efforts is evident in the words of its first president:

The humanitarian policies in regard to the treatment of the defective, the incompetent, and the criminal classes seem to tend to increase the burdens carried by the normal and industrious portion of the population; and these burdens react on the vigor and happiness of the normal people. (Eliot, 1913, p. 16)

Of particular relevance to sex education, the mental measurement movement had "scientifically," as measured by intelligence tests characterized by historians as race- and class-biased (Gould, 1981; Karier, Violas & Spring, 1973), identified "feeblemindedness" as a fundamental factor in prostitution, criminality, pauperism, and drunkenness. Viewing "feeblemindedness" as a major factor in prostitution helped to impose a scientific discourse over class and gender distinctions related to sexual behavior. Thus, prostitutes (predominantly working-class women) were construed as "defectives," while their predominantly middle-class male customers could still be seen as "normal and industrious" (Eliot, 1913, p. 16). A concern with "rapid breeding of the defective, irresponsible, and vicious" (Eliot, 1913, p. 16) permeated the writing and speeches of the early sex education campaigners, and prominent eugenics advocates including W. Clarke, C. A. Ellwood, H. H. Goddard, W. W. Hall, and E. L. Thorndike were featured in *The Journal of Social Hygiene*.

Like the newly prominent curriculum theorists of the period, school sex education proponents anchored their educational solution to the social "deterioration" problem in objective and scientific curriculum.

The Politics of School Sex Education

In the words of one speaker at the Fourth International Congress on School Hygiene in 1913:

> The country is now suffering from a great scourge, a physical, mental, and moral unfitness, most of which might be prevented by careful scientific training, first in the normal facts of life and then in the reproductive organs and their functions in connection with the racial instinct. (Garrett, 1913, p. 62)

However, this "scientific training" and "facts of life" represented a particular selection based on the middle-class and morally conservative Victorian ideals of its proponents—a notion that sex is legitimate only within marriage and that the purity and nobility of the marital sex act should transcend both passion and the disgusting physical nature of sexual activity (Imber, 1982; Strong, 1972). Sexual curiosity on the part of young people was characterized by these campaigners as strictly intellectual in nature and, therefore, best satisfied by scientific explanations. Thus, the "facts" being advocated largely concerned the union of reproductive cells in plants and animals and very limited descriptions of human anatomy: "detailed descriptions of external human anatomy are to be avoided ... descriptions of internal anatomy should be limited" (Bigelow, Balliet, & Morrow, 1912, p. 3).

That moral injunctions also masqueraded as "facts" is best illustrated by the campaigner's reaffirmation of the nineteenth-century semen theory as an argument against male masturbation and premarital sex. This theory suggested that cells within the semen were reabsorbed into the blood, enabling heightened physical and moral development; therefore, a young man's semen should not be wastefully expended (Hall, 1914). Although there was increasing medical awareness during this period of the significance of the endocrine glands on physical development, these proponents molded medical facts to their own morality by continuing to evoke the semen theory (Strong, 1972, pp. 145–46).

These early campaigners also generally agreed that parents, particularly mothers because they were considered innately pure and the moral cornerstone of the family, were primarily responsible for instilling purity in their children, both by example and by keeping their children's curiosity minimally satisfied. However, the only mothers thought capable of this important task of transmitting Victorian dominant group morality belonged to the educated middle-class (Strong, 1972). The exemplary efforts of these parents were featured in a regular "How Shall We Teach?" section of *The Journal of Social Hygiene*, while other parents were described as "too ignorant" (Eliot, 1913, p. 18), "not equipped by nature or art," or "doing more harm than good" (Cabot, 1913a, 43; 1913b, 101). In outlining "Points of Attack in Sex Education" Thomas Balliet, Dean of the School of Pedagogy at New York University, maintained that local boards of education should not make public announcements before sex education was included in the curriculum to avoid negative reactions from "classes of persons who are neither intelligent nor high-minded, and whose attitudes towards questions of sex is wholly wrong" (1913, p. 31).

Thus, scientific child study experts along with other educators and physicians had the major role in developing sex education curricula. Although these early campaigners continually affirmed the parents' role in sex education, the bulk of their efforts continued to focus on school sex education as a solution to the societal problems that concerned them (Imber, 1982). Parents were seen as a means to the campaigners' ends, persons to be favorably influenced so sex education could be introduced first into high schools and then elementary schools (Balliet, 1913, p. 27).

Recent Political Context

Those familiar with efforts to promote school sexuality education during the past two decades will readily recognize that this generation of advocates (also primarily white, middle-class professionals in health and education) offer justifications and strategies strikingly similar to their earlier counterparts. Both maintain that school sexuality education can solve complex social problems, with the current "problem" initially defined during the 1970s and early 1980s as teenage pregnancy and, more recently, as HIV/AIDS. Key issues in both the earlier and current educational and political debates include school vs. family as sanctioned providers of sexuality information, which topics to include in the curriculum, and effects of school sex education on young people's sexual behavior (Trudell, 1985).

Constructing the Teenage Pregnancy "Epidemic"

Lee and Berman (1992) describe the conceptualization of teenage sexuality, pregnancy, and childbearing that emerged during the 1970s as a "well-structured problem," one with a singular correct solution determined by applying explicit rules within a closed system in which relevant information is narrowly defined. Context as well as interper-

13

The Politics of School Sex Education

sonal and intrapersonal knowledge are excluded from consideration, and the solution then derived from a linear, mechanical process. Two publications from The Alan Guttmacher Institute (an affiliate of Planned Parenthood Federation of America), which were widely circulated among health care professionals, educators, and policy makers, are illustrative of this "well-structured" approach. Both were instrumental in initially elevating teenage pregnancy to the status of "epidemic" and promoting sex education and family planning services as the solution.

The first, *11 million Teenagers: What Can Be Done about the Epidemic of Teenage Pregnancies in the United States* (Alan Guttmacher Institute, 1976), utilized 1971 national survey data on heterosexually active females ages 15 to 19 (sexually active meaning intercourse at least once). Adolescents at risk of pregnancy were calculated by applying survey data to the current female population and making "very rough 'guesstimates' " for males (Dryfoos, 1990, p. 70). Aggregate statistics (differentiated only by age, not race or income) were displayed in graph format. According to the report, 4 million females and 7 million males ages 15 to 19 had already experienced sexual intercourse and were thus at risk for pregnancy. It also documented about 1 million teenage pregnancies per year in the U.S. and delineated the ways these pregnancies damage the young mother (dropping out of school, poverty, divorce, pregnancy complications, maternal death), her infant (lower birth weight, death in first year), and wider society (welfare dependency).

The second Guttmacher report, *Teenage Pregnancy: The Problem That Hasn't Gone Away* (1981), utilized data from subsequent surveys to update and elaborate on the first. Rates of teen premarital sexual activity, marriage, out-of-wedlock births, and some problematic outcomes of teen childbearing (e.g., marriage disruption) were displayed in graph format by both age and race. Although the rate of sexual activity among black teen women was shown to be about twice that of whites, the rate among 15- 17-year-old white women was shown to have increased most dramatically—doubling from 15 percent in 1971 to nearly 30 percent in 1979 (p. 9). Similarly, the number of births per thousand unmarried teens was much higher for black women ages 15 to 17 (seventy per thousand), than for whites (eleven per thousand). However, birth rates among this age group of white young women was shown to have increased 27 percent, while the rate for blacks decreased 10 percent (p. 25). This rising rate of premarital (hetero)sexual activity and birth among young white women were two findings that received considerable public attention. Negative outcomes of teen childbearing were again reported in *Teenage Pregnancy: The*

Problem That Hasn't Gone Away, including more specific references to the economic burden on taxpayers (e.g., dependence on government for cost of delivery (p. 60) and AFDC (Aid to Families with Dependent Children) payments of $4.7 billion to families in which mothers had given birth as teenagers (p. 32). Both Guttmacher reports recommended the same ameliorative strategies: sex education, family planning, and related health care services for teens.

While this statistical formulation of the teenage pregnancy "problem" and its commonsense "solution" appears neutral and objective, it actually embodies particular economic and social interests as well as normative assumptions about cultural meaning and what constitutes legitimate sexual expression. First, reliance on aggregate statistics for documentation focuses on individuals in isolation from their history, culture, and economic circumstances and neglects structural inequities as contributing factors to the teenage pregnancy "epidemic." For example, categorizing teen women only by age and race neglects such important factors as social class and poverty. It also inhibits consideration of the ways that inequitable social relations (systematic discrimination against women and people of color in employment opportunities and wages) might contribute to pregnancy for teenage women, especially in a society that sanctions motherhood as the ultimate goal of female sexuality. Thus, teenage pregnancy is depicted as an individual and moral "problem," a notion that was reinforced by the conservative resurgence taking shape during this period as far right politicians and ministers joined forces (Reissman & Nathanson, 1986).

Furthermore, it seems beyond coincidence that teenage pregnancy first began to be defined and accepted as a more urgent social concern as research suggested earlier and higher rates of sexual activity for *white* young women and greater percentages of births to unmarried white, middle-class teens (Reissman & Nathanson, 1986). At the same time, the ongoing higher rate of such births to black teens began to be promoted as an economic problem for taxpayers.

In addition to neglecting structural inequities, this statistical/individual formulation of the teenage pregnancy problem obscures the role of cultural differences in the meaning of this event and tacitly focuses on individual young women rather than men. Finally, it assumes intercourse as the only legitimate expression of human sexuality; "sexually active" and heterosexual coital activity (at least once) are synonymous. Other forms of sexual expression such as masturbation, oral sex, gay and lesbian sex, are invisible and thus not legitimate.

In short, given this exclusion of the wider social context from analysis of this "well-structured problem," educating individuals via school sex education becomes the solution preferred over changing inequitable social and economic structures. Thus, the privilege of dominant groups remains largely undisturbed, while essentially moral, ethical, and political considerations are reduced to technical considerations of efficiency and cost effectiveness:

> There are few avenues available to society to prevent unintended teenage pregnancy and childbearing. Sex education is one that has many advantages: it can reach all boys and girls before they become sexually active and information can be provided to them at relatively low cost through school systems and other facilities. (Alan Guttmacher Institute, 1983, p. 1)

In contrast to this formulation of teenage pregnancy as a "well-structured problem" with one correct solution, Lee and Berman assert that problems related to teen sexuality are more appropriately conceptualized as "ill-structured." Such problems consider the impact of context and require simultaneous attention to several interconnected factors. They have multiple causes and demand multiple responses, based on consideration of both interpersonal and intrapersonal knowledge. Over the last several years, teenage pregnancy has begun to be conceptualized as an "ill-structured" problem (Children's Defense Fund, 1986; Dryfoos, 1990; Edelman, 1987). In the words of Faye Wattleton, former President of Planned Parenthood Federation of America:

> But we must also recognize that the teen pregnancy problem cannot be solved through sexuality education and family-planning services alone. If our efforts are to succeed, society must provide all our young people with a decent general education, tangible job opportunities, successful role models and real hope for the future. (1990, p. 111)

In spite of this growing awareness, school sex education and availability of protective devices to adolescents are still the most widely promoted aspects of a solution to the complex problems of teenage pregnancy and sexually transmitted disease, as evidenced by increased government mandates to provide some form of sexuality and HIV/AIDS education. Nevertheless, as I shall document later in the chapter, a conservative resurgence has meant that even mandated course offerings are brief, noncomprehensive, and frequently promote "just say 'no' " approaches.

Emergence of the New Right

During the 1970s, while teenage pregnancy was being constructed as an individualized problem with education the preferred solution, a national nexus of conservative political and religious groups, the New Right, was gaining coherence.[8] This elite and well-financed interlocking network was founded by leaders of such conservative organizations as the Heritage Foundation, National Conservative Political Action Committee, and Conservative Congress. Its purpose was and is to foster a conservative economic and social agenda at the level of national policy and electoral politics (Hunter, 1984). These leaders also organized conservative religious groups and helped to form new organizations such as the Moral Majority and Religious Roundtable which were instrumental in Ronald Reagan's 1980 landslide election (Reissman & Nathanson, 1986). Leaders of the New Right established connections with local backlash social movements, such as those opposed to school sex education, coordinated electoral/lobbying activities through the offices of their organizations, and formed coalitions around a variety of issues. For example, the Pro-Family Coalition, which includes such groups as Phyllis Schlafly's Eagle Forum, James Dobson's Focus on the Family, and Beverly LaHaye's Concerned Women for America, was organized during the late 1970s. A major purpose of the coalition is to promote a monolithic definition of *the* family: people related by heterosexual marriage, blood, or adoption. It coordinates activities of groups opposed to the ERA, feminism, abortion, gay rights, busing, school prayer, and, of course, school sex education (Hunter, 1984). In short, since its emergence around 1974, the New Right has played a major role in the current conservative resurgence in government, policymaking, and public discourse about education and other issues.

With regard to sex education, its traditional definition of the family was reinforced legislatively with passage of the Family Protection Act in 1981. One of the act's provisions prohibited federal funding for schools whose curriculum "would tend to denigrate, diminish, or deny the role differences between the sexes as they have been historically understood in the United States." Another provision denied government benefits, including social security, to persons who presented homosexuality "as an acceptable alternative life style or suggests that it can be an acceptable life style" (D'Emilio & Freedman, 1988, p. 349).

The Office of Adolescent Pregnancy Prevention (OAPP), which was created in the same year to administer federal grants to educational programs, adopted an increasingly hard-line conservative approach to funding decisions throughout the 1980s. Responsible sexual behavior was defined by then President Reagan as "based on fidelity, commitment, and maturity, placing sexuality within the context of marriage" (U.S. Dept. of Education, 1987). Provision of *any* contraceptive information in curricular materials—even those that stressed abstinence— was attacked for conveying a "mixed message" while abstinence-*only* materials that advanced the New Right's ideological agenda received substantial federal funding (Kerr, 1992a). Religious connections were so evident in major abstinence-only curricula funded by OAPP that a legal challenge was mounted in the mid 1980s to the program's constitutionality as a publicly funded endeavor (Kerr, 1992a).

In spite of educational shortcomings (Trudell & Whatley, 1991, 1992), *Sex Respect* is reportedly being used in about sixteen hundred districts nationwide (Kerr, 1992a), and *Teen-Aid* officials say their curriculum is being used in all fifty states (Greenberg, 1992). The inflated promises[9] (Reynolds, 1991) of New Right promoters that these abstinence-only curricula will solve complex social problems have considerable appeal to concerned parents and educators (Trudell & Whatley, 1991). However, this level of adoption seems to be less the result of spontaneous grassroots movements than of the systematic efforts, sophisticated strategies, and coordinated national linkages of Christian fundamentalist and far right groups (Kantor, 1993; Sedway, 1992).[10]

Similarly, such groups orchestrate challenges in districts across the U.S. to curricular or library materials that do not endorse their narrow sectarian or ideological views. According to *Attacks on the Freedom to Learn: 1990–91 Report* (People for the American Way, 1991), New Right groups are currently retaking the offensive in an increasing number of broad-based censorship attacks on classic literature, reading texts, peace education, biology instruction, drug abuse prevention materials, and self-esteem development projects as well as sexuality education. Furthermore, the New Right has also stepped up efforts to elect fundamentalist Christians to state and local offices, especially school boards, where such candidates won over 30 percent of school board elections they entered last November (Kantor, 1993).

Internal connections within this New Right network are extensive but often obscure, especially at the local district level (People for the American Way, 1991; Kerr, 1992b). Referring specifically to sex education, Mark Sedway, coordinator of a People for the American Way project that monitors school censorship, says:

Indeed, what at first seemed to be isolated challenges in towns around the country take on the shape of a nationally coordinated movement as objections, tactics, and materials repeat themselves in incident after incident. (1992, p. 13)

These tactics include lobbying state legislatures to mandate abstinence-only approaches; a network of paid speakers "invited" into local districts that experience controversy; offers to provide curriculum, staff training, or legal advice free of charge; presentation packets complete with transparencies; publications with instructions for setting up private curriculum review committees, pressuring textbook adoption committees and/or school board members, and taking over school boards; organizing anonymous phone and mail campaigns; and making allegations (sometimes false) against comprehensive school programs (Greenberg, 1992; Hennessy, 1992a, 1992b; Sedway, 1992; Whetstone, 1992).[11]

Although New Right groups represent a minority viewpoint, their "disturbing and saturating" cloud currently permeates school sex education (Phillips & Fine, 1992, p. 242), most notably in narrowing the parameters of official course content and in creating a climate in which educators censor themselves (Whatley, 1992). As these national organizations share information and orchestrate tactics in individual districts, word of their divisive effect on communities has spread; local school board members and educators have become increasingly "wary of a disruptive battle, and much more likely to capitulate to requests to remove or restrict [more comprehensive] materials" (Sedway, 1992, p. 16). Thus, as I shall document in the next section, although state mandates for sexuality and HIV/AIDS education have increased, most course offerings are brief and consist mainly of "safe" content that heavily emphasizes negative consequences of sexual behavior and promotes abstinence.

Current Status of School Sex Education

Prevalence

Both the proportion of U.S. students receiving some form of school sexuality education and the number of separate courses have increased during the 1980s. Seventeen states, including the District of Columbia, made school sex education mandatory in 1992 (Haffner, 1992), while only Maryland, New Jersey and the District of Columbia made such instruction mandatory in 1984 (Kirby, 1984). In addition, thirty other state departments of education currently recommend that local districts offer some form of school sexuality education (Haffner, 1992). No state prohibits it (Haffner, 1990), and only four—Massachusetts, Mississippi, South Dakota, and Wyoming—take no official position. Thirty-three states mandate HIV/AIDS education at some grade level, with another fifteen recommending it (Haffner, 1992). Among the country's largest school districts, two-thirds require some sexuality education and less than two percent discourage or prohibit it; eighty percent require HIV/AIDS education (Kenney, Guardado, & Brown, 1989). It is estimated that about fifty thousand public school teachers offer sexuality education in grades 7–12 (Forrest & Silverman, 1989).

Most school offerings in sex education are a relatively brief unit of study (Kirby, 1984; Sonenstein & Pittman, 1984), presented in the context of other classes such as physical education, health, biology, or home economics (Donovan, 1989; Orr, 1982; Sonenstein & Pittman, 1984); teachers are most frequently trained primarily in these areas rather than human sexuality. Such offerings are typically begun at the ninth or tenth grade (Forrest & Silverman, 1989), with less than one-third of large metropolitan school districts providing at least 75 percent of students with sexuality instruction for at least one class period before ninth grade (Sonenstein & Pittman, 1984). Of the fifty thousand public school personnel providing this instruction, 60 percent describe sex education as accounting for 10 percent or less of their total teaching time and do not identify themselves primarily as sexuality educators; 80 percent report they need help with factual information as well as teaching strategies and materials. Nevertheless, 90 percent believe they were adequately trained, with 72 percent recently attending some form of sexuality inservice and almost none having graduate preparation in human sexuality (Donovan, 1989).

Content

In spite of this increasingly mandated public school instruction in human sexuality and the widespread public approval cited earlier, it has been estimated that only about 10 percent of U.S. students receive what could be termed comprehensive instruction in human sexuality (Kirby, 1984). As defined by a SIECUS-sponsored national colloquium on the future of sexuality education, a comprehensive program would address the following four primary goals (National Guidelines Task Force, 1991, p. 3):

Information: To provide accurate information about human sexuality, including: growth and development, human reproduction, anatomy, physiology, masturbation, family life, pregnancy, childbirth, parenthood, sexual response, sexual orientation, contraception, abortion, sexual abuse, HIV/AIDS and other sexually transmitted diseases.

Attitudes, Values, and Insights: To provide an opportunity for young people to question, explore, and assess their sexual attitudes in order to develop their own values, increase self-esteem, develop insights concerning relationships with members of both genders, and understand their obligations and responsibilities to others.

Relationships and Interpersonal Skills: To help young people develop interpersonal skills, including communication, decision-making, assertiveness, and peer refusal skills, as well as the ability to create satisfying relationships. Sexuality education programs should prepare students to understand their sexuality effectively and creatively in adult roles. This would include helping young people develop the capacity for caring, supportive, non-coercive, and mutually pleasurable intimate and sexual relationships.

Responsibility: To help young people exercise responsibility regarding sexual relationships, including addressing abstinence, how to resist pressures to become prematurely involved in sexual intercourse, and encouraging the use of contraception and other sexual health measures. Sexuality education should be a central component of programs designed to reduce the prevalence of sexually-related medical problems, including teenage pregnancies, sexually transmitted diseases including HIV infection, and sexual abuse.

In contrast, a recent SIECUS review of state-mandated curricula or guidelines shows that sex education classes focus mostly on such issues as relationships among family members, dating, child development, and gender role socialization while they avoid directly addressing sexual issues. Nearly half have limited contraceptive information. Overall, researchers conclude that only one in six of these state curricula provide for comprehensive sexuality education. A similar review of HIV/AIDS state-mandated curricula presents an even more restricted picture. Abstinence is covered in 85 percent of the curricula, while only 9 percent

21

include detailed coverage of safer sex practices. Seventy-four percent mention condom use, while only 9 percent explain how to use or obtain condoms (de Mauro, 1990).

According to other survey research (Alan Guttmacher Institute, 1983; Forrest & Silverman, 1989; Kenney, Guardado & Brown, 1989; Orr, 1982; Sonenstein & Pittman, 1984), facts about the negative social, emotional and economic consequences of teenage pregnancy and abstinence are among topics most emphasized in the classroom. Other topics more likely to be included are physical changes of puberty, reproductive anatomy and physiology, and sexual decision making related to dating, marriage and parenthood. Topics that might realistically be effective in preventing pregnancy and disease (contraception and abortion) are more often considered "controversial" and included with less frequency and/or depth. Similarly, sexual activities other than heterosexual intercourse (masturbation, other safer sex activities, and homosexuality) are covered less frequently (Forrest & Silverman, 1989; Orr, 1982; Sonenstein & Pittman, 1984). Finally, the pleasures of sexuality are usually omitted from school sex education classes altogether (Fine, 1988; Haffner, 1990).

Survey research, however, cannot reveal what actually occurs in the classroom (the curriculum-in-use), including the extent to which a topic is discussed. For example, respondents in one study (Orr, 1982) claim to cover an average of fifteen topics with fewer than five hours of instruction, suggesting that some topics might merely be mentioned rather than covered in any depth. Furthermore, such research cannot describe the context in which a particular topic is discussed. Abortion, for example, might be described quite differently as either an informational or moralistic concern (Orr, 1982). In contrast to most existing studies of school sex education, the qualitative research methods used in *Doing Sex Education* offer insight into this wider context of a specific topic.

Conceptual Framework

Doing Sex Education draws upon theoretical and empirical work in the sociology of knowledge, feminist and critical cultural analysis, and organizational theory. Broadly interpreted, this critical scholarship situates school knowledge in its economic, cultural, and political context and recognizes the important role of the curriculum in shaping cultural values. Although they seriously disagree about the process by which this occurs, those engaged in this appraisal of education share a conviction that the content and form of classroom knowledge is not neutral but privileges the interests of particular groups over others. They see the educational system as structurally related to power and control in the wider society and involved in the continued dominance of certain class, gender, and racial groups.

Economic and Cultural Reproduction

Early theoretical work from this general critical perspective conceptualized schools as reproducing wider social inequities, emphasizing a mechanistic connection between the economic and ideological requirements of powerful groups and day-to-day life within schools. Students and teachers were viewed as passive subjects who internalize the attitudes and knowledge that enable them to take their place in a capitalistic social system. For example, Bowles and Gintis (1976) characterized the educational system as a primarily economic institution and pointed out structural similarities in the organization of schooling—hierarchy, authority relations, and bureaucratization—that replicate the division of labor in the workplace. According to them, the underlying components of school organization (the "hidden" curriculum) socialize students by class into the consciousness, dispositions and traits—respect for authority, obedience, punctuality, and so forth—essential to the capitalistic system. Thus, Bowles and Gintis saw schooling as a major force in the reproduction of inequitable social relations.

Subsequent investigators have maintained that schools are cultural as well as economic institutions (Apple, 1979; Bernstein, 1977; Bourdieu & Passeron, 1977) that reproduce and legitimate the knowledge and communicative forms of dominant groups. These theorists have focused their inquiry on the structural and interactional aspects of cultural practices within schools, including curricular content, organization, and evaluation. Like economic reproduction theorists, they argue that the underlying structural reality of these seemingly neutral practices actually serves the needs of dominant groups, generating unequal social relations which go largely unquestioned by the dominated.

The Selective Tradition. From this perspective, schools act as agents of "cultural incorporation" by making available to students a particular selection from a wider pool of knowledge, with certain information chosen for emphasis and other information excluded, a process Raymond Williams (1977) calls the "selective tradition." Both the content

23

and form of this chosen knowledge tacitly support or at least do not contradict the interests and views of dominant groups, helping to create citizens who do not question current economic and social arrangements because their consciousness and whole process of living is thoroughly saturated with knowledge and values of the dominant culture. Williams uses the term "hegemony" to describe this saturation of consciousness, a concept that must be understood on a deeper level than simple opinion:

> It is a whole body of practices and expectations over the whole of living: our senses and assignments of energy, our shaping perceptions of ourselves and our world. It is a lived system of meanings and values—constitutive and constituting—which as they are experienced as practices appear as reciprocally confirming. (1977, p. 110)

Thus, the pressures and limits of particular economic, political and cultural systems are common sense aspects of the process of living, so it is difficult for most members of a society to move beyond these "absolutes" in most areas of their life. Nevertheless, Williams' concept of hegemony is more complex than simple manipulation or internalization of dominant views. He asserts that hegemony is a lived process that is continually resisted and challenged; therefore, it needs to be continually renewed and defended (1977, p. 112).

These concepts, cultural and economic reproduction and hegemony, can help make visible some of the interests and assumptions inherent in the current commonsense notion of teenage pregnancy as a "problem" and school sex education as a "solution." While this formulation appears neutral and objective, I have shown how it actually embodies particular economic and social interests as well as normative assumptions about cultural meaning and what constitutes legitimate sexual expression.

Similarly, questions raised by theories of cultural and economic reproduction are central to making visible the interests and values embodied in the sex education curriculum-in-use in a particular classroom. Such questions are a major aspect of *Doing Sex Education* and include the following: What are the official purposes and content of the sex education curriculum? What specific information is conveyed and omitted? What tacit and explicit values about sexuality and the nature of gender relations are presented? In particular, what constitutes "responsible" sexuality for males and females? In what form is school sex education knowledge conveyed?

Cultural Production

In general, theoretical work on the role of schooling in reproducing inequitable economic and social relations takes the important step of situating the school in its larger social context and making visible its latent function in serving the needs of dominant groups. Because reproduction theories of education largely ignore the actual day-to-day interactions within schools, including the perceptions and activity of students and teachers, they provide little insight into the specific *process* by which relations of domination and subordination are perpetuated. Furthermore, such theories assume too mechanistic a correspondence between macrosocietal economic and cultural forms and individual consciousness by conceptualizing students and teachers as passive subjects who then internalize attitudes and knowledge that serve the interests of dominant groups.

Some educational researchers (Everhart, 1983; Hudak, 1985; McNeil, 1981, 1986; McRobbie, 1978; Valli, 1986; Willis, 1977) have taken the previously ignored day-to-day activities within the school as their starting point for analyzing the school's role in perpetuating unequal social relations. Instead of proceeding "downward" from a theory of cultural reproduction, these researchers work "upward" from everyday cultural practices in the school itself. From this perspective, they identify a more active and complex process than that described by reproduction theorists, a process Paul Willis (1977) first labelled "cultural production." This growing body of ethnographic work suggests that ongoing domination by particular groups is not a passive process of internalizing the ideology of dominant groups. It is an *active* process in which students (for whom the school is an arena for collective social life) and teachers (for whom the school is a workplace) have power to mediate, reinterpret, and contest dominant cultural meanings embedded within the curriculum and organization of the school. Furthermore, according to this research, the activity of students and teachers is characterized by rationality, collectivity, accommodation, and resistance.

Thus, although the "selective tradition" is operative, the perspectives of dominant groups are not simply passed on by teachers and passively absorbed by students. Instead, the process by which ongoing relations of domination/subordination in the wider society are partially produced within the school is complex and permeated with contradiction. Since teachers and students are themselves members of various gender, class, and racial groups, the contradictions and tensions within and between these groups work their way through daily school life. Further-

25

more, because material and ideological conditions at a given moment set limits on the potential of teachers and students to act, behavior which may be liberating at one level may reproduce subordination at another. In other words, resistance to one form of domination may mean submission to another.

Student Resistance and the Curriculum-in-Use. As an illustration of this concept, working-class students in some of these studies actively construct their own informal group culture around humor to make the school a more livable institution, i.e., "having a laff" (Willis, 1977), "playing up the teachers" (McRobbie, 1978), "goofing off," and "bugging the teacher" (Everhart, 1983). In so doing, they generate fun and collegiality but neither confront nor critically analyze the lack of meaning of the school's knowledge and procedures for them. Thus, while these students disrupt the flow of classroom activities, they do not substantially modify the teacher's agenda. In long-range terms, this cultural response may ultimately contribute to their own subordination in that they are learning not to challenge inequity in an organized or political way.

Similarly, students in three high school social studies classes studied by McNeil (1981) settle into "polite silence" during lectures and offer little or no outward resistance to the teachers' information, methods, or evaluation. Nevertheless, subsequent interviews revealed that an overwhelming majority of students resist "at the point of believing or internalizing the content of lectures" (1981, p. 317). Although the origins of this resistance vary, the reason most frequently offered by students is a discrepancy between information the teacher presented as fact and knowledge the student had gained from another source such as personal experience, parents, television or books read outside the school. Once a discrepant fact or generalization is noted, students become suspicious of subsequent lecture content. While the overt acceptance of teacher-supplied material leads students to the short-term gain of obtaining credit toward graduation, the long-term outcome of this response is alienation. At the wider social level, the value of acquiescence—of not questioning or being actively involved in changing the system—is confirmed, and dominant groups retain their status.

This active process of negotiation by a particular teacher and students in the area of sexuality and gender relations is a major concern of *Doing Sex Education*. The concept of student resistance and its impact on the curriculum-in-use is embodied in the following questions: What are student responses within the classroom to presented information and values about sexuality and the nature of gender relations? Are they accepted, rejected, contested? How are student reactions similar or different across gender, race, and class lines? How does this classroom knowledge contradict or reinforce the lived experience of students in their families and informal peer groups? What impact do student cultural responses have on school knowledge about sexuality and the nature of gender relations? In addition to an interest in student cultural responses, the study poses similar questions about the impact of a teacher's active negotiations, as a gendered worker within the school, on curricular and pedagogical choices.

Teachers and the Curriculum-in-Use. The school as a workplace is characterized by bureaucratic arrangements that emphasize management and control, and teacher responses to such arrangements have a significant impact on the construction of school knowledge (McNeil, 1986). For example, administrative priorities are a major factor affecting classroom knowledge about social studies in four schools studied by McNeil; the more a given administration focuses on order and detail, the less it focuses on academic teaching quality. Teachers calculate how much of their own considerable knowledge of subject matter to risk in the classroom, weighing both the potential for student dissent and disorder and the probable backing they would receive from school administration should discipline problems occur. Given pressure on them to "cover the material," their perceptions of generally inadequate administrative support and monetary compensation, dwindling energy, widely varying student ability, and the minimal effort students seem willing to exert, teachers in these schools choose primarily to lecture and to utilize what McNeil calls "defensive teaching" strategies in order to maintain their authority over curricular content and classroom process. Such strategies include: 1) simplifying content into easily transmitted, answered, and graded fragments and lists; 2) mystifying complex or controversial topics by making them appear important but unknowable; 3) omitting certain topics or aspects of topics; 4) promising that concepts not amenable to lists will not be difficult or explored in much depth (1986, pp. 165–75). In addition, the observed teachers required almost no reading assignments or written work from students. The underlying rationale for these strategies seems to be "control students by making school work easy" (1986, p. 184). Thus, according to McNeil, the bureaucratic needs of the school, working their way through teachers, transform potentially rich and diverse "real world knowledge" into "school knowledge", which she defines as:

an artificial set of facts and generalizations whose credibility no longer lies in its authenticity as a cultural selection but in its

27

mental value in meeting the obligation teachers and students have within the institution of schooling. (McNeil, 1986, p. 191)

The outcome of such teaching is contradictory for teachers as well as students (McNeil, 1986). In accommodating organizational demands of the school, teachers' expressed ideals about content (broad, in-depth inquiry and discussion) are divorced from what actually occurs in the classroom. Their years of training, experience, and extensive knowledge of subject matter are reduced to a bland recitation of oversimplified content. Thus, they participate in their own "deskilling" (Apple, 1982), and their wider teaching skills, including curricular deliberation and planning, begin to atrophy from disuse.

In addition to its bureaucratic organization, the school as a workplace is also characterized by a sexual division of labor and patriarchal authority relations, with classroom teachers predominantly female and administrators predominantly male. Apple (1983) maintains that these factors—along with class dynamics—are crucial to understanding why state bureaucrats, industry, and (largely male) academics have attempted to restructure and "proletarianize" teachers' work through technical procedures such as management by objectives and competency-based instruction, as well as behaviorally oriented and prepackaged curricula.[12] However, teachers have not been passive in their acceptance of this increased technical control over their labor. While partially accepting this process under the rubric of "professionalism," they resist in political and cultural ways, including changing or refusing to teach certain prespecified objectives and holding more relaxed discussions with students on topics of their own choice (Gitlin, 1980).

Considering teaching as a labor process adds another dimension to understanding the curriculum-in-use. These findings suggest that teachers as workers make active choices about content and presentation based on a variety of factors, including administrative priorities for control, labor intensification pressure, and the sexual division of labor. Thus, *Doing Sex Education* asks the question: What practical considerations influence teacher selection, organization and presentation of information on sexuality and the nature of gender relations?

Drawing on these concepts from critical educational scholarship on the role of schooling in perpetuating inequitable social relations, my examination of the school sex education curriculum-in-use calls its commonsense perspectives and activities into question. I conceptualize knowledge conveyed in the classroom about sexuality and gender relations as representing a selective tradition; that is, it is selected from a larger pool of possible knowledge and is likely to reflect perspectives of the most powerful groups in the society. Furthermore, I conceptualize this classroom knowledge as actively constructed by teachers and students in a particular context. Thus, *Doing Sex Education* describes and analyzes this process of construction, addressing an issue largely ignored in the school sex education literature. It investigates factors, particularly the bureaucratic organization of schools, that influence teacher selection of material for classroom presentation and explores the lived responses of students to this material. In setting forth the day-to-day process by which sexuality and gender relations are actively constructed within the school and classroom, I will illuminate opportunities for progressive social action and public policy aimed at bettering present conditions while leading to eradication of wider social and economic inequity, action referred to as "non-reformist reform" (Apple, 1982, p. 134).

This in-depth exploration of the day-to-day process in one sex education classroom grows out of my own involvement for two decades in sex education as classroom teacher, curriculum consultant, community educator, and workshop facilitator, as well as the theoretical orientation just described. Both experientially and theoretically, I conceptualize teachers and students as active agents in the educational process. This conceptualization served as a lens through which I observed and recorded classroom events, formulated interview questions and heard responses, and decided what significance to attach to what I saw and heard. Thus, just as I do not assume curriculum to be neutral, I do not view my selection of certain events for closer scrutiny and subsequent interpretation as a neutral, objective process. I reject the fact-value dichotomy of positivism; I accept the "theory-laden dimensions of observation and the value-laden dimensions of theory" (Lather, 1986a, p. 260).

However, I made every effort to keep the theoretical framework from blinding me to alternate interpretations. I attempted to hold my theoretical perspective in constant tension with what I saw and heard and to construct an analysis in which theory was informed by observation as much as observation by theory. A concrete example of how this occurred will be instructive. *After* observing for several weeks the classroom teacher's presentation of what I called "bits and pieces" of information, I encountered Linda McNeil's discussion of "defensive teaching" in a prepublication draft (1986). Thus, I did not initially enter the classroom looking for data to fit the *a priori* category of "defensive teaching," although this construct proved useful in my interpretation. Similarly, Robert Everhart's notion of "reified knowledge" (1983) provided a framework for discussing my observations, although I did not have this construct in mind while collecting the data.

I also openly acknowledge that my research, like the critical theoretical perspective from which it emerges, has a particular value stance and emancipatory purpose. Simply put, the study grew out of my commitment to both understand and change the unequal distribution of power and resources in our society and the role of schooling in this process. Although gender/sexuality issues are the major focus of my attention here, I try to remain conscious of my own simultaneously privileged and oppressed statuses as a white, middle-aged, middle-class with working-class roots, feminist, heterosexual, physically able woman. Given the multiplicity of intersecting and contradictory positions which inform my own life and that of the classroom, I recognize that this description and analysis is my interpretation of what I saw and heard and represents at best only a partial understanding of classroom process. I also recognize, as pointed out by Deborah Britzman, that "my dilemma as a researcher is to construct and critically re-present the voices of others, and, in so doing, care for their integrity, humanity, and struggles" (1990, p. 12). In short, I take seriously my responsibility as a researcher to minimize possibilities of distortion from personal bias, to maximize data credibility (Lather, 1986b, p. 65), and to make my own process of investigation visible in such a way that readers can assess for themselves whether or not my interpretations are warranted. I refer readers to the Appendix, which describes the ethnographic methodology I used in collecting, organizing, and recording my data.

The next chapter of *Doing Sex Education* explores the context of the classroom I observed, with particular emphasis on the sexual values and gender relations of the community and school, and describes the district and school health education program of which the classroom is a part. The next two chapters focus on Mrs. Warren, the classroom teacher. Chapter 3 documents her working conditions, including school organization and labor intensification, and Chapter 4 discusses her accommodation and resistance to feminine ideology and demands of the workplace. Chapter 5 introduces the students in Mrs. Warren's second period health class and describes their social groupings and overall classroom dynamics. Chapter 6 focuses on the content and form of the sex education curriculum as selected, organized, and presented by Mrs. Warren and analyzes points of view about sexuality and gender relations with which students were invited to identify. Chapter 7 documents students and the process by which they actively participated in the construction of the sex education curriculum-in-use. It details their classroom cultural responses and, on the basis of interview data, demonstrates how they weighed their own interests in acquiescing to or resisting course content and format. Chapter 8 summarizes major findings and explores implications for classroom practice and research.

2

The Informal Sexuality Curriculum: "A Lot of Eyes and Ears Out There"

"Social interaction is a normal part of the education process, but physical displays of affection are considered inappropriate at school or at school-sponsored activities."—*Van Buren Student, Parent, and Staff Handbook*

"Yes, she's got some real good tricks—does some great moves on the floor."—Male gymnastics coach introducing female gymnast at Van Buren pep rally

"For all the times we did it in the basement when your parents weren't home." "I wanna have sex with all the blond chicks."—Student messages from "Junior Wish List" bulletin board in Van Buren hallway

The classroom in which Mrs. Warren and her students came together to teach and learn about sexuality does not exist in a vacuum. The terrain upon which it is situated encompasses a specific school, district, and community in which various groups of people live, work, and play. The dominant values and patterns of interaction around sexuality and gender relations that make up everyday lived experience on this broader terrain also affect the classroom, with a certain kind of sexuality appearing as a normal, taken-for-granted part of ordinary life rather than a specific ideology to be questioned. In short, formal instruction is by no means the only student source of school messages about sexuality and gender relations. Therefore, before describing the dynamics of sex education in Mrs. Warren's classroom, it is essential to illuminate this larger context.

This chapter offers a brief portrait of the community of Woodland and Van Buren High School. It makes visible the internal organization of the school, the underlying dominant adult values regarding sexual behavior and language, and student contestation of them. It describes the hierarchical gender code as manifested in school ritual and faculty gender arrangements and explores the impact of staff gender relations on the issue of sexual abuse and assault in everyday student life. It also demonstrates how racial dynamics work their way through these situations.

Van Buren High School

Van Buren is one of four large comprehensive public high schools in Woodland, a midwestern city with a population of about 175,000. Education is highly valued in the city, and the local school system is perceived by most Woodland citizens as doing a high-quality job of educating its young people. Statewide, the district has a similar reputation among professional educators. Van Buren, with an enrollment of about eighteen hundred, is located on the less affluent side of Woodland in a residential area of relatively modest homes (most in the $45,000 to $65,000 range) near the city's edge. Most households are supported by state/city government, small business, or blue-collar workers, including many women who work outside the home.

Mr. Gray, who has worked in the Woodland system for twenty-eight years and has been principal at Van Buren for seven, characterizes people in that part of the community as "hardworking" and economically, socially, and ethnically "homogeneous":

It's a middle-class community with great pride in homes and interests in education. . . . It does not have—*certainly* does not have—the upper end of the spectrum. There are some students who come from quite low socioeconomic backgrounds—although a limited number of students. The great share of the students are white and come from a middle-class background.

33

The Informal Sexuality Curriculum

Mr. Gray also describes the community as religiously homogeneous, with "overwhelmingly Christian" church affiliation and attendance prevalent among Van Buren families. He offers the word "traditional" as the most encompassing descriptor of the community's religious beliefs and says that Van Buren serves this majority very well:

> The prevailing view [in the community] is that the school is doing a good job. We are not constantly fending off these (pause)—I guess, splinter groups or these attacks people are making. We just have relatively little of that.

Mr. Gray's perspective that the surrounding area is relatively homogeneous and traditional is shared by other staff members, who also perceive Mr. Gray himself as a religious and traditional man. Some staff also use the word "conservative" to describe the community; they mention the presence of a large number of students from "fundamentalist" religious backgrounds, and a general community emphasis on such values as hard work and strict discipline. Other school personnel also lend support to Mr. Gray's assertion that their constituency regards the school as "doing a good job"; parental complaints about their activities are rare. Finally, some staff suggest that preserving this harmonious relationship with a largely homogeneous community is a major, if infrequently verbalized, concern of Van Buren administration.

With regard to Mrs. Warren, both she and Mr. Gray report there have been "no problems" with parent complaints about her teaching of the health course and sexuality unit. In fact, she says she gets little feedback of any kind from parents. When I was at Van Buren, a mother told Mrs. Warren she did not want her son to participate in the health class the next semester because of sex education (nonparticipation in school sex education is an option parents may legally choose in the state where the research was conducted). Mrs. Warren simply referred the woman to Mr. Gray, and never learned how he handled it. She also mentioned receiving a phone call about four years earlier from a parent who was "concerned" that a condom had been passed around the male health teacher's (Mr. Austin) class for students to examine during a discussion of birth control. Mrs. Warren said she told the parent that abstinence is "obviously the best method," but it was also important for students to know how to prevent pregnancy. In Mrs. Warren's words, the parent "wasn't so upset" after this conversation and the complaint did not go further.

Although the community is largely homogeneous, racial homogeneity at Van Buren is changing as increased numbers of students of color, many from large urban areas relatively near Woodland, have recently enrolled at Van Buren. According to the Coordinator of Minority Services (a position created by district and school administration in response to this situation), the number of these mostly African-American students at the school had increased by 50 percent during the previous year (from 85 to 126), with students of color making up about 7 percent of the total school enrollment.[1] In the words of one teacher, "Van Buren is no longer a lily white school." Mr. Gray describes the effect of these changes on school staff:

> We are finding difficulties in terms of the background that they [students of color] bring to the school. . . . Having been used to serving this homogeneous [white] population and being very successful at it, we are finding some difficulties in serving this new population. But we're working at finding ways to do that.

While this issue will not be pursued in detail here, interracial dating is one of its manifestations that is particularly salient in administrative discourse on student sexual behavior and will be more fully explored later in this chapter. In addition, racial dynamics as they work their way through the sex education classroom I observed will be discussed in Chapters 4, 5, and 6.

Pride in Excellence

As the following quote from Mr. Gray illustrates, administrators—as well as most teachers and parents—are proud of Van Buren:

> I would say that it's a hardworking area and, again, the pride in the community and the pride in the school I think is evident. Certainly it's evident to me, and it's evident to everyone who comes here. I think that's important, valuable from a school standpoint.

Administrators and other school staff agree that Van Buren parents are mostly content to leave school decisions to professional educators. In the words of Mr. Gray, "There is good interest. There's support of the school, but there is not an avowed interest in telling educators how to do it."

There is justification for this pride and confidence because Van Buren had been recognized the year before as one of 262 outstanding secondary schools in the country by the U.S. Department of Education—an honor still proclaimed a year later in a large glass display case near the school's main office. The display, "Excellence in Education," features a commendation plaque, citations by the Governor and state legislature, and a large American flag. Van Buren's brochure (with "Excellence in Education" on the cover) also cites the award, along with "outstanding programs" in reading-study skills, integrated services for special need students, media facilities, and opportunities for gifted students.

Administrative Concern with Procedure and Discipline

Administrators and staff also seem proud of the school's generally firm approach to discipline. For example, one of the assistant principals announced during faculty orientation that Woodland's daily newspaper had just reported Van Buren as having the highest suspension rate (10 percent) of any high school in the city.[2] When he explained to the assembled staff that Van Buren's high rate of suspension meant that "this administration backs up teachers," his statement was greeted by a loud and sustained burst of applause. He also reported that approximately five thousand detentions had been served the previous school year. Over the course of the semester, several teachers and other school personnel expressed without solicitation their appreciation for this generally firm administrative stand on discipline.

In fact, communication from administration to teachers (daily bulletins, faculty meetings, and so on) was concerned primarily with disciplinary and procedural issues. Faculty orientation was mostly spent on such topics as ninth-grade orientation procedures, daily silent reading mechanics, scheduling, handling classroom discipline, detention and attendance/tardiness procedures. The largest single block of time was devoted to an explanation of the new computerized attendance system, during which an assistant principal distributed a handout ("Tattle Tale Report") to illustrate how teachers with such imaginary names as "Dumbensky," "Boring," and "Loop Olse" would be noted daily by the office if they failed to turn in attendance cards.

In addition, administrators placed a high value on respect for school property as a manifestation of school pride, and many positive references to the tidy appearance of the building were made by staff as well as administrators during the course of the semester. The Van Buren Student Council (which several teachers characterized as a mouthpiece for the administration) has been nationally recognized for its antivandalism program, and any destruction or defacement of school property is immediately repaired—and rendered invisible—by the maintenance staff.

On the surface level of day-to-day interactions, authority relations between students and staff seem amicably maintained at Van Buren. In general, students move to and from classes and socialize with friends with typical adolescent exuberance in an atmosphere free of visible coercion. For the most part, school personnel adopt a genial preventive presence; however, in the words of one teacher, "Behind every smiling adult is a cop." Mr. Gray and his assistant principals (Mr. Brunswick, Mr. Tony, and Mr. Carnegie) are important elements in this continual, low-profile watchfulness and could frequently be seen in the halls or Commons (an approximately $50' \times 50'$ area, with groupings of tables and upholstered couches and chairs, where students can informally congregate) before school, during lunch time, or between classes when students were present. They rarely obviously "monitored" students; they simply walked casually and unexpectedly through an area—speaking to students, picking up litter, or generally making their presence felt.

Students are not allowed in the hallway without a pass during class time or at all during a fifteen-minute required reading break; during these periods, most teachers also function quietly in a monitoring role. Those who have a preparation period during reading break are assigned to the hallways and Commons area, where they question any student who appears; I saw teachers asking students for passes on numerous other occasions as well. The extent to which students expect and comply with this amiable adult supervision is revealed in a brief interaction I had with a male student I met in the hallway during class time: I smiled at him as we walked past each other; he smiled back and then reflexively turned to hold out his signed pass slip so I could see it.

However, Van Buren students do contest adult authority and find their own creative ways to circumvent it. School personnel have to constantly work to maintain an acceptable level of student conformity to adult-set standards. For example, I observed an intense fifty-minute struggle for control involving a female teacher and nearly one hundred students (mostly ninth-grade males) in a study hall. The room was never quiet, and students steadily employed a variety of tactics to irritate the teacher (mostly behind her back)—yelping; fart sounds; throwing paper wads, corn nuts, and paper airplanes; spitting in the wastebasket, and so on. At the end of the study hall, she told me that this is a particularly difficult group, since many students have academic difficulty and/or have already had a study hall during the day. She added that she was going to talk with Mr. Gray about the situation that same day. Later in the semester, when I asked her whether things had changed, she said they were "much better"; the principals had started to drop in periodically, and the reading consultant regularly took a fairly large group to work with him. Genial preventive presence as a strategy for dealing with student contestation seemed more effective for male administrators than for this female teacher.

Administrative Distance from Classroom Instruction

While functioning visibly in the realms of discipline and control, Van Buren administration was more distanced from curriculum and instruction. More specifically, Mr. Gray and Mr. Brunswick (the assistant principal who has formal responsibility for supervision in health and physical education) verbalize a belief in allowing teachers considerable autonomy in the classroom—a policy also espoused by Woodland District. In Mr. Brunswick's opinion, this policy enables individuals "to work from strengths." As principal, Mr. Gray maintains that teacher "competence and professionalism" should be assumed unless there is evidence to the contrary. While taking care to clarify that he does *not* believe that "no news is good news," he says he relies on a "lot of eyes and ears out there" to evaluate instructional quality. In his words:

> My basic feeling is that if there is something going on in the classroom and we hear about that—either through a parent, students or observation of colleagues—we then would get to that and try to—I guess in some cases, depending on the situation—indicate to the teacher this is something that shouldn't happen.

However, he adds that "not many" of these situations actually occur.

Mrs. Warren, who is regarded highly as a health teacher by district and school administrators as well as her peers, perceives that an absence of parental complaints and procedural difficulties are valued more highly by Van Buren administrators than curriculum planning and classroom pedagogy. In contrast to Mr. Gray's statement, she volunteered without solicitation during an interview that she thinks the administration's attitude toward teaching is "no news is good news."

Furthermore, Mrs. Warren sees school administrators (particularly Mr. Gray and Mr. Brunswick,) as being supportive of the health education program in general, largely because the class "has gone real smoothly" in terms of such procedural arrangements as scheduling freshmen and coordinating use of facilities.

She reports that Mr. Brunswick last visited her class to evaluate her teaching (to "actually come in and sit down and write stuff") about four years earlier, quickly adding, "He's always around; it's not like he's not doing his job." However, Mrs. Warren noted later that he had observed only a physical education class, never her classroom teaching. Finally, Mrs. Warren comments on her evaluation by Mr. Brunswick:

> Even if he does evaluate, I don't think he's really being fair, 'cause he always over-rates. In my opinion, he always over-rates. I mean, like all fours [the highest rating], and I just don't think that's right. I can't imagine that I'd have perfect in everything. There's got to be something [to improve]—organiza-tion—(pauses).

> But, see, I just think he realizes that as long as everything's going well and he doesn't see any problems with me and parents, then that's probably his sign that things are going OK.

It should be clarified that organizational arrangements of the school, not necessarily individual administrators, are the issue here. For example, Mr. Brunswick (along with other administrators) has a wide range of responsibilities that go well beyond classroom evaluation. As summarized from a list provided to Van Buren teachers, these include: (1) budget and curriculum development, coordination, and scheduling for social studies, art, music, physical and health education, driver's education, industrial technology, home economics, and special education; (2) coordination of student teachers; (3) administration of student activities programs, e.g., "Master Calendar" of activities, Student Council, field trips, Pep Club; (4) liaison for Woodland/Van Buren public information efforts; (5) liaison with local police department; (6) coordination of Parent-Student Advisory Committee. Overall, I do not suggest that Van Buren administrators were unconcerned with academics but that their interest in procedural and disciplinary "excellence" was most visible to Mrs. Warren.

The Informal Sexuality Curriculum

Informal Student Culture

Because of my interest in sexuality and gender relations, I was particularly cognizant of adult efforts to sustain their versions of acceptable sexual behavior within the school and of student resistance to these efforts. Two such areas of contestation between students and staff at Van Buren, physical demonstrations of affection and sexual language, are particularly noteworthy.

"Physical Displays of Affection"

When asked what they saw as major sexual issues for students, both Mr. Gray and Mr. Brunswick mentioned inappropriate displays of affection near the top of their lists; Mr. Gray added that parents who visit the school are also concerned about such displays. Given administrative concern with maintaining the school's good reputation in the community, such parental perceptions are taken seriously. However, what actually constitutes acceptable physical displays of affection is an ongoing area of contestation between students and staff at Van Buren, with students continually acting on their own definitions rather than on the following school rule:

> Social interaction is a normal part of the education process, but physical displays of affection are considered inappropriate at school or at school-sponsored activities. (*Van Buren Student, Parent and Staff Handbook*, 1985–86, p. 21)

Based on my conversations with administrators, guidance personnel and teachers, as well as my own observations, there seems to be general agreement among adults at Van Buren that this rule is not strictly a "hands-off" policy. Therefore, they usually ignore hand holding, a quick kiss, or brief hug. However, the following behaviors are mentioned by various staff as inappropriate and subject to adult intervention: "tight embrace," "kissing at length," "French kissing—the wet lip routine," "smooching or rubbing hips together," "having each other by the cheeks [buttocks] with body motion," and "groping." There is disagreement about the propriety of lap sitting, with the degree to which the couple is "entwined around each other" an apparent factor. Furthermore, one assistant principal is opposed to lap sitting as a cause of chair breakage in the Commons. It is significant that heterosexuality is assumed in these descriptions of couples and behavior.

For the most part, adults function as amiable monitors of these less acceptable kinds of "social interaction"—telling students to move on to class or to stop—rather than as agents of punishment, although such conduct is listed in the handbook as a "detentionable offense." Furthermore, this adult monitoring is uneven because what might elicit a response from one adult, for instance, lap sitting, might be ignored by another. Thus, various versions of student physical displays of affection (mostly those generally ignored by adults) are commonly seen before school, whenever students pass between classes, lunch periods, and so forth. This is not to say that *most* students engage in such outward demonstrations of affection, but that at any given moment in a particular area of the school, at least two or three couples are visible who do. The "tight embrace" or "wet lip routine" is less frequently visible but not uncommon, particularly if one chooses to look behind open locker doors or into obscure corners.

With regard to behavior at a school-sponsored activity, "tight embrace" accurately characterizes the way most couples danced to slow music at the Student Council-sponsored dance I attended. Most couples danced with the male's arms linked around female's waist, her arms linked around his neck, bodies pressed together. A much smaller number of couples (mostly freshmen) had their arms around each other in the same way but maintained a distance of about six inches between their bodies. Although there were several adult chaperones (administrator, teachers, and parents), I saw none of them approach students about the inappropriateness of these "displays."

Sexual Language

Although specific instances of students' contesting adult versions of acceptable sexual language will be documented more fully in later chapters, it is clearly not confined to the sex education classroom. In their verbal exchanges with each other throughout the school, I daily heard students use language that their parents and school personnel would probably have found objectionable, including frequent use of "fuckin'" as both adjective and verb. It was not uncommon, however, for a student to stop in midexpletive if he or she realized that I or another adult was within earshot.

Graffiti was, for the most part, absent from the school. Whenever it appeared on furniture or in the rest rooms, it was quickly removed.

The Informal Sexuality Curriculum

On one Friday in midDecember, students were unwittingly given an opportunity to make their language visible in the form of graffiti, without risking charges of vandalism, when the junior class president put up a blank sheet of newsprint on one of the large bulletin boards. It was titled "Junior Wish List" and invited students to write their Christmas wishes. By the following Monday morning, I observed several explicit sexual messages, for instance, "I wanna have sex with all the blonde chicks," "For all the times we did it in the basement when your parents weren't home," "Eat me, (male coach's name)." Some of the messages had been covered with black ink. After school that same Monday, Mr. Gray took down the "Junior Wish List" and replaced it with a glossy poster—"A Student's Guide to Army Benefits."

In contrast, when a similar sexual message was publicly delivered by a male teacher, it was perceived as humorous, not unacceptable. At the gymnastics pep rally, the newly appointed male coach of the girls' team made the following comments while introducing one of the team members:

> Coach: "She competed all around for the first time last night—with me anyway." (Realizing the possible double meaning, he goes on) "Ooh, groan!"
>
> Students and faculty in attendance laugh; some—including Mr. Gray, who is standing in a visible spot with other coaches at the front of the gym—also applaud.
>
> Coach (apparently realizing his "slip" has been well-received): "Yes, she's got some real good tricks—[more laughter]—does some great moves on the floor."
>
> Students and faculty laugh uproariously, and many applaud and hoot.

These everyday language habits at Van Buren, including the remarks of the gymnastics coach that were applauded rather than challenged by several hundred staff and students, illustrate the omnipresence of one form of sexual harassment. As is the case in the wider society, these taken-for-granted communication forms reflect a power structure preoccupied with sexuality and sexual domination (Linn et al., 1992, pp. 108–9).

Student Gender Codes in School Ritual

In addition to employing their own versions of physical affection and sexual language on an informal basis, students at Van Buren witness and enact dominant cultural forms of gender relations as they participate in the "expressive order" of the school. According to Bernstein, this expressive order "controls the transmission of the beliefs and moral system" of the school and is frequently conveyed in such rituals as assemblies and extracurricular activities (1977, p. 55). These rituals contain messages that are, in Bernstein's words, "highly predictable":

> The messages themselves contain meanings which are highly condensed. Thus, the major meanings in ritual are extraverbal or indirect; for they are not made verbally explicit. (1977, p. 62)

He adds that rituals function simultaneously to bind various participants in the school together in behavior reinforcing the dominant value system of the wider society ("consensual rituals") and to deepen attachments to specific groups within the larger framework ("differentiating rituals"). The Van Buren Homecoming pep rally was an example of this simultaneous function, having both the goal of building school loyalty and grade level identification through competition to determine which grade can yell loudest during the "Battle Cry" cheer, sell the most "spirit links," and build the best float.

Official school ideology is imparted through these rituals; however, as the informal cultural productions of students interact with official ideology during school rituals, contradictions to official ideology can also emerge. Since students are members of various other broad social groups (class, race, gender), the imposition of grade level as a primary school category can create conflict for some students. For example, before the pep rally began, I saw one of the black students from the ninth-grade health class dancing with two other black young women in front of the section where freshmen traditionally sit. About fifteen minutes later, I noticed that all three of them had moved to join about twenty other African-American students sitting between the sections of juniors and seniors. As the two black football players are introduced, the students in this "minisection" jump up and cheer wildly; one of the black players raises a fist to the group in acknowledgment. However, when an assistant principal announces that the "Battle Cry" competition will be next, members of the African-American group join their respective grade levels (as do band members, athletes, cheerleaders and others). Thus, these students of color demonstrate both accommodation and resistance to the group identity imposed by official school ideology.[3]

Similarly, black students would congregate at the few tables and chairs in the middle of the Commons area rather than the traditional grade level corners. An incident arose at the end of the semester when a group of these students decided to occupy the freshman corner in response to vandalism of a Martin Luther King commemorative bulletin board put up by the Human Relations Club. Rumors of black students having weapons began to circulate, and administrators, male teachers, and plainclothes police monitored the Commons on the day designated for the takeover. Freshmen continued to occupy their corner, and no violence occurred; however, the black student who was a central promoter of the effort was suspended for three days. He was reinstated after his parents met with school officials, and he subsequently wrote an article on Black History Month that was featured as the lead story in the February issue of the school newspaper. The effects of this incident on Mrs. Warren and one of the African-American young women in her class will also be detailed in Chapter 5.

Because the overall planning and supervision of the rituals I observed at Van Buren were done by adults, their messages can be understood, for the most part, as school ideology. Nevertheless, some aspects that were planned and/or controlled by students can be regarded as representative of informal student culture. It should be noted that informal student culture is not always visible to the outside observer of ritual. For example, at the Homecoming pep rally, winners of the election for Homecoming Court (all white) were revealed. Names were announced in pairs, with the male name first. Each young man was then given a brief verse to read about the young woman whose name he revealed at the end. Finally, he presented a carnation to the young woman. All six "couples" gave each other a hug and kiss as the carnation was presented, reinforcing the notion of heterosexual "coupleness." Later, I overheard one of the young women tell a friend that she "didn't even know the guy" but kissed him anyway. Furthermore, in contrast to the couples image, I heard the father of one of the young women tell a teacher that five of the six female court members do not have a date to the Homecoming dance that evening, and they're considering going together to make a "social statement."

In addition to the events already mentioned, I observed several other assemblies and extracurricular activities at Van Buren. These included the Homecoming musical variety show and parade, talent show, and three additional pep rallies. In general, a traditional stratified gender code, with women relegated to positions subordinate to men and judged on different criteria, was clearly visible in the structure and content of these events. More specifically, according to this code, young women are primarily defined by their appearance and sexuality, while young men are defined more by their accomplishments. Thus, female "poms" and cheerleaders (all white and the most popular and prestigious group of young women at Van Buren) serve a decorative and supportive function for mostly male athletes during pep rallies and athletic events. They are dismissed from class fifteen minutes before the pep rallies, at which time they converge on the girls' locker room with curling irons, hair spray, and makeup to prepare themselves for this role. During pep rallies they dance and cheer, lining up in front of the male teams to salute them or (in keeping with traditional female domesticity) to present them with a large decorated cake. Although female athletes are introduced at pep rallies, they are not accorded these honors. In addition, at the first pep rally the inherent female frailty of the "poms" is emphasized by the football coach in acknowledging their hard work during the summer in preparation for state level competition, at which they won top honors for originality and execution. He says to the audience, "Do you know what's the first thing they do [at practice]? They take 'Fem-Iron plus Minerals' and then they go to work."

Pep Rally Routines

The "poms" work out their own choreography with minimal adult supervision and, although the routines clearly incorporate some vigorous and athletic elements, sexuality is a major component. For example, one pep rally routine begins with the young women (in pleated miniskirts and sweaters) lying on their backs on the floor, feet pointing to the center of a circle formed by their bodies. They slowly rise to an inclined plane, with feet on the floor and pelvises thrust upward; at this point clapping and whistling from males in the audience begins. Gyrating hips, as well as bumps and grinds, are a significant part of the rest of the routine; male voices calling "wiggle it" and whistles frequently accompany these moves. The fact that poms prepare their own routines and obviously enjoy this audience response suggests that this emphasis on sexuality is not imposed on them. Instead, considered in the light of Angela McRobbie's research (1978), it may be one way these young women contest their previously described decorative and frail female role. McRobbie sees this accentuation of female sexuality as an oppositional cultural form that challenges the traditional and unexciting lives that young working-class women in England observe in the older women they know. However, given their own material realities, they realize that marriage is an economic necessity for them. Thus, they achieve some degree of power over the behavior of male peers by emphasizing their own sexuality. Nevertheless, they are sexually exploited by the young men, and their actively constructed "culture of femininity" (as McRobbie labels it) ultimately reproduces the limitations already inherent in their gender and economic roles.

Different criteria for athletic performance on the basis of gender is visible at the gymnastics pep rally, where several male and female gymnasts (all white) demonstrate their skills. In general, the young men's routines could be characterized as strong and vigorous, and the young women's as graceful and sexy. In keeping with the tone set by the previously described introduction, whistles and "whoo-whoo's" from males in the audience accompany the female performances, some of which are done to slow music; both males and females applaud male efforts, which are not done to music. Furthermore, female gymnasts regularly get assistance (a hand at the small of their backs during back bends) from the male coaches while male gymnasts do not.

In spite of the honor accorded the pom-pom squad at state competitions, the group seems to be valued less as actual representatives of Van Buren than male athletes—particularly those in the most prestigious sports of football and basketball. Thus, male athletes in these sports are not merely representatives of the school, they *are* the Van Buren "Vikings," as conveyed by the coach's introduction of the football tri-captains: "the biggest Viking of them all," "the strongest and stubbiest of all the Vikings," "the meanest and best-looking of all the Vikings." Although their appearance, e.g., "big"/"good-looking," is also part of the introduction of these young men, it is situated in the wider context of their football skills rather than functioning as a primary definition. Furthermore, cheers and applause for male individual athletes and teams are always louder than for females at the pep rallies I observed.

Homecoming Variety Show

The Homecoming musical variety show, one of the most important and well-attended assemblies of the year,[4] offers further evidence of a dominant gender code in which young women are primarily valued for their attractive appearance and sexualized performances. About 180 students are involved in the production, with females comprising about 80 percent of the cast (only two young women of color were visible). These students (particularly the young women) are among the most popular in the school; they get good grades and participate in a variety of other extracurricular activities, including many who are "poms" and cheerleaders. With the exception of one football player, male athletes did not perform in this event. Furthermore, at the two school-time performances I observed, the football team sat together in a visible and noisy group, prompting me to wonder to what degree they and the largely female cast regard the show as a performance *for* these athletes.

Music selection and overall direction of the show is done by Mr. Handel, the vocal music teacher, who puts considerable effort and after-school time into this endeavor. As is the case with pom-pom routines, most of the choreography is done by female students. The student singers and dancers perform in an extremely polished and confident way, and the production is enhanced with professional look-ing sets, special effects, lighting, and colorful costumes. In short, on a technical level it is a most impressive production.

The Homecoming theme, "Back to the Future," is a perfect vehicle for the show's depiction of traditional gender relations prevalent in the 1950s. Such songs and lyrics as "I Am Woman; You Are Man" ("Let's kiss"), "Rock and Roll Party Queen" ("Baby baby, can I be the one to love you with all my might?"), "Summer Lovin'" ("Did he get very far?/Did she put up a fight?"), and "You're the One I want" ("I got chills/they're multiplyin'/I'm losin' control/'cause the power you're supplyin' ") are included in the first section of the program. The songs in this generally upbeat initial segment are accompanied by female disco dance routines. The featured dancers are dressed in tights and leotards and—in my opinion—are both competent and blatantly sexual. This opinion seems to be shared and acknowledged by many males in the audience (especially the football players), who punctuate the performance with whistles and cat calls.

The second segment is more sexually sedate but, for the most part, reinforces stratified and stereotypical gender roles. It features Walt Disney songs, which earn considerable applause but no whistles or shrieks from the audience. During one selection, several young women (dressed in demure long white dresses with ribbons in their hair and holding small stuffed animals) sing "Never Smile at a Crocodile." Meanwhile, a smaller number of young men making fierce faces menac-ingly slither like crocodiles from the edges of the stage to surround the helpless and childlike young women. The young women begin to sing (in increasingly high-pitched and frightened voices) and to move with tiny steps to the middle of the stage to get away from the croco-diles. At the end of the song, the young women are completely sur-rounded; the crocodiles lunge toward the singers, who shriek, drop their stuffed animals, and mince offstage.

The next selection, a rendition of "Someday My Prince Will Come," seems to simultaneously poke fun at and reinforce traditional gender arrangements. The song is sung by a group of young women while the former crocodiles—minus their fierce faces—watch them from an elevated position on risers at the back of the stage. As they finish singing, a slight dark-haired young man appears at the top of the risers and begins to walk toward the singers, smiling and fluffing his curls (in a way that reminds both another female teacher and me of Michael Jackson). He blows an exaggerated kiss to the singers, and they all fall to the floor in a swoon. This selection garners howls of laughter and wild applause from the audience. Even less stereotypical but stimulating less applause, an all-female chorus sings a selection from "Mary Poppins" that centers around women's suffrage and contains the lines: "We're soldiers in petticoats/We adore men individually/But as a group they're rather stupid."

Immediately after the Walt Disney segment (as the strains of "Bippity-Boppity-Boo" are fading), the scene changes dramatically for the final disco number—"Red Light, Hard Night." The stage is dark except for red strobe lights, and whistles and long shrieks begin as the red lights reveal female dancers in flashy disco leotards and tights. As in the first segment of the performance, the dancing is obviously sexual and punctuated by whistles and cat calls. Lyrics to this song describe females competing for a man: "Worked so hard to get me a man/Don't try to take him away/I don't want you hangin' around/My man is too hard to hold/If you plan to, I'm stoppin' you cold."

Thus, while a traditional code portraying stereotypic gender arrangements is clearly visible in the structure and content of the variety show, this code is also contested—particularly in the sexually emphatic choreography by female students, which contradicts dominant school ideology. While this blatant assertion of sexuality does challenge the image of a frail, submissive female, it reinforces female identification primarily on the basis of sexuality rather than achievement.

Faculty Gender Relations

Faculty gender relations are another aspect of the day-to-day school terrain upon which the sex education class I observed is situated. Both Mrs. Warren and her students experience hierarchical gender arrangements as part of everyday lived culture at Van Buren. In the following sections I shall describe these gender arrangements and the conflict that emerges among staff, particularly around their divergent perceptions of sexual abuse and assault as distinguished from "horse-play" in student interactions. Finally, because race is an integral part of administrators' discourse on this issue, I will discuss how racial dynamics work their way through such situations.

Men are clearly in charge at Van Buren, with women involved more frequently in support roles. All four principals and most department heads are male. Staff is about 60 percent female and 40 percent male, with women clustered in traditionally feminine or nurturing fields such as special education, business education, social work and counseling, and home economics. Men are clustered in more technical fields as science and mathematics. All clerical staff are female, while nearly all coaches (including those involved with women's sports) are male. One notable exception is the female coach of boys' volleyball, whose team won the state championship that year.

These structural arrangements exist beneath a surface atmosphere of collegial congeniality and good humor. Nevertheless, underlying tensions and anger regarding gender issues occasionally erupted through the apparently collegial informal interactions I observed in the lunch room and at faculty meetings.[5] The most visible of these centered around "Women's Week," an annual event coordinated for the last several years by a group of primarily female staff, who might be generally described as having some degree of feminist awareness, and officially supported by the Van Buren administration. During the week, all teachers are encouraged to take their classes to a series of films, displays, and speakers from the community on such topics as changing male/female roles, educational equity, sexual abuse and assault, women's history, and so forth. I heard early in the year from several sources that many male staff denigrate "Women's Week" as "just another flaming feminist" event.

The perception was partially validated in mid-semester, when a male teacher sent a "humorous" four-page typed memo to one of the assistant principals. The teacher requested equal time for "Men's Week," listing such potential topics as: "Barefoot and Pregnant—A Success Story," "Where to Buy Those Kickin' Boots," "Hiring a Teenage Maid—a Primer," "Reasons for Male Superiority," and "Getting the Most Out of Your Inflatable." As copies of the memo began to circulate throughout the school, a few female teachers who had been involved in "Women's Week" and were most visible as feminists made their objections known privately to Mr. Gray and publicly at a faculty meeting. Angry verbal tirades occurred from both sides (males who saw the memo as a joke and female feminists who saw it as an intolerable insult). However, the visibly angry women seemed to be judged most harshly by their peers, and the predominant staff feeling appeared to be, "Can't you feminists take a joke?"

Mr. Gray's role in this situation was (in the words of one teacher) to "keep everybody happy—good ole boys and feminists—" and to smooth over the conflict by stressing mutual tolerance and inclusive *human* relations that transcend gender. He later told one of the Women's Week organizers to remove a sticker from her door that said, "Pornography Free Zone: Women and Children Are Safe Here," on the grounds that it was divisive in its exclusion of men. In a subsequent discussion with Mr. Gray (during which this incident was not mentioned by either of us), he described similar staff divisions regarding the dynamics of sexual abuse and assault among students. He says that some staff are "very involved and get violently angry about it," while a "small segment think it's laughable." Furthermore, he recognizes a need to sensitize staff to this "educational problem" and offers the following analysis of its underlying dynamics:

> Implicit in this whole thing is the idea that girls—especially girls—*can* say "no," that they don't have to take the kind of mauling they take because they think that's what being a girl is.

Although he does not address mutuality of responsibility (the young man must actually stop when the young woman sets limits), he does take the issue seriously enough to have arranged a brief (thirty-minute) presentation to staff that focused mainly on legal definitions of sexual assault and their responsibility to report it. The broader concept of sexual harassment and the fact that it constitutes sex discrimination under Title VII of the Civil Rights Act of 1964 (amended 1972), Title IX of the Education Amendments of 1972, and state statutes was not addressed at the in-service. Nor did school personnel bring up the concept of sexual harassment during my other interactions with them, including discussions of the "Men's Week" memo. At the time, the Woodland District Gender Equity Committee was in the process of developing informational brochures for staff and students and planning mandatory inservices for district staff, which were subsequently required yearly for those newly hired. Hopefully, there is now greater awareness of the concept, and situations such as those described in this chapter might be recognized and challenged as forms of sexual harassment.

My observations at the after-school presentation suggest that the segment of staff who do not take sexual harassment seriously may not be so small as Mr. Gray believes. For example, a woman teacher asked the presenter to clarify what body parts are included in the legal definition of fourth degree sexual assault. The presenter answered, "Buttocks, genitals, and breasts," to which the woman responded with another question, "Not kissing?" At this point a male staff person called out, "Not unless they're doing it right," and a large contingent of males in the room laughed heartily. After the session, I heard several male teachers making jokes with each other ("Let's turn out the lights; we're all going to experiment," "You better watch out or I'll report you," etc.). Nevertheless, although their various analyses of the nature of this problem may differ, the majority of Van Buren staff at the presentation seem to regard sexual abuse/assault as a serious issue, including some whose primary concern is protecting students from erroneous accusation. Many voiced a need for more time and information on the topic during and after the brief inservice.

Next, I shall delineate the impact of staff gender relations and these divergent perceptions on the issue of fourth degree sexual assault as it is distinguished from simple "horseplay" in the day-to-day life of Van Buren students. I shall also demonstrate how racial dynamics work their way through these situations.

"Horseplay" or Sexual Assault?

Differentiating between student "horseplay" and sexual assault is another aspect of monitoring student behavior at Van Buren. Fourth degree sexual assault is defined by state law to include nonconsensual sexual contact. Specifically, in the state in which Woodland is located, it involves:

> any intentional touching . . . either directly or through clothing by the use of any body part or object, of complainant's or defendant's intimate parts if that intentional touching is either for the purpose of sexually degrading; or for the purpose of sexually humiliating the complainant or sexually arousing or gratifying the defendant or if the touching contains the elements of actual or attempted battery.

Nearly every day I was present at Van Buren, I saw instances of a young man "playfully" overpowering a young woman—pulling her onto his lap or against him, pushing/pulling her down a hallway, while she "playfully" resisted, saying "Stop it" (usually with a smile or laugh)

51

or pushing him away. It was difficult to determine whether such contact was nonconsensual. For a small number of staff at Van Buren (primarily women who consider themselves feminists) and for me, such behavior cannot be assumed to be mutual fun. Instead, it may represent part of a continuum of sexual and gender-based harassment, ranging from subtle to overt, which Bogart et al. describe as a matrix of actions that may be both verbal or nonverbal and exert psychological or physical control:

> Sexual and gender-based harassment may involve *overt* actions as extreme as physical threats, sexual assault, and rape, as well as *subtle* interactions that communicate condescension, hostility, or invisibility. Harassment may be expressed in *verbal* comments, jokes, innuendoes of a sexual nature, as well as in *nonverbal* communications such as suggestive looks or [un]wanted touching. *Psychological* as well as *physical* in its power over others, sexual and gender harassment may exert control through disapproval or rejection as well as through the use of physical strength to overcome or subdue an individual. (1992, p. 194)

Feminist staff with whom I talked expressed greater willingness to intervene in this more subtle "playful" overpowering, especially (in the words of one) "if it is prolonged," than the administrators I interviewed, for whom it seemed more likely to represent "horseplay."

During the semester I was at Van Buren, a relationship between two white students re-erupted into violence at school (the young man had been suspended the previous year for a similar incident). Both incidents were clearly not "horseplay." In the most recent, he spit on her, shoved her against a wall, and hit her; she also hit him. Her wrist was sprained during the altercation. School counselors as well as community agencies became involved in the incident, and both students were suspended—he for two days and she for one.

Racial Dynamics

Without solicitation from me, both administrators I interviewed (Mr. Gray and Mr. Brunswick) brought up the issue of race in their discussion of appropriate and potentially abusive sexual behavior. Based on their remarks, it would seem that a given situation would be less likely to be perceived by them as "horseplay" when the couple is interracial.

Mr. Gray asserts that interracial couples (these consist mainly of black male and white female at Van Buren) tend to be "more visible" in this regard, a remark that illustrates how various forms of status (in this instance race) interact with gender to heighten the perceived vulnerability of some individuals (Linn, et al., 1992). He says that nearly every fight involving the two racial groups grows out of such relationships and cites other problems: the young woman's parents "can't cope with it," she begins to cut herself off from the rest of the population, and usually she is not doing well in school. The Minority Services Coordinator sees these relationships as problematic in a different way; black young women are "left out" when black males date white females, since white males at Van Buren do not date them.

Mr. Brunswick estimates about six incidents a year arising from relationships between black males and white females, perceiving a particular "psyche" (the black male's sense of property rights over a woman) that can result in abusive behavior. He acknowledges the conflict that such situations generate for the four white male administrators and describes a recent incident that ended in suspension for the black male student involved. After observing the young man "grabbing and shoving" the young woman and "rushing her down the hall," Mr. Brunswick says he told the male student to stop and come to his office. The student then told Mr. Brunswick he had no right to interfere in this private matter between him and "his woman." When Mr. Brunswick persisted, the student shoved him, and Mr. Brunswick called the police. The student was subsequently suspended and his father required to come before he was readmitted. The young woman was only "warned" because, according to Mr. Brunswick, "her behavior was not the problem."

A different version of the incident was offered to me by another staff person, who perceived that insensitivity to cultural differences and racism were factors in the black student's suspension. This person's perception was that Mr. Brunswick initially confronted the student for simply "talking with his girlfriend." While the "truth" of this encounter cannot be ascertained, it does illustrate the complex and potentially volatile interactions among race, gender roles, and sexuality.

In this chapter I have described the community, district, and school contexts within which Mrs. Warren's health education class is situated, with particular emphasis on the sexual values and gender relations of the community and school. In Chapter 3, I shall describe Mrs. Warren, the institutional arrangements that affect her classroom teaching, and her active negotiation of contradictory gender expectations and organizational constraints.

3

Mrs. Warren's Working Conditions: "Runnin' on Empty"

"It would be nice to be recognized as a health teacher and that I'm important from some other teacher in the school, but it's—like, phy ed takes care of study hall—you know—shit jobs. That's the way they look on a lot of us. We're phy ed people, and health is phy ed. . . . so it's not important."—Mrs. Warren

"I'm always behind and rushing around; I'm runnin' on empty."—Mrs. Warren

The concept of teaching as a labor process has been explored by Michael Apple (1983) and will provide helpful background for this discussion of Mrs. Warren, her working conditions, and their effect on the sexuality curriculum-in-use. In his analysis, Apple describes the steady encroachment of technical control procedures on teachers' work, a process related to the role of the state during economic and ideological crisis, the interests of capital, and the male-dominated gender relations typical of education. The needs of industry for technical knowledge and suitably trained personnel has resulted in more power for those in technical and middlemanagement positions, reassertion of academic dominance in the curriculum, and a restructuring and loss of autonomy in teachers' work over the past two decades. More specifically, in a long and steadily increasing process, more "efficient" technical control procedures—reductive behaviorally-based curricula, prespecified objectives, curricular packages prepared by "experts" outside the classroom—have been instituted. This has been accompanied by labor "intensification," defined as a "chronic sense of work overload that has manifested over time" (Apple, 1983, p. 618). Thus, the everyday practice of the largely female work force in education has been altered, and Apple argues that gender is a significant but often overlooked factor in this. Nevertheless, he asserts that teachers have not accepted such encroachments passively but have resisted at a cultural level, sometimes with contradictory outcomes. These broad concepts (teaching as a gendered labor process, restructuring of teachers' work, labor intensification, cultural resistance, and contradictory outcomes) provide reference points for analyzing Mrs. Warren's work life at Van Buren and its connection to the sexuality curriculum-in-use.

Also relevant is research by Linda McNeil (1986), which demonstrates how the administrative context of schools mediates and transforms classroom knowledge. She maintains that dominant forms of school organization (which began early in this century when schools were rationalized more explicitly as a means of social control) split administrative personnel from teachers and subordinate educative ideals to efficiency and control. Her comparative analysis of four secondary schools reveals that the higher priority a particular administration gave to maintaining a "smooth running" school, the less it focused on and rewarded the quality of classroom instruction. Nevertheless, as long as procedural standards were met, teachers in such settings had considerable authority over subject matter content. Given an administrative value on efficiency and discipline, teachers observed by McNeil experienced a tension between managerial and educational ideals. They actively negotiated their own best interests, acquiescing to administrative priorities yet simultaneously resisting this erosion of classroom autonomy, and they exerted greater classroom control on students by engaging in what McNeil calls "defensive teaching." That is, they selected mostly noncontroversial topics, presented easily transmitted and graded fragments of technical details, limited student discussion, and required little written work. McNeil conceptualizes such teaching as a logical outcome of school organization rather than a failure of planning, lack of training, or political position of an individual teacher.

One ramification of defensive teaching identified by McNeil is the transformation of rich, complex and relevant "real-world" knowledge into bland, oversimplified and irrelevant "school" knowledge. This knowledge alienated students and led to their creation of oppositional knowledge forms, which prompted further defensive teaching. Defensive teaching also generated a contradictory outcome for teachers. In negotiating the organizational demands of the school, their expressed pedagogical ideals (discussion, in-depth inquiry, and so on) were split off from what actually occurred in the classroom, while their training, experience, and knowledge were reduced to simplified content.

With these concepts in mind, I shall document in this chapter the specific, yet largely invisible and taken-for-granted institutional arrangements that affect Mrs. Warren's classroom teaching. These include requirement of ninth-grade health instruction for graduation; a long and ever-expanding district syllabus; location of the health class within physical education, with alternate classroom/activity sessions; a fragmented, heavy teaching schedule; and a hierarchical, male-dominated school and department power structure. I shall then describe Mrs. Warren herself, including her familial roles as wife and mother. I shall assert that conditions in her workplace, along with her gendered status, result in a non-nurturing work environment and chronic work overload.

Woodland District Health Education

One-half credit of health education is a requirement for high school graduation in the state where Woodland is located, and the district conforms to this requirement by offering a full-semester course at the ninth-grade level. This course is part of an interdisciplinary K–12 health education program that conceptualizes learning experiences for students into seven interrelated "curriculum strands" (physical health, community and environmental health, nutrition, mental and emotional health, human sexuality, personal safety and emergency care, alcohol and other drugs) that are derived from five overall health-related goals.[1] These curriculum strands and goals provide the framework around which the official curriculum of the ninth-grade health course is organized. Furthermore, Woodland District places great emphasis on involving teachers in curricular decisions that affect them, including curriculum development, textbook and audiovisual selection, and so on. The three members of the Van Buren health staff were active in the ongoing health and physical education evaluation process, including that year's revision of comprehensive and specific K–12 student behavioral objectives.[2] Mrs. Warren worked on the alcohol and other drugs, "healthy lifestyles," mental health, and nutrition content committees; she was asked to be part of the overall evaluation committee but declined.

District Syllabus

Woodland's ninth-grade health courses are divided into alternate-day activity and classroom sessions. The physical activity component encompasses eleven objectives that emphasize cardiorespiratory fitness and includes swimming, jogging, biking (optional with jogging) and weight training. The classroom components (making up 50 to 60 percent of total course time) encompass sixty-seven objectives in the following areas: "healthy lifestyles, physical fitness, nutrition, personal safety/emergency care, human sexuality, mental health, substance use and abuse." Mr. Cox, Woodland District's coordinator of health and physical education, described these to teachers as "fundamental topic areas addressed by all schools—possibly with varying amounts of time."

Mr. Brunswick, the assistant principal who supervises health and physical education and also serves on the district health education evaluation committee, says that the health education objectives "encourage consistency across the program" while permitting individual teachers to work "from their strengths." Thus, one teacher at another high school spends considerably more time on first aid and less on sexuality than most, while another incorporates coverage of chewing tobacco. In terms of comprehensiveness ("spectrum of topics, in-depthness, and balance"), Mr. Cox regards Van Buren as one of two top quality health education programs in the district, an assessment shared by other ninth-grade health teachers. While Mrs. Warren takes the lengthy syllabus seriously, she says she can only "touch on" most of the topics if she is to "get through" all the objectives.

In response to new health-related information or concerns in the community, district administration sometimes recommends additional items for inclusion. Sexual assault, AIDS, and suicide were three such topics that Mrs. Warren felt obliged (because she took her role as leader of the Van Buren health team and meeting district objectives seriously) to incorporate into the curriculum the semester I observed. More specifically, with regard to sexual assault, Mr. Cox sent a memo to all ninth-grade health teachers, saying that incidents of student sexually abusive behavior appeared to be increasing in Woodland schools. He enclosed a copy of legal definitions of varying degrees of sexual assault and urged them to explain legal consequences of such behavior as follows:

> Though all of you cover sexual assault in your classes, few talk about the law—especially as it defines fourth degree sexual assault. Students need to know the legal consequences of such behavior, and what their rights are. The ninth-grade health curriculum needs to accommodate this need.
>
> If you would like information about community resources available to help with this in the classroom, call me.

Mrs. Warren took this memo seriously but felt she was the only one of the three health teachers who did, telling me, "I'm the only one who feels this. It's all on my shoulders." Mrs. Warren's actual coverage of the topic involved laws and a newspaper clipping about previous incidents in Woodland schools.

> Ed knows that I will do what he says, and I will try my best to present it as best I can to the kids. . . . We'll attempt to do the job we're supposed to be doing and keep all of this new stuff in the program and keep all the old stuff going.

Nevertheless, she did tell Mr. Cox and other district health teachers at a meeting that "there's no way to get this in without cutting [other topics]."

Human Sexuality Objectives

The overall human sexuality goal, as stated in the official district ninth-grade health curriculum, is to help students understand the basic characteristics of human growth and development from conception to death and learn to make informed and responsible sexual decisions. Broad topic areas include: (1) Relationships and Lifestyles; (2) Reproductive Anatomy and Sexual Function; (3) Emotional Development; (4) Responsible Decision Making; (5) Family; (6) Sexually Transmitted Diseases; (7) Issues; (8) Family Planning. Specific student behavioral objectives are as follows:

1. examine values and other factors in choosing friends, dating partners and potential mates;

2. be accepting of an individual whose sexual orientation differs from his/her own;
3. use appropriate terminology to describe reproductive anatomy and physiology;
4. describe the menstrual cycle, conception, fetal development and birth;
5. recognize how characteristics are transmitted genetically including such birth abnormalities as Down's Syndrome, Sickle Cell Anemia, Tay-Sachs Disease, Cystic Fibrosis;
6. recognize and practice appropriate reproductive hygiene and health care, e.g., breast self-exam, testicular self-exam;
7. accept the importance of regular medical examination of the reproductive system and know the procedures used;
8. recognize parents as an important source of information and support regarding adolescent sexual development;
9. recognize that mature love and sexual expression is based on mutual trust, responsibility and encouragement of both persons to develop fully as individuals;
10. analyze the responsibilities of parenthood and the skills needed for parenting;
11. acknowledge and respect an individual's right to say "no" in situations involving sexual decisions;
12. know that conception can generally be prevented by various birth control methods;
13. recognize the signs and symptoms of pregnancy and identify community resources for pregnancy testing;
14. identify the signs, symptoms and treatment of the prevalent sexually transmitted diseases;
15. describe how both sexes become disadvantaged when sex role stereotyping is part of behavior;
16. recognize various sexual lifestyles alternatives encountered in contemporary society; and
17. recognize the economic and social consequences of teen-age pregnancy.

These objectives were last reviewed by teachers four years earlier and revised as part of the previously described evaluation process.

Although a lengthy critique of the process is not warranted here, it is important to comment that this widely used technical and positivistic approach to curricular planning and evaluation has been criticized for its linkage to ongoing control by dominant social and economic groups

(Apple, 1979). Among other criticisms, Apple asserts that reducing complex human cognitions and feelings to abbreviated behavioral specifications "substitutes the slogan of manipulation for the awesome task of making moral choices" (p. 111). Furthermore, conceptualizing curricular decision making as a technical problem to be solved by rational procedures obscures the political and ethical nature of the decisions as well as the ambiguity, uncertainty, and conflict inherent in the process.

As a participant in the working group that developed the original human sexuality objectives, I can attest to vigorous argument as individuals with vastly different life experiences and values tried to reach consensus about what information is essential for young people of varying ages to know about sexuality and what constitutes "informed and responsible sexual decisions," one of the district's overall goals for health education. At the end of the process, we did not agree on the issues; nevertheless, we had completed our assignment of constructing several objectives that were more or less acceptable to all members of the group. These objectives were then considered by an entirely different group—the Health Education Evaluation Committee—in which no one from the sexuality content committee was included, and they were further debated; in the neutral language of the final intent document, the objectives were "distilled." Furthermore, as the district health coordinator, Mr. Cox, explained to members of the various content committees assembled to see the final document, the evaluation committee was faced with the dilemma of making the intent document "manageable and readable," by selecting only a small number of objectives—"a trade-off between readability and specificity." In fact, the evaluation committee's selection of key objectives so vastly altered, both in spirit and substance, the human sexuality content committee's consensus that two original committee members (myself included) successfully argued with Mr. Cox and the head of the evaluation committee that the original focus should be reinstated if the process was to have substantive meaning. As this brief chronology suggests, the district's neutral description fails to illuminate the complexity, conflict, and politics of this so-called objective process.

Finally, although the official district sexuality curriculum encompasses grades K–12, the reality is that as the focal point of the district's sex education efforts, ninth-grade health has been the only required course in which teachers in all schools across the city actually teach toward the stated objectives. Because classes at lower grade levels receive less emphasis and their coverage of sexuality information is inconsistent across schools, students enter the ninth-grade health classes with a wide range of classroom sex education experience and knowledge levels.

Ninth-Grade Health at Van Buren

Health within Physical Education

Like other high schools in the district (and many across the country), Van Buren's health education program is part of the physical education department. Altogether, six full-time members of the department (three men and three women) teach nearly fifty classes per week, over twice as many classes and students as most other Van Buren teachers. These include eight in freshman health, eight in freshman physical education, thirteen in sophomore physical education, eight "adaptive" classes for special education students, and nineteen electives (general junior and senior level classes as well as specialized classes like weight training, basketball, aerobics, lifesaving, and so on). Although health classes meet daily, physical education classes are scheduled on an odd-even calendar date basis. For instance, Mrs. Warren teaches an eleventh/twelfth-grade class during fifth period on odd-numbered dates and teaches a ninth-grade class during the same period on even-numbered dates.

Low Status

Although they appreciate the excellent physical education facilities and acknowledge ongoing administrative support at Van Buren, Mrs. Warren and the physical education staff I interviewed also perceive their curricular area to have lower status than academics at Van Buren. Teaching large numbers of classes and students (with class size approaching forty in the afternoon, a fact Mrs. Warren attributes to academic department heads scheduling most of their classes in the morning), having to give up classrooms for special academic testing, and having parents and other teachers question the worth of required physical education courses are cited as evidence of this lower status. In the words of one physical education department member: "In physical education there's nothing you can do about it because academics do come first."

Mrs. Warren also reports that she feels a lack of respect from teachers of higher-status subjects:

Mrs. Warren's Working Conditions

It would be nice to be recognized as a health teacher and that
I'm important from some other teacher in the school, but it's—
like, phy ed takes care of study hall—you know—shit jobs.
That's the way they look on a lot of us. We're phy ed people,
and health is phy ed so it's not important. [Other teachers
think] you just got lucky, and it had to be a required class.

She believes that the informality of her usual attire (athletic shoes,
shorts, sweat pants, T-shirt) when teaching physical education and
interactions with students are elements in other teachers' perceptions
of her:

The teachers—a lot of them—think that I'm a little person and
I'm not acting my age because of the way I dress and the way I
am with the kids. . . . There's a lot of old fogies that don't like
some of the stuff I do.

She takes pride in her difference from "lots of traditional physical
education teachers who sit there and watch" but don't participate in
the activities and says, "I don't really care what they [other teachers]
think." Nevertheless, sometimes being perceived as "a little person"
by other teachers seems to bother her. For example, there was a note
of sadness in her voice when she told me about the following incident:

Mrs. Jones stopped me the other day when I was in running
clothes and said, "You look just like a little kid." I didn't
know if it was a compliment. I kinda felt bad. I'm a human being and a woman. . . . I don't really want another image, but—
[she stops in midsentence and looks away].

Possibly to better convey the image of "grown-up" classroom teachers,
all three health teachers (Mrs. Warren, Mrs. Crocker, and Mr. Austin)
dress more formally for classroom days. The women wear skirts, dressy
slacks, nylons, and so on (although Mrs. Warren says she doesn't
"have the money to go out and buy suits and heels and nylons and
look like fancy Mrs. Jones"), and Mr. Austin wears a dress shirt and
tie.

Fragmented and Heavy Teaching Schedule

Mrs. Warren teaches three health classes daily, alternating classroom
and activity sessions (periods 2–4); an eleventh/twelfth-grade physical

education class (period 5 on odd-numbered days); a ninth-grade physical education class (period 5 on even-numbered days); an adaptive class for special education students that she coteaches with Mrs. Crocker (period 6 on odd-numbered days); and a tenth-grade physical education class (period 7 on even-numbered days). Altogether, she met with about 225 students per week during the semester I observed. This large number of classes and students contributed to a fragmented and rushed teaching day as well as making classroom control more difficult (Mrs. Warren says class size—nearly forty for afternoon classes—is the single largest factor in control problems). Furthermore, when asked about what she would like to change about her teaching situation, she listed having fewer different classes and not teaching the adaptive class (for which she is not certified but coteaches with Mrs. Crocker, who is).

I understood more fully the impact of such a diverse and heavy schedule after accompanying Mrs. Warren for two full days through both an odd- and even-numbered day. It was a fast-paced exercise in fragmentation—a dizzying kaleidoscope of requests and questions from students and other teachers, cumbersome physical activity equipment and teaching paraphernalia, constant incidental interruptions, and noise (student locker-room conversation, laughter, shouting, boom box, bouncing balls, thwacking hockey sticks. The ten-minute reading break was the only silent period of the day, although Mrs. Warren spotted three students illegally in the hallway and used part of the time to escort them to the main office.

Even Mrs. Warren's preparation periods (period 1 daily, period 6 on even-numbered days and period 7 on odd-numbered days) were filled with constant noise and interruption, partly because of the location of her office, (which she shares with Mrs. Crocker), in the girls' locker room (since she also shared classroom space with other teachers, this was not available during preparation periods). On one of the full days I spent with her, Mrs. Warren used these two periods to grade exams, give makeup exams (written and swimming), review physical agility scores, call the nurse to check on an injured student, search for a video, look through records of adaptive students, call a sporting goods company about purchasing cross-country ski equipment for next semester's classes, help another teacher put up an archery net, respond to a guidance counselor's request for information about a student from four years before (going back through drawers of old records), confer with Mrs. Crocker (in person) and Mr. Austin (by phone) about a health filmstrip for the next day, eat a quick lunch and snacks, use the bathroom, fill out attendance cards and take them to the office, check in with her children, and talk with me. At the end of the day just outlined, Mrs. Warren attended a faculty meeting, which included (as listed in the daily bulletin) "a presentation on policy and responsibilities relating to child abuse," and conferred with Mr. Brunswick about a student. Just before she left the building at 4:30, she realized she had completely forgotten about a 10:00 a.m. meeting.

Clearly, there was little time or space in Mrs. Warren's schedule during most school days for reflective curriculum planning. For example, I was present in her office while she hurriedly prepared to cover sexual assualt, as suggested in the memo from Woodland's health and physical education administrator. In her words, she "got it together twenty-five minutes before class." Before school she had discovered a handout on state sexual assault laws that someone left on the xerox machine, and Mrs. Crocker showed her a newspaper clipping about previous incidents in Woodland schools. After further discussion with Mrs. Crocker and a few questions directed at me, Mrs. Warren spent nine minutes in the classroom that day on sexual assault, mostly reading aloud from the memo, clipping, and handout.

Authority and Gender Relations

At the district level, formal organizational guidelines call for yearly election of a department chairperson by physical education staff at each school, pending the principal's final approval. The chairperson's role according to Mr. Cox, is "facilitator and coordinator—not evaluator." At Van Buren, Mr. Austin has been functioning in this role for the last several years. His primary duties are scheduling classes, ordering equipment, and communicating with Van Buren's administration and the district about department issues. However, when major internal department conflicts arise, teachers seem to look to Van Buren's principal, Mr. Gray, not Mr. Austin, to work them out. As one teacher who consulted Mr. Gray about such a situation explained: "He [Mr. Austin] wouldn't have done a thing. I mean—he doesn't have any authority really. We had to go higher up."

Mrs. Warren and Mrs. Crocker regard Mr. Austin as doing, in the words of one, "an excellent job of making health a priority within physical education," an accomplishment about which Mr. Austin also expresses pride. Thus, Van Buren's physical education facilities (particularly the pool and weight training room) are scheduled around needs of the health classes. All three health teachers have first period available for joint planning, and one male and one female teacher are scheduled back-to-back during a given period to allow locker-room supervision of both sexes during activity days. Finally, classroom sessions are scheduled in a large room separated by a movable divider, so audiovisuals can be shown to both classes at once.

On the other hand, Mrs. Warren and Mrs. Crocker have some criticisms of Mr. Austin's efforts as department chairperson. They believe he does not keep department members adequately informed or solicit their input; for example, no department meetings were held the semester I observed, although (as will be discussed later) major decisions were being made about Van Buren's compliance with Title IX, a 1972 federal law mandating equal opportunity in education. Also, they perceive the teaching schedule Mr. Austin assigned himself as more advantageous than the schedules of other department members, including their own. Specifically, Mr. Austin has two daily planning periods and three preparations—the lowest number of preparations in the department. In contrast, Mrs. Warren has five preparations (including health, physical education, and the adaptive class). Although Mr. Austin told me early in the year it has been his policy for everyone in the department to be involved in teaching *either* health or adaptive physical education, Mrs. Warren and Mrs. Crocker are the only staff who teach both.

As is the case in the wider school milieu, traditional gender roles prevail among members of the Van Buren physical education department. Although they complain among themselves about it, the three women in the department mostly accommodate the men regarding schedules, requests, and so forth; most departmental decisions are made by men. The following are selected examples: (1) Mr. Marine (a long-term department member and successful boys' basketball coach) asks Mrs. Warren during first period to take his seventh-period class that same day because he has a dental appointment. She agrees, although it means teaching for six straight periods before attending an after-school faculty meeting. Later she tells me she wonders why he waited until the last minute if he knew he had the appointment; however, she feels she can't refuse. (2) When I ask why she is teaching an adaptive class for which she is not certified, she replies, "Because I got stuck with it. Mr. Austin asked me to do it, and he knows me well enough to know I wouldn't refuse." (3) Mr. Austin doesn't let Mrs. Warren know she will have to supervise a physical education bike ride because of his absence. The next day, when she asks him why, he tells her, "You'd only worry if you knew." (4) Mr. Austin frequently writes, "See Mrs. Warren" on his substitute orders instead of writing up plans. (5) Mrs. Crocker and Mrs. Warren's adaptive class is disrupted when Mr. Austin's weight training group moves into their part of the gym to have their pictures taken. Mr. Austin does not ask the women for space; he tells them he needs it. They do not protest.

However, Mrs. Crocker and Mrs. Warren find more subtle ways to subvert male authority within the department. For example, on one occasion the principal, Mr. Gray, came into Mrs. Warren's class to ask if she knew where he could find Mr. Marine. She playfully directed him to the gymnastics room, where she knew Mr. Marine frequently took a nap during that period:

> Mr. Gray: (putting an arm over Mrs. Warren's shoulder) "Where's Mr. Marine?"
>
> Mrs. Warren: "Upstairs sleeping, I betcha."
>
> Mr. Gray: "I'm not gonna pay you much if you're right."
>
> Mrs. Warren: "Betcha a quarter."

Mr. Gray leaves and Mrs. Warren turns to me with a grin and says, "Now I'm in trouble."

Female accommodation to male decisions is particularly visible in dynamics surrounding the department's ongoing noncompliance with Title IX in scheduling classes grouped by sex. Similarly, traditional gender assumptions seem to underpin the resolution of a seniority dilemma involving Mr. Austin and Mrs. Warren. Because these situations are important aspects of the context in which Mrs. Warren works and illuminate some of the personal gender assumptions that influence her teaching, I shall briefly describe them.

Title IX. According to Title IX of the Educational Amendments of 1972:

> No person . . . shall on the basis of sex, be excluded from participating in, be denied the benefits of, or be subjected to discrimination under any education program or activity receiving Federal financial assistance.

As applied to treatment of students in physical education classes, compliance with Title IX requires that all instruction and participation be offered on a coed basis, with some allowances made for separate competition in such contact sports as football, wrestling, etc. Separation or sectioning is legal only if done for documentable reasons, such as skill level, that are not based on sex.

According to Mr. Austin, required physical education courses in the ninth grade had traditionally been separated by sex but were first offered on a coed basis at Van Buren during the 1980–81 school year in response to requirements of Title IX. This resulted in problems, particularly with locker-room supervision and different expectations between male teachers and female locker-room supervisors. Mr. Austin says that at the end of that year all teachers in the department wanted to return to same sex classes. Thus, since 1981, Van Buren's required ninth-grade physical education classes have been grouped on the basis of sex; classes are either all-male or all-female and are taught by a department member of the same sex. These classes meet separately but, according to Mr. Austin, students get instruction and practice in the same curriculum—touch football, basketball, soccer, and gymnastics. As chair, he justifies these arrangements to district and school administration on the basis of the previously mentioned contact sports exemption. He asserts that Van Buren meets the "spirit of the law" because the same instruction is offered to both males and females and that such issues as safety, discipline, and staffing are a higher priority than equal opportunity as defined by law. For example, he expresses a concern for safety in gymnastics because boys and girls use separate equipment, and it is more difficult for an instructor to supervise safe procedures on several pieces of equipment at once.

Nevertheless, these arrangements were judged by state and district officials to be in violation of equal opportunity rulings, with Mr. Gray and Mr. Austin both being informed of this finding during the semester I observed at Van Buren.[3] All members of the department, including the women, seem satisfied with current arrangements and largely agree with the assertions put forth by Mr. Austin. In short, they feel that other pragmatic priorities such as safety and discipline are more salient than the equal opportunity ruling; although the women seem somewhat more willing to go along with scheduling coed classes than the men, I never heard any of them argue for the principles behind the ruling. As one of the women said in reference to Title IX, "It's just a technicality." Mr. Marine, on the other hand, is emphatically opposed to coed classes and was both vocal and sarcastic in expressing his opposition (based on his attempt to conduct coed wrestling classes) at a district in-service on Title IX implementation. No teachers spoke in support of Title IX, and no women spoke at all during the in-service.[4]

According to Mrs. Crocker, Mr. Austin's initial response to district notification of noncompliance was to tell her and Mr. Marine to "work something out" about gymnastics; however, Mrs. Crocker and Mrs. Warren felt everyone should be involved in this decision-making process.

Mrs. Warren's Working Conditions

One day while I was in their office, they suggested to Mr. Marine that the department get together to discuss this issue. He responded by telling them not to worry about it for next semester. Furthermore, he said, "We don't have to tell what we do. If we can't do anything, we won't." No department meeting on this (or any other) matter was held during the entire semester, and the women made no further effort to push for one. Toward the end of the semester, Mr. Austin told Mrs. Warren that he had received no pressure from Mr. Gray to change the schedule for the second semester, so the same sex classes would continue.[5]

The Seniority Dilemma. The interaction of Woodland District's curricular organization (with health education as a component of physical education) and Van Buren's traditional gender hierarchy created a complex job retention dilemma involving Mrs. Warren. Specifically, the union contract provides for teachers being surplused (assigned to other schools on a percentage or full-time basis) or laid off, contingent upon school enrollment and based on seniority. However, since teaching health requires different licensure than physical education, there is lack of clarity in the contract about whether physical education seniority applies to health teachers. The following seniority situation existed among the health teachers at Van Buren a year prior to my study: Mrs. Warren, who was certified in health and had been teaching the course since 1976–77, could be considered to have health seniority, while Mr. Austin, who had not obtained health certification but had been teaching the course since 1977–78 under provisional certification, had physical education seniority, since he joined the Van Buren staff two years before Mrs. Warren. Mrs. Crocker, the third health teacher, had both health certification and more physical education seniority than the other two.

Because of an anticipated decrease in health enrollment at Van Buren a year prior to my fieldwork, a four percent cutback in health teachers seemed necessary; therefore, the decision was made by school and district administration to surplus Mrs. Warren on the basis of having least physical education seniority. Mrs. Warren felt the decision was unfair and discussed her feelings at some length with a union steward. The two of them subsequently met with Mr. Gray as a contract-mandated first step before filing a formal grievance. At this meeting, Mr. Gray reaffirmed an interpretation of the contract based on physical education rather than health seniority.

The union steward believes that this decision went beyond contract interpretation to possible gender discrimination; she speculates that "the administration preferred not to have Mr. Austin traveling at the end of the day because he needed to be at Van Buren for coaching." Furthermore, since Mrs. Warren had been instrumental in developing and teaching the health class and Mr. Austin had been warned and had promised repeatedly to complete his health certification, and had not, she feels the administration was willing to jeopardize the quality of the health program (as will be described later, Mrs. Warren had taken leadership for developing the health curriculum and had been functioning as unofficial "health coordinator") and the spirit of certification largely because they considered Mr. Austin, a male coach/teacher, more valuable. The steward was also confident, at the time, that Mrs. Warren would win the grievance because this aspect of the contract was unclear and subject to various interpretations.

Nevertheless, although several people encouraged her to take the next step and file a formal grievance, Mrs. Warren decided not to do so. In her words: "Technically, I should've grieved it, and I would've won. But I think it would've hurt more people than it needed to." Mrs. Warren added at a subsequent reading of this narrative that, although she lost her seniority, the administration agreed that she and Mr. Austin should share equally in being surplused.

Fortunately, the anticipated health enrollment decrease did not materialize, so no one was surplused. Although he describes certification as the bureaucracy forcing experienced teachers to "jump through hoops," this incident made Mr. Austin realize that he must obtain health certification or, in his words, be "aced out" of health teaching. Thus, he secured special approval from the state department of public instruction to teach one Van Buren health class as a "student" (at his regular salary), with Mrs. Warren agreeing to serve as his school-based cooperating teacher. Although she now expresses bitterness at the way he obtained certification, she was instrumental in his getting it. However, Mrs. Warren feels she made a principled choice based on her assessment of the situation at the time.

The union steward sees female socialization and male dominance at the heart of this seniority dilemma. She describes the treatment meted out to Mrs. Warren by Mr. Austin and the administration as "insensitive and deplorable," describing her as "tromped on" by these men. In addition, she sees Mrs. Warren as conditioned to assume a traditional female role secondary to men and, therefore, unable to "stand up and say, 'No . . . you can't treat me like this,' " particularly since teachers have the right to refuse to take a student teacher. Whatever the factors involved, the practical result is Mrs. Warren having lowest job retention status in both physical education and health.

Mrs. Warren's Working Conditions

Health Classes

Altogether, eight health classes are offered at Van Buren: Mr. Austin teaches four (periods 2–5), Mrs. Warren teaches three (periods 2–4), and Mrs. Crocker teaches one (period 5); two classes are scheduled back to back (with male and female teacher) during a given period. As previously described, classes meet daily for a full semester on an alternate activity/classroom basis, that is, even-numbered days in the classroom and odd-numbered days in physical activity.

All three teachers attach considerable importance to following a similar health syllabus; they pride themselves and are praised by peers and district administrators for this emphasis on consistency. Although the Van Buren health teachers take the official district curriculum seriously and attempt to address all topic areas, Mrs. Warren seems to be the most invested in it. Her commitment emerges partly from serving on the original district health curriculum committee in 1975–76 (at that time, she was the only Van Buren teacher certified in health), teaching the course the first year it was offered, and continuing to teach it and to be actively involved in the district evaluation process. This combination of early licensure, commitment to the districtwide health program, and accumulated teaching experience has resulted in her acknowledgement as the unofficial "health coordinator" at Van Buren by all three health teachers as well as Van Buren and district administration. In Mrs. Warren's words, "I've been kind of in charge." She regards the Van Buren health program as a reflection of her hard work and points out:

> I'm proud of what we're doing here; I really am. It's been a lot of hard work for me. I think Ed [Mr. Cox] has said that . . . he likes what we're doing here, and he has made that a point to people. If you want to see a health class, go see Van Buren's and Hancock's.

More specifically, Mrs. Warren's role includes such tasks as planning and typing the written semester schedule, taking leadership for incorporating new content based on district directives, and arranging for audiovisuals. Judging from her frequent mention of this "kind of in charge" role to me, it is one she takes seriously. For example: She feels responsible for "keeping track of" what the other two teachers are doing and says her "hardest job is trying to keep everybody in line so we can kind of stay together so we can get everything done." For example, with regard to the inclusion of sexual assault in the curriculum, Mrs.

70

Warren feels she was the only one who took it seriously and says, "It's all on my shoulders." The schedule Mrs. Warren prepared for all three teachers at the beginning of the semester is a brief topical outline of the broad concepts to be covered on various dates, subject to ongoing revision by individual teachers. They show audiovisuals on the same day to all classes, use the same textbook as well as several of the same student handouts (particularly in the healthy lifestyles and nutrition units), and try to adhere to similar schedules. However, no substantive joint planning or actual classroom team teaching is done. Except for days they showed the same audiovisuals, the three covered classroom material differently. Thus, in practice "staying together" seemed to mean beginning and ending major units at roughly the same time and showing audiovisuals on the same schedule.

Although all three are scheduled for preparation time first period to facilitate joint efforts, most planning for the health class takes place informally as teachers perceive its need, rather than on a regular or prearranged basis. Most frequently, this involves Mrs. Crocker or Mr. Austin initiating brief questions or "check-ins" with Mrs. Warren during first period. Because the two women have shared an office within the confines of the girls' locker room for seven years and are friends, such communication occurs on a daily basis between them. In fact, Mrs. Crocker seems to rely substantially on Mrs. Warren for guidance in teaching the health class, with Mrs. Warren attributing this to Mrs. Crocker's teaching only one health class among six daily preparations and her lesser familiarity with some of the recently incorporated topics. Since Mrs. Warren also relies on Mrs. Crocker for major planning of the adaptive class they coteach, this arrangement seems reciprocal. In contrast, Mr. Austin is geographically isolated from the women's informal communication because his office is within the boys' locker room. With young women often changing clothes in the girls' locker room, he cannot simply walk into the women's office. Therefore, he uses the phone to communicate (generally once or twice weekly) during the latter part of the first period. My observation that both Mr. Austin and Mrs. Crocker usually initiate these contacts with Mrs. Warren (frequently to ask what she is planning or to otherwise "check in") seems to further confirm her central role in the health program.

This current level of teamwork represents, according to Mrs. Warren, a decrease from earlier practice: "We used to meet all the time way back at the beginning." While increased health teaching experience may be a factor, the level of communication also appears to have been adversely affected by the seniority dilemma of the previous year, particularly the special arrangements for Mr. Austin's health certification and Mrs. Warren's role as his cooperating teacher. Although I heard the two of them make a joking reference to it, this situation was referred to in a resentful way in several remarks between Mrs. Warren and Mrs. Crocker.

Labor Intensification

These organizational factors add up to labor intensification for Mrs. Warren. Her heavy and escalating workload means that she is constantly "running on adrenalin. I don't dare stop." Lack of time was the most frequent complaint I heard from her, with resultant fatigue and stress. This labor intensification, increasingly found in schools dominated by reductive and strict management systems and prespecified behavioral objectives (Apple, 1983), has other effects on teachers, including Mrs. Warren. First it tends to decrease leisure and collegial sociability and increase the risk of isolation in the workplace. Thus, as I have documented, when her seniority was in jeopardy, it was difficult for Mrs. Warren to accept support from the union steward and other colleagues who attempted to give it. Mrs. Crocker, who shares Mrs. Warren's office, is the only peer with whom she has substantive interactions on a given day, and these exchanges are frequently interrupted by students because of their office location. Mrs. Warren regards Mrs. Crocker as her best friend, but by the end of the semester Mrs. Warren told me that she found herself withdrawing more at school. It seems possible that this sense of isolation was to some degree a factor in Mrs. Warren's consenting to be involved in the present study; she let me know on several occasions that she enjoyed our conversations and found them useful, although I was clearly one more addition to an already hectic schedule. As will be shown later, one of Mrs. Warren's strategies for coping with alienation and isolation was to become more involved with students and an active promoter of "school spirit," which also had the contradictory outcome of adding to her workload.

Second, by increasing the quantity of work expected, labor intensification can work against quality; thus, "getting done becomes more important than what was done or how one got there" (Apple, 1983, p. 619). For example, topics in the class can only, in Mrs. Warren's words, be "touched on" rather than covered in depth, and "staying on target time-wise" becomes a major concern. Similarly, in the context of a school administration that values procedure over pedagogy and a lengthy district syllabus, Mrs. Warren is particularly proud of the *form* of Van Buren's health program:

> I think we've got the best health program in the city—the way we run it, the way we do things. Now obviously the material is not always presented the best, but I think as far as organization—as far as what the kids are getting—it's the best one in the city because we do biking and running; we do weight training and swimming; we do all the lecture areas. . . .

With little time for reflective thinking in her daily schedule, Mrs. Warren feels tension between organizational ideals of efficiency and control and her own ideals of good teaching. Thus, there is a dichotomy between her expressed teaching philosophy and actual classroom practice. On many occasions she expressed a goal of helping students make their own decisions about various topics, by providing "enough background to make healthy choices" or developing their "ability to deal with life situations." Nevertheless, as we shall see, the reality of her classroom practice was quite different. Instead of student discussions about a range of choices, most of the class material was technical, teacher-presented information geared toward passing the exam rather than selected for its relevance to students' lives. While Mrs. Warren says she would "like to get away from talking," it represents the most effective way to "get through" the lengthy syllabus and control students.

Furthermore, early in the semester Mrs. Warren told me that her lectures were part of a progression, culminating in small work groups at a later time when students would be more "comfortable." However, she never used this teaching method, for reasons she relates mostly to time constraints (small groups "take a lot of time to prepare"), discipline ("kids play and fool around in small groups"), and efficiency ("a lot doesn't get done"). Thus, at the end of the semester Mrs. Warren acknowledged that students had not had enough time to talk, and added:

> I feel they got enough at least to make some good decisions, healthy decisions. I'm sure they need more but I think it was a good introduction. . . . Maybe they'll make some changes with just the little bit of information they might've gotten, and that's all I can hope for. I can't expect miracles.

Mrs. Warren's Working Conditions

Labor intensification also means that Mrs. Warren has trouble keeping up-to-date in her field—especially crucial with a subject like health, in which new developments are constantly occurring. She feels ill prepared to deal with such emerging and complex topics as sexual assault and AIDS, relying increasingly on outside experts for these curricular materials and reading them verbatim to students. Thus another contradictory outcome was generated: the more she relies on reading other people's words or utilizing formula activities, the more her own ability to utilize essential teaching skills atrophies. For example, Mrs. Warren says she seemed to have "forgotten" ways to teach that would "keep everyone involved."

These aspects of labor intensification, which are outcomes of the organizational arrangements of the school and district, provide the context in which Mrs. Warren's classroom efforts can be most fully understood. The school environment is non-nurturing, and she feels overburdened by a hectic teaching schedule and continually expanding syllabus that allows little time for reflective thinking. In contrast to her educative ideals, she can only "touch on" various topics if she is to cover the district objectives and has too little time to stay updated in her field. In this context, the teaching strategies I describe in Chapter 6 can be seen as partial solutions to the structural dilemmas she encountered and as active attempts to negotiate these organizational constraints. Before the content and form of the sex education curriculum-in-use is presented, it will be helpful to discuss in greater detail the agents in the process of its construction—Mrs. Warren and the students in her second-period health class.

4

Mrs. Warren: Nurturing Mom, Cheerleader, and One-of-the-Girls

"She's top-notch in her field—really great with kids and dedicated. She's got a young family too. She should—could—be home with her family, but she's here."—Mr. Brunswick, Van Buren Assistant Principal

"My mothering instincts come out a lot in teaching."—Mrs. Warren

"I've always respected teachers I've had who have gotten involved, showed me they have ability. Kids are more likely to pay attention to and respect a teacher like that."—Mrs. Warren

In addition to teaching physical education and health, Sally Warren is a wife and mother. She says she does not consistently think of herself as defined *first* by teaching or either of her familial roles; each is part of her self-identity. She is white, in her mid-thirties, and takes particular pride in her physical strength and ability. She dislikes being perceived and treated as potentially fragile because she is a woman; for example, she told me that in floor hockey she likes to demonstrate to the "big guys" in her classes that she can do as well as they even though she is "little and a girl." However, Mrs. Warren (as she is referred to by students and staff) does not consider herself a feminist. In short, she has several "layers of identity" (Randall, 1987) where gender, class, race, or any other categories by which individuals define themselves or are defined intersect, sometimes in contradictory ways. The following discussion offers a brief map to some of the intersections which seem most relevant to her work as a physical education and health teacher.

From the time she was in ninth grade, Sally Warren knew she wanted to be a physical education teacher because, in her words, "It was what I was good at." At the end of ninth grade, she transferred from a Catholic girls' high school to a public school because the latter offered more physical education opportunities. While her high school grades were average, she was one of the best female athletes and a cheerleader. She wanted to major in physical education at the large state university in Woodland, but her father (a blue-collar worker) refused to allow her to attend due to Vietnam War–era student protests occurring at the time.

Therefore, she enrolled in a smaller branch of the state university system that offered a physical education program, where she was determined not to fit the prevailing stereotype for physical education majors: "Men are men and women are too." Instead, Sally wanted to be good at physical skills but "look like a woman and be feminine"— goals she feels she achieved. In general, she did well in college, winning medals on the track team and earning an A average during her last semester. She minored in health education, accumulating twenty-five credits (just two short of a major) and earning teaching certification. Her minor courses included basic health information, philosophy of health education, teaching methods, emotional health, community resources, and sex education. She student taught for four weeks in health and a full semester in physical education at the elementary and middle school levels. Her primary work interest after college was in teaching elementary physical education—not high school health.

She met her husband (a shot-putter on the track team) in college, and they were married at the beginning of her final semester. He dropped out of school to work, and she worked part-time. When Mrs. Warren graduated in 1972, she had "interesting" job offers from three neighboring states; however, she decided to accept none of them. Instead, she and her husband moved to Woodland, where he had a summer job and they would be closer to their families. The city also seemed large enough for her to eventually find a teaching job.

She began coaching gymnastics at the Woodland YMCA, which led to a part-time coaching position at Van Buren in the fall of 1973. Fortunately for her, a physical education teacher there went on maternity leave after Thanksgiving, so Mrs. Warren sat in on this teacher's classes for a few weeks and then took over her teaching duties for the remainder of the semester. Because the other teacher decided not to return after the baby was born, Mrs. Warren was hired on a permanent basis. With the exception of two maternity leaves (in 1977 and 1981), she has been teaching high school health and physical education at Van Buren for the past twelve years.

At Van Buren she initially functioned as both physical education teacher and coach (girls' gymnastics, golf, and track); however, after giving birth to a daughter in 1977 and subsequently developing an ulcer, she decided the hectic schedule "wasn't worth it" and quit coaching. That same year she began to supervise the pom-pom squad, a job she continued until 1984, when she gave it up because of "too much time, too little appreciation." Because she was already certified in health, she was asked to assist with development of the original Woodland District ninth-grade health curriculum in 1975–76 and first taught the course in 1976–77.

Teaching health was hard for Mrs. Warren at the beginning because she had no classroom teaching experience beyond four weeks as a student teacher. She never thought she would actually be teaching health and describes her first classroom experience at Van Buren as being "in another world" from teaching physical education—in ways ranging from learning to write on the board to dressing and relating differently to students. In particular, some of the "bigger guys" in her classes gave her "a hard time" at first; however, she says she "made a point of being authoritative," an approach that has now given way to being "more comfortable and laid back." In short, she says she "learned [classroom teaching] by doing."

Since her employment at Van Buren began, Mrs. Warren has earned the major share of her family's income (her husband was a seasonal landscaper and began a night shift at the post office during the final weeks of my observations). She has been primarily responsible for domestic duties, including meal preparation, housework, and child care arrangements (both their eight-year-old daughter and four-year-old son have been in day care since they were babies). She describes a typical day as beginning at 6 a.m. After getting herself and the children ready to leave, she drives them to day care at 7:15 (the oldest is bused to school from day care) and arrives at Van Buren by 8:00 to begin her official paid work day. She leaves school by 4:00 p.m., picks the children up at day care, prepares the family dinner by 6:00, and rarely gets to bed before midnight.

Nurturing Mom, Cheerleader, and One-of-the-Girls

Contradictory Gender Role Expectations

As this brief sketch suggests, Mrs. Warren's accommodation to the traditional female roles of daughter, wife, and mother have had a significant impact on her paid work as a teacher. However, given her decision to major in physical education, and the fact that she placed her children in day care and earns the major share of family income, it would be inaccurate to describe Mrs. Warren as having passively accepted a traditional female role.

Instead, as Jean Anyon (1984) suggests, Mrs. Warren might be more accurately characterized as actively struggling to deal with the social contradictions and role conflicts involved in being female. In her analysis, Anyon describes two inconsistent social messages that young women attempt to resolve. First, appropriate feminine behavior is widely depicted as nurturing men and children and being submissive, noncompetitive and domestic. In contrast, the appropriate means of achieving recognition and self-esteem in U.S. society occurs in the nondomestic, competitive work world. Anyon further suggests that the contradictions between femininity and self-esteem are particularly rigid for working-class and lower middle-class women; the demands of their daily struggle for economic survival are in sharp contrast to the submissiveness of femininity. Drawing on Genovese's (1972) discussion of the dialectic of accommodation/resistance among black slaves in the antebellum South, Anyon maintains:

> Most females neither totally acquiesce in, nor totally eschew, the imperatives of "femininity." Rather, most females engage in daily (conscious as well as unconscious) attempts to resist the psychological degradation and low self-esteem that would result from total and exclusive application of the approved ideologies of femininity such as submissiveness, dependency, domesticity and passivity. Females' attempts to offset these demands with those of self-esteem (that is, to mediate the contradiction between femininity and competence as it is socially defined) exhibit both daily resistance and daily accommodation. . . . (1984, p. 30).

The following incident, which occurred at the first all-school dance of the year where Mrs. Warren was a chaperone, graphically illustrates the inconsistent social expectations she faces on a daily basis:

Nurturing Mom, Cheerleader, and One-of-the-Girls

Mrs. Warren introduces me to Mr. Brunswick, the assistant principal who supervises the physical education/health program and is also a chaperone. After the three of us talk briefly about my research project, he tells me that I am "lucky" to be working with Mrs. Warren because: "She's top-notch in her field—really great with kids and dedicated."

Mrs. Warren blushes and looks down at her feet.

Mr. Brunswick continues, "She's got a young family too. She should—could [recovering smoothly from his slip]—be home with her family, but she's here."

Since Mr. Brunswick's remark about her teaching is based on only a few teaching observations (none of her classroom teaching), and since Mrs. Warren regards it as over-inflated in any case, this compliment might be construed as related more to gender than to teaching performance. When I asked Mrs. Warren about the remark the following week, she said she had not noticed it and that colleagues at Van Buren "know I take my family seriously too." Thus, her dual involvement in what Acker (1983) calls two "greedy institutions" (familial and educational) requiring a high level of commitment and productivity puts her under the same pressure experienced by many female teachers and academics

> to demonstrate unequivocally that they have indeed come to terms with this dilemma and that their successful performance in one of these institutional life forms is not being achieved at the expense of underperformance in the other. (Walker & Barton, 1983, p. 12)

Throughout the semester, I observed Mrs. Warren incorporate aspects of a socially acceptable definition of femininity (being a nurturing "mom," cultivating school spirit as a "cheerleader" or creating fun by behaving like "one-of-the-girls" with students) into her paid work as a teacher. Although these informal cultural practices give the surface appearance of passive acquiescence to traditional feminine expectations, in Anyon's terms they represent both accommodation and resistance to feminine ideology. These patterns of behavior may actually represent an active appropriation of "femininity" to deal with the demands of an alienating, non-nurturing school environment and to maintain student control. Furthermore, they can be seen as manifestations of the "fundamental social tension between demands for conformity at a collective level and the struggle for self-fulfillment at an individual one" (Walker & Barton, 1983, p. 15). Thus, these strategies can be understood as gendered and contradictory cultural practices. They may be personally liberating while simultaneously reproducing dominant societal gender arrangements; they may make the alienating work environment more livable at one level while increasing difficulties at another. I wish to make clear that my description of Mrs. Warren's patterns of behavior does not imply that she consciously thinks of her actions as mediating the demands between femininity and competence in the work place, as attempting to negotiate institutional constraints, or as contradictory cultural practices. Instead, these concepts serve as heuristic lenses through which her strategies may reveal alternate meanings.

Being a Nuturing "Mom"

Mrs. Warren's status as "Mom" was a salient feature of her interactions with students and colleagues, although it is worth noting at the outset that hers, like other female teachers', is a professional motherliness. As such, it is accompanied by a need for impartial evaluation and assessment of students, enforcement of school regulations, and other teaching obligations (Acker, 1983). She often mentions her own children and mothering role in the classroom and uses these experiences to illustrate course material. She sometimes refers to herself as "Mom" with students and had been called "Mom" by students on the pom-pom squad and teams she coached. The day of the Homecoming pep rally ("Hat Day" at Van Buren), she wore a "Viking Spirit" hat with "Mom" printed on the visor, and brought her eight-year-old daughter (wearing a Viking sweatshirt) to the pep rally and parade.

Mrs. Warren says that her "mothering instincts come out a lot in teaching." Thus, she treats students like a stereotypical good mom—baking cookies for the second-period Christmas party and maintaining steadfast patience and cheerfulness in dealing with the myriad of student requests she must continually address. Because the office she shares with Mrs. Crocker overlooks the girls' locker room, Mrs. Warren's work space and time (including planning periods and lunch break) were nearly always accessible to students; they borrowed clothes, used the teachers' bathroom and curling irons, obtained tampons, had minor injuries attended to, stored packages, or just visited.

Like a nurturing mom, she is alert to signs of potential problems among students, and one of the school psychologists told me that Mrs. Warren and Mrs. Crocker are major sources of student referrals. On one occasion when Mrs. Warren and I were discussing types of students with whom she feels most effective, she told me that she "look[s] for the challenging ones." She was particularly involved with one young woman, Andrea, who had been in her health class a few years before. According to Mrs. Warren, Andrea's family had a long history of problems, including alcoholism, institutionalization for mental health reasons, and violence; Mrs. Warren first became aware of these problems when Andrea was injured during activity period, and she accompanied the student in the ambulance to the hospital. Since then, Mrs. Warren has perceived and referred to herself as a mom to this young woman, with Andrea coming to Mrs. Warren's office to talk nearly every day before or after school or during her lunch period. Mrs. Warren notified a school psychologist about Andrea's situation; however, she remained a major support person in this student's life.

Mrs. Warren also functions in a motherly way with less "challenging" students—those who, in her words, "aren't bad kids yet." She believes that the "good kids need help just as much as the bad kids" (those with academic, family, or social problems), and she sees her role as providing "positive reinforcement" to them in the form of rewards for effort as well as personal warmth and accessibility. Therefore, she and Mrs. Crocker keep their office door open so that students will "know they can come in and feel welcome." In addition, given a school environment that offers, they feel, little "positive reinforcement" for good teaching, this personal contact with students provides feedback to them that their efforts are worthwhile. Mrs. Warren commented about the large number of students who took advantage of this opportunity for more personal interaction:

> It ties us up a lot, but I think that if we can see the good happening in kids, it sure makes our jobs a lot easier. It's worth working then. You tend to get stuck in all the negatives and you just wonder, "why do I bother?" So that feeds back to us—as far as positive—that we can feel good, that we can see we're actually doing some good. They know the office door is open if we're there. Thy know they can come in and feel welcome, and I think a lot of kids take advantage of that.

Mrs. Warren's grading practices also reflect the nurturing qualities of a traditional mom. She likes grading least of all her teaching duties, especially the "tedious paperwork stuff" (mostly because there is too little time, a rationale that makes sense with 225 students) and the decision-making process involved. She says she usually ends up being subjective and "giving the higher grade," partly because she knows the course is required for high school graduation and partly because she sees grades as a form of encouragement: "Anything that's positive may be one more step in the right direction," "You want to help the kid, help that person feel good about themselves." Therefore, most of her students got A's and B's, and no one failed. As Dawn, one of the second-period students, put it: Mrs. Warren "sees that you get a good grade."

Along with being informed by the traditional division of labor in which woman's role is to provide emotional nurturance and security, Mrs. Warren's grading practices can also be seen as gendered resistance (Apple, 1983) to labor intensification, technical procedures, and bureaucratic control. Thus, she offers the following rationale for giving Toni, a sophomore who had been failed by Mr. Austin the year before, a passing grade:

I don't think the kids get enough positives. I think they're torn down too much. I mean, they're always getting yelled at. They're always getting in trouble, and there's not a lot of good things happening in a lot of kids' lives. If I can make one nice thing happen to them, that might be just enough to keep them going.

She is aware that her grading approach, also shared by Mrs. Crocker, is very different from that of the men in the department. She perceives them as using failure to motivate a student to try harder, while the two women believe that failure is more likely to make a student "give up."

Mrs. Warren's nurturant approach to students as well as her grading philosophy clash with administrative priorities, as illustrated by an incident that occurred near the end of the semester. This incident encapsulates the tension between Mrs. Warren's educative ideals and administrative priorities, along with her resistance to them. It involved Toni, who had never been in the water during the swimming unit because she was either absent or told Mrs. Warren she had her period; she had failed the previous semester in Mr. Austin's class for not going in the water or taking the test of swimming ability. Mrs. Warren told Toni she had to at least take the test to pass. After vain attempts by Mrs. Warren over several weeks (personal appeals, phone calls to parents, and two missed makeup sessions), Toni had still not taken the test by Monday of the last week in the semester. At that time Mrs. Warren told me she was going to talk with Mr. Brunswick, an assistant principal, to let him know that Toni was "trying." The following exchange occurred after a faculty meeting that day:

> Mrs. Warren tells Mr. Brunswick that she wants to talk about Toni (well known to him because of her record of trouble in school) "just to let you know what's happening." She goes on to say that Toni has not shown up for two makeup swimming tests; she is "really borderline about passing," having also failed her sex education test.
>
> Mr. Brunswick says that Toni has been using swimming makeup as an excuse to not serve detentions, so "she's playing both ends against the middle." He thinks that Mrs. Warren "has given her every opportunity," and Toni "needs to suffer whatever consequences."
>
> Mrs. Warren repeats that she "just wanted to keep you informed," and tells me as we leave that she is "glad to know Toni is playing games."

Nevertheless, by Friday (the last day of semester exams) Mrs. Warren scheduled another makeup exam with Toni over the noon hour. This time, Toni showed up and passed the course.

Finally, Mrs. Warren interacts with colleagues in a correspondingly nurturing and supportive way. Like a stereotypical mom, she is frequently more concerned with the wider emotional climate than with getting her personal needs met, as illustrated by her previously described refusal to file a grievance when she was surplused and her agreement to supervise Mr. Austin's student teaching. In fact, she described herself to me on several occasions as being a mom to both Mr. Austin and Mrs. Crocker, looking out for their emotional needs and "keeping things together" in the health course.

Cultivating School Spirit

Similarly, within the wider context of the school, she functions as a background cultivator of school spirit. Mrs. Warrren states that she is well known within the school as an "athletic supporter"—"People know I'm a Viking fan. I push as much as I can as far as spirit". Thus, Mrs. Warren painted numerous banners during the semester ("Watch Volleyball Girls Win at Regional," "Everything Points to a Victory— Girls/Boys Buckets") and was a behind-the-scenes coordinator/helper at pep rallies (contacting individual coaches to speak, making signs, setting up the sound system, setting up and taking down gymnastics equipment), while the (mostly male) coaches and administrators played more visible roles in these events.

At Homecoming she functioned as, in her words, a "picker-upper" who "helped out" wherever she was needed—backstage during Skit Night, judging homeroom door decorations, coaching girls' "Powder Puff" football. Although I was aware of no visible or official acknowledgement of her efforts during the semester I observed, it should be pointed out that Mr. Gray, Van Buren's principal, had sent her a personal letter of appreciation at the end of the previous school year, which was taped to the supply room door in her office. Furthermore, she had been named Grand Marshall of last year's Homecoming parade. As announced at the Homecoming pep rally, the honored person (usually an older male teacher, which was the case at the rally I attended) "exemplifies the spirit, fight, and enthusiasm of Van Buren." Although the choice was made by a faculty committee, Mrs. Warren perceives her selection the year before as the result of student efforts—particularly from Andrea, the cheerleader for whom she functions as a second mom. According to Mrs. Warren, "She [Andrea] knew that it would be a nice pay-back for all the stuff that I did—a nice thanks. She knew that I really wanted it. . . ." After being named Grand Marshall, she feels she has "let people down because I'm not doing as much as I used to—like going to games and stuff like that." Nevertheless, school activities beyond teaching still occupy a considerable portion of Mrs. Warren's time.

Thus, although Mrs. Warren maintains an active interest and involvement in Van Buren athletics, her largely supportive role (like that of mom in a traditional nuclear family) has little status and visibility. The following incident reveals Mrs. Warren's awareness of her less-valued background role:

A male student asks Mrs. Warren during the weightlifting activity if she has a key to the varsity locker room.

Mrs. Warren: "I'm not privileged enough to have a varsity locker room key."

Student: "Are you a coach?"

Mrs. Warren: "I'm just a 'mom.' I used to be a coach, but I've become a keeper of sorts—a troubleshooter."

In addition to recognition from students, this role offers her a chance to participate in an activity highly valued by Van Buren administration:

promotion of school spirit. Mr. Gray allows school time for six pep rallies a year, and athletic "excellence" is a major part of the Van Buren tradition. Mr. Gray himself is known among students and faculty as something of a "jock," and coaches (mostly male) are a high-status group at Van Buren. Thus, Mrs. Warren's role at pep rallies—even though it is mostly behind-the-scenes—makes her at least a peripheral part of the inner circle. Finally, as I shall elaborate next, such participation is actually fun for Mrs. Warren and serves to counteract the alienating aspects of her work environment.

Behaving Like "One-of-the-Girls

Finding ways to create fun, including interacting on an informal "one-of-the-girls" basis with students, is another of Mrs. Warren's active attempts to negotiate the heavy demands of the workplace and to make it more livable. Physical activity is what she enjoys most about teaching, a fact that is evident to anyone watching her participate exuberantly in a floor hockey game or run across the finish line with arms in the air and a big grin. She performs the various physical fitness tests (sometimes racing with Mr. Austin) with obvious enjoyment and enthusiasm. Before and after activity sessions, she is usually surrounded by a cluster of students of both sexes chatting informally with her. Furthermore, Mrs. Warren's boom box (played loudly enough to satisfy ninth-grade student volume requirements) is a regular accompaniment to weight training sessions, and, as evidenced by her finger snapping and occasional dance steps, Mrs. Warren seems to enjoy the music herself.

She says that being with kids is part of the enjoyment and getting a good work-out is vital for her: "I'm not as good a person if I don't work out. Teaching is a big part of my life—especially activity." On a personal level, she consciously uses physical activity as a way to relieve stress. For Mrs. Warren, knowing how to play ("getting in touch with your crazy side") is an important aspect of mental health for herself and students. With regard to the latter, she comments, "Finding their play is the only thing that will keep them straight." Furthermore, because activity is fun for her, she regards it as the easiest aspect of teaching and also believes that it "keeps the kids going": "It's one less thing to worry about for the kids. I think they know that it's the easier part of it [the class] in most cases."

Finally, Mrs. Warren uses her participation in physical activity as a teaching tool. First, it demonstrates her skills to students, making it clear that she is "practicing what I'm preaching." Second, she says it enhances students' respect:

> I've always respected teachers I've had who have gotten involved, showed me they have ability. Kids are more likely to pay attention to and respect a teacher like that.

Third, it motivates students to try harder themselves; as Mrs. Warren says: "The more active I am, the more kids do." She is aware that the "teacher-student barrier drops when you run and swim with kids" and uses this to relate to students on a personal level and get them to try "for" her. Thus, informality, enthusiasm, and willingness to be one-of-the-girls serves the useful purpose of helping her gain compliance in physical activity, in which most students have considerably less interest than their teacher.

As will be evident later, Mrs. Warren's classroom interactions with students are generally less casual, although still relatively informal and characterized by bantering interactions. However, constraints of the classroom mean that Mrs. Warren cannot be one-of-the-girls to the degree she can before, during, and after activity period. As I shall elaborate more fully in upcoming chapters, students constantly tested the boundaries of informal interactions with Mrs. Warren in the classroom.

At such times, being a mom enabled Mrs. Warren to regain adult status and maintain benevolent authority and classroom control. For example, Carrie, an African-American student who occupied a central role as classroom humorist, frequently called Mrs. Warren "buddy" during activity and classroom sessions, an informality that Mrs. Warren accepted and even seemed to enjoy. However, as the following incident reveals, when the student became even more personal and informal in the classroom, Mrs. Warren modified her initial stern teacher reaction to being a mom.

> About a minute before the bell is to ring, students noisily begin to pack up their notebooks. Four students stand up and inch toward the door while Mrs. Warren is occupied talking with others. In the hubbub, Carrie calls out loudly, "Mrs. Warren." Failing to get her attention, Carrie calls, "Sally" [Mrs. Warren's first name]. At this, Mrs. Warren's face becomes very stern. She points her finger at Carrie and says, "Don't do that. Call me 'Mrs. Warren.' [pause] Or call me 'Mom.' I'll answer

to that." The bell rings, and Carrie moves quickly out the door.

As I have demonstrated, Mrs. Warren appropriated aspects of a socially acceptable definition of femininity—behaving like a stereotypical mom or one-of-the-girls—in her role as teacher at Van Buren. These strategies were useful as a benevolent means of eliciting student compliance, maintaining control, and motivating students to perform on a physical level (getting nonswimmers who are afraid of the water to try swimming, those who hate running to do a timed mile run, and so on). Partly because she is a woman who is smaller and less strong than many of her students (especially the males), this last task is easier if students like rather than fear her. As observations and interviews will reveal more fully, most students seemed to genuinely like her; this was most dramatically illustrated by the impeccable behavior of a large archery class of mostly juniors and seniors that collectively surmised (I learned later) that my presence meant Mrs. Warren was being evaluated.

Mrs. Warren's informal cultural practices can also be thought of as accommodating to the administration's emphasis on school spirit and the alternate day format of the health class. At the same time, although they make the non-nurturing school environment seem more livable, these strategies may also have contradictory outcomes and serve to make her workplace even more alienating. First, Mrs. Warren's participation in what she called other "projects" (banner painting, door decoration judging, and so on) further increase the fragmentation and frantic pace of her teaching day. Furthermore, there are some occasions when, she says, "I find myself getting too involved [in projects], and I end up not doing my [classroom teaching] work." Finally, her obvious enjoyment and exuberance may also contribute to the image some other teachers have of her as a "little kid."

Similarly, by using grades as a form of encouragement (being an "easy" grader), cultivating supportive personal interactions with students, and promoting school spririt, Mrs. Warren resists technical and alienating bureaucratic arrangements of the school. Nevertheless, these strategies of gendered resistance also may have contradictory outcomes. They may contribute to a reproduction of traditional gender roles that can keep women in subordinate positions in a workplace that values efficiency and rational technical procedures, and convey the notion that women's personal and work needs (a quiet place, time to think) are secondary to the needs of young people to be nurtured. As Mrs. Warren puts it, she sometimes gets "walked on" and "taken for granted by the kids." Just as Mrs. Warren takes little satisfaction from Mr. Brunswick's "over-rated" assessments of her teaching, interviews suggest that students who regarded the class as easy may view their good grade as a meaningless credential toward the graduation requirement. Moreover, Mrs. Warren's mostly behind-the-scenes role at pep rallies, painting victory banners, assisting at athletic events, and so on may contribute to a traditional view of women as athletic *supporters* rather than athletes. However, it should also be noted that her active participation and skills in the context of physical education classes might counter this perception.

In summary, I have shown that Mrs. Warren does not passively acquiesce to the organizational priorities, patriarchal power relations, and labor processes that characterize her workplace. Instead, she negotiates them, accommodating and resisting in complex, cultural ways that are influenced by gender and can have contradictory outcomes. Given these contradictory outcomes, it is important not to romanticize or view these cultural practices as necessarily progressive. As we have seen, what may be liberating at one level may serve to increase subordination at another. I will demonstrate in Chapter 6 how these organizational constraints interact with student lived cultural responses to influence Mrs. Warren's selection and presentation of classroom sexuality information. Before doing so, the students in her second-period health class will be introduced.

5

The Classroom as Social Arena: "Good Kids," "Dirts," and Black Students

"I Can't Get No Satis-fuck-tion."—Sung by Carrie and Dawn

"Can we list things we *really* like to do and not get in trouble?"—Toni

"You gonna call me a nappy-headed reject from Africa?" "You nappy-headed reject from Africa."—Exchange between Carrie and Andrew

"You tend to say too much too often."—Mrs. Warren to Carrie

There were twenty-seven students (seventeen females and ten males) enrolled in Mrs. Warren's second-period ninth-grade health class. They embodied in appearance the wide range of physical development typical of early adolescence. Most young women had developed adult body contours and were taller than many of the young men. Furthermore, several female students looked older in other ways, wearing a considerable amount of makeup, stylish clothing, and sophisticated hair styles. In contrast, most of the male students looked more like gangling boys than adult men. Their clothing (jeans and shirts or sweaters) and hair tended to be less styled than the young women's. Most students had come to Van Buren from two nearby middle schools in Woodland. Two had attended Catholic schools, and two had transferred into the district—one from a large urban area and one from a rural area.

Social Groupings

"Good Kids"

About three-fourths of the students typified the school's standards of "excellence"; they took their academic work fairly seriously (many had grade point averages of 3.0 or better during the first quarter, with seven named to the 3.5 Honor Roll), participated in extracurricular activities, and generally followed school rules. The students' choices of organized extracurricular activities seemed to be divided along stereotypic masculine/feminine lines; a higher percentage of young men were involved in organized school sports, while several young women were involved in more traditionally feminine activities. More specifically, half the young men in the class (Matt, Ian, Doug, Ed, and Russ) participated in such organized school sports as football, track, and basketball. On the day of a game or meet, they could be distinguished from other male students by their clothing—shirt, tie, and dress pants. Andrew was a member of the Woodland Scouts Drum and Bugle Corps and frequently wore his satin jacket to class.

In contrast, less than a third of the young women (Linda, Tammy, Kristi, Jodie, and Carrie) participated in organized school sports such as basketball, track, volleyball, and gymnastics. Dawn participated in the freshman "powder puff" football team at Homecoming. Several young women in the class were involved in other activities: Dawn and Carrie were members of the Human Relations Club (a small group of mostly black students); Carrie participated in forensics (winning a gold medal in an eight-school meet for her humorous monologue); Tammy and Lauren were in the freshman chorale and performed at the Homecoming Show; Lauren was elected one of eight freshman representatives to the Student Council; Carol performed in the Variety Show (lip-syncing two Madonna songs, a performance she did regularly at local lip-syncing competitions); and Sharon was selected to dance in a Woodland civic ballet production.

In short, most students in the class generally met the expectations of Van Buren administrators and teachers, and Mrs. Warren referred to them as the "good kids." Within this broad category, the most highly regarded were "jocks" (those who excelled in sports) and "preppies" (those who were attractive, well-dressed and relatively affluent). The former label was usually associated with males and the latter with females, although not exclusively. Although there were a few jocks and preppies in the health class, most students were more ordinary good kids.

Nevertheless, a smaller contingent of students in Mrs. Warren's classroom did not fit school expectations and norms so well. For example, Mike was a "loner" in the classroom. He was a tall, thin, nonathletic young man who missed school often because of illness that, according to Mrs. Warren, was a result of family problems; he was not at all athletically inclined. He sometimes interacted in a friendly way with a quiet young woman who sat beside him at the front of the room; however, as I will describe in Chapter 7, he was more frequently isolated and ridiculed by others—particularly male jocks—as, in their words, a "fag."

"Dirts"

One group that did not fit prevailing school expectations and norms was the "dirts," as they were referred to by both students and physical education staff. These students took academic work less seriously, had their own version of cocurricular activities (including smoking and "partying"), and were less inclined to follow the rules. Mrs. Warren had privately used the word dirts to describe such students in the wider Van Buren population, and I asked her early in the semester whether she would characterize any second-period students as dirts. She identified Toni (a sophomore who was repeating the health class after failing the previous year) and Paula, largely because they smoked and drank. Both came from working-class families; Paula had been picked up by the police during that semester for juvenile drinking, and Toni (as well as her older siblings) had a record of encounters with school and law enforcement authorities. Mrs. Warren also mentioned Joan and Michelle as possible dirts. They had long, bleached blond, bouffant hair and wore heavy makeup, tight blue jeans, and sometimes high-heeled boots. Although they were quiet and compliant in class, their appearance seemed to be a factor in Mrs. Warren's saying she was not sure about whether they were dirts.

Although not identified as a dirt by Mrs. Warren, Carol, who was new to Van Buren, told me that she had been a "dirtball" at the smaller school from which she had transferred. There, she was part of a visible group who smoked openly just outside the school building. However, at Van Buren she concluded after attending a few parties that being a dirt meant greater involvement in alcohol, drugs, and sexual activity than she wanted, so she did not wish to be categorized in that group (although "preppies aren't my style either"). She also had bleached hair and wore heavy makeup and tight jeans, but she did not associate with anyone else in class and generally looked quietly bored.

Black Students

Three black students (Andrew, Carrie and Dawn), were another visible group in Mrs. Warren's classroom that did not fit prevailing norms at Van Buren (where only 7 percent are students of color), although they shared characteristics of good kids. During the previously mentioned conversation about dirts with Mrs. Warren, she also said that Carrie and Dawn were "sort of different," adding that the label dirt didn't really apply "because they are black." Nevertheless, Carrie and Dawn did share the more openly sexual appearance and behavior that characterized most of the female dirts.

Andrew was a gregarious and witty student who was a vocal participant in the classroom, calling out questions and comments that suggested a high level of interest and awareness about most health topics. Because he had a knee problem that warranted a medical exemption, swimming (at which his skill level was excellent) was the only activity in which he participated fully. During other activities, he usually remained in street clothes, kept himself mostly separate from male classmates, and stayed near Mrs. Warren (sometimes serving as her assistant) or other nonparticipating students, mostly young women. In the classroom, I heard only one put-down directed at him by a male student, who said, "That's Andrew," as a picture of a third trimester fetus' face was being circulated while Mrs. Warren was briefly out of the room.

Andrew and Carrie frequently engaged in humor and mutual insults that symbolized their bond of intimacy and understanding around race. For example, while students were copying definitions from the textbook, Andrew made a silly face at Carrie, who began to laugh:

> Carrie: "Owie. Don't make me laugh. My ribs are sore."

Andrew repeats the face.

Carrie:	"You Negro."
Andrew:	"You gonna call me a nappy-headed reject from Africa?"
Carrie:	"You nappy-headed reject from Africa."
Mrs. Warren:	(grinning) "What did you say?"
Carrie:	"I called him a nappy-headed reject from Africa." (To Andrew) "You're an African boody-scratcher."

Although they laughed, neither Mrs. Warren nor white students engaged in similar interactions with Andrew, Carrie, or Dawn. This suggests the fine line between insults representing a joke among members of a social group and hostility from an outsider.

Carrie and Dawn usually exhibited similar racial solidarity—"boogeying" in the aisle, sitting together, referring to themselves as "two Negroes," and doing "high fives." However, on some occasions an undercurrent of tension seemed to exist between them, as typified by the following caustic exchange that occurred while students were matching drugs and their effects on a worksheet:

| Dawn: | "What's [the reaction to] glue?" |
| Carrie: | "Are you dumb! What do you do when you breathe? Does your mama still whup you? If you was mine, I'd whup you everyday 'cause you're so stupid." |

Dawn looks angry but continues to work silently for a few minutes and then says to Carrie, "Your lips look crusty because you don't have lipstick."

| Carrie: | "Between your legs is crusty." |
| Dawn: | "Ooooh, oooh." She returns to work. |

Although Carrie and Dawn shared two aspects of identity (gender and race), differences of physical appearance and family income may have accounted for some of the tension between them. First, Carrie's father is white, and her skin is golden brown—dark enough for her to be considered black by the overwhelmingly white student body and staff, but not as dark as most other black students, including Dawn. Carrie was, in her words, "mixed." Thus, her skin color put her outside both the dominant white culture and minority culture at Van Buren; she was not a full-fledged member of either "community." For example, during an incident near the end of the semester when a group of black students decided to occupy the freshman corner of the Commons area in response to vandalism of a Martin Luther King commemorative bulletin board, Carrie told Mrs. Warren that the leader of the occupation effort asked the few Hispanic and "mixed" students to demonstrate "what color they were" by their participation. Carrie did not join the occupation and told Mrs. Warren she felt "scared shitless" by some of the black students who did. During a confrontation with these students, Carrie was "backed up" by some white male seniors, including the star basketball player who regarded her as a freshman "buddy," while she had a "crush" on him all semester.[1]

Furthermore, Dawn's slim body, stylish hair, and more expensive clothing (spike heels, wide leather belts, and so on) fit dominant definitions of attractiveness more than Carrie's fat[2] body, unruly hair, and loose tops and jeans. Carrie occasionally made ironic remarks about her appearance in the classroom ("I'm out for Miss America,") although, after one relay race, she confided in Mrs. Warren that she felt embarrassed running in front of others. On that day, Carrie said that her friends (Dawn, Paula, and Toni) were "giving [her] a hard time," and Mrs. Warren told her to just ignore it and run with other people. Dawn's demeanor also reflected her well-educated, middle-class family background (her mother was a teacher in the Woodland school system), while Carrie's bearing, loud voice, and humorous (often outrageous) remarks reflected her working-class roots.

Carrie, Dawn, Paula, and Toni

Along with Paula and Toni, Carrie and Dawn were part of an all-female social grouping that played the most prominent role in classroom dynamics. They usually sat near each other, frequently saving seats for one another and occasionally getting other students to move to accommodate this. When not sitting next to each other, they would simply talk over another student who was between them. Furthermore, at least one or two (sometimes all four) of them were excused by Mrs. Warren to use the bathroom every classroom session, while very few other students asked for such permission.

Like the working-class British young women of the same age described by McRobbie (1978), this group of female students asserted a particular form of "femaleness" in the classroom that emphasized sexuality and sophistication. Paula wore heavy makeup, had long bleached blonde hair, and polished her long manicured nails in class. Both she and Dawn dressed in ways that accentuated their sexuality, frequently wearing high-heeled boots or pumps and tight pants and sweaters. Furthermore, during nearly every class session Dawn engaged in a slow, hip-gyrating stroll to the front of the room (to sharpen a pencil, get a tissue, use the wastebasket, adjust a window shade, get a book), sometimes accompanied by a long leisurely arm stretch. Toni dressed mostly in tight jeans, a T-shirt (including one with the words "I got this body from lifting weights—12 oz. at a time") or hooded sweatshirt, and sneakers, although she got up very early to "do" her bleached blonde hair. These three and Carrie (who wore looser clothing) interjected their sexiness into the classroom in other, audible ways. The following represent numerous examples: When Mrs. Warren asked students to list their favorite activities, Paula asked with feigned innocence, "Can we list things we *really* like to do and not get in trouble?", to which Carrie whispered to Toni, "She'd write 'give blow.' " A few sessions later, when Mrs. Warren solicited qualities looked for in a date, Toni quipped, "We *could* get into details, but I don't think you'd like it." On another occasion, Carrie and Dawn burst into a spontaneous chorus of "I Can't Get No Satisfaction" (with "satis-*fuck*-tion" laughingly substituted by one). During the entire semester, Carrie kept up a steady stream of humorous digressions and risque quips that perpetuated a sexy image. For example:

I'm a sex fiend (in response to Toni's comment that she had seen Carrie at a shopping mall with several guys).

Doug (one of the most popular jocks), there's a nasty rumor goin' round that you and I are layin' down.

Carrie, Dawn, Paula, and Toni resisted participation in activity sessions in a variety of ways—walking instead of running, forgetting their gym clothes or swimsuits, skipping and otherwise fooling around, recording inflated scores for each other during the physical fitness tests. On "Fun Days" (Mrs. Warren's term for a few sessions when the class played volleyball) or rainy day sessions (when she had them do relay races), these young women would arrange themselves on the same team. Then they would maximize the "fun" aspect of the activity by gossiping, fooling around, playfully giving each other "the finger" after a missed serve, and so on. They did not try to hide their dislike for activity, and they participated mainly because they were required to in order to pass. In contrast to most other students (boys in general, jocks and good kids of both sexes), these four clearly shared less in Mrs. Warren's valuing of athletic competence or even "trying hard"; they were there to get through the required course with as little effort as possible. In addition, none of them was very good at most activities. As Carrie said to the other three after a paced run: "If I frickin' ran around the world, I couldn't get my pulse over twenty." Their lack of interest and skill, minimal enthusiasm, and occasional sullenness during activity was a concern for Mrs. Warren, who saw them as a real "challenge," frequently offered words of encouragement, and genuinely tried to help them pass the course. For Dawn, this meant Mrs. Warren's allowing her to retake a failed exam; for Paula, ignoring her skipping during activity. In addition, Mrs. Warren agonized much of the semester over Toni's lack of compliance with swimming. Toni professed an allergy to chlorine although she never produced the required official medical exemption and skipped every swimming session. As previously described, Mrs. Warren finally convinced her to do the swimming ability test on the last day of the semester—several weeks after the swimming unit was over and a matter of hours before semester grades were due in the office.

As I shall subsequently describe in more detail, these four played a major role in influencing classroom process. They contested school knowledge about sexuality and classroom control by engaging in a variety of visible, interactive, and collective activities. Their attempts to make the classroom more relevant and livable took various forms, including accentuating female sexuality, making humorous quips, initiating conversational eruptions, and interjecting their own cultural experience and language into the classroom. However, their contestation and Mrs. Warren's responses were generally good-natured and humorous rather than belligerent. I shall also document that keeping these activities under control was an important factor in Mrs. Warren's teaching strategies.

This brief introductory sketch demonstrates that students in Mrs. Warren's ninth-grade health class generally exemplified the racial homogeneity and traditional gender code of the wider Van Buren community with the majority typifying the school's standards of "excellence" as characterized in Chapter 2; they took academic work fairly seriously, participated in extracurricular activities, and followed school rules. In short, more of them were "good kids"—students who entered to some degree into school activities and generally met the expectations of Van Buren administrators and teachers.

Nevertheless, this profile also suggests that Mrs. Warren's second-period health class was made up of individuals with membership in various social groupings that have differing levels of status in the wider society and school. Students were not members of a unified, coherent group but of smaller groups with a variety of identities related to gender, class, race, sexual orientation, appearance, and so on. Like Mrs. Warren, her students have several "layers of identity" and points at which categories by which they are defined or define themselves intersect (Randall, 1987). Furthermore, membership in these categories can overlap. Thus, the classroom may be thought of as a social arena permeated by the contradictions and tensions within and between these groups. Whatever the information given about sexuality and gender relations and the form of its presentation, this school knowledge is interpreted through and altered by students' varied and sometimes contradictory cultural responses and thus may acquire alternate meanings. I will maintain that students are active participants in constructing the sexuality curriculum. For now, I will generalize classroom dynamics and students' roles in negotiating an overall classroom bargain—an easy grade for acceptable behavior.

The Classroom Bargain

Mrs. Warren's Role

As discussed in the last chapter, Mrs. Warren's selection and organization of the curriculum emerged within the context of certain working conditions, including state and district health requirements for graduation and an alternate-day classroom/physical activity schedule. Thus, she was faced with the dilemma of achieving a balance between maintaining classroom control and being enough of a "buddy" to secure student participation in physical activities, between creating an atmosphere for having fun and encouraging students to take the class seriously, between covering material on a lengthy district syllabus and making the work easy enough for students to do well in the required course. In the context of these tensions, Mrs. Warren gained student compliance and maintained her congenial authority by making the class easy. I will describe in detail in Chapter 6 how she utilized "defensive teaching" strategies—selecting mostly noncontroversial topics, limiting substantive student discussion, presenting easily transmitted and graded fragments of technical details essential for passing the exam, and requiring no written work. These had the effect of reducing the complex and value-laden topic of sexuality to simplified and irrelevant school knowledge.

However, different strategies were required during alternate-day activity sessions. There, Mrs. Warren had to relate more informally with students to gain their compliance in physical activities in which most (especially the young women) had little interest. Enthusiasm, informality, and good humor became essential teacher qualities, and Mrs. Warren was more likely to behave like "one-of-the-girls" during activity sessions. Her informality and sense of humor was enjoyed by students (even Carrie, Dawn, Paula, and Toni) and seemed to be a factor in their thinking she was a nice person and, in Paula's words, "cool". Thus, she was able to gain compliance during activity by asking students to "try for me" or to "be good for me."

This informal and personal aspect of relating to students carried over into the classroom, where Mrs. Warren exercised a genial authority. For example:

> The class has taken a quiz which includes a question on body changes during puberty. As papers are being passed to the front, Andrew (who has been eating Gummy Bears candy while taking the quiz) says to a nearby student, "My Gummy Bear is going through puberty. He's getting taller."
>
> Mrs. Warren hears this remark and moves to his side of the room saying, "You're not eating Gummy Bears?" When she is actually standing in front of Andrew, he looks her in the eye, pops another Gummy Bear in his mouth, smiles, and says, "No."
>
> Mrs. Warren playfully raps him on the head with the rolled-up quizzes she is carrying. She is smiling and says, "Not in my class—not unless you bring enough for everyone." She turns to the rest of the group and announces in a loud voice, "Andrew's bringing treats for everyone on Monday."
>
> Mrs. Warren then begins to provide correct answers for the quiz.

Although the classroom atmosphere was informal and bantering, most students did not offer straightforward challenges to information Mrs. Warren presented or her agenda. While there were a few very noisy days during which she seemed marginally in control, no second-period student openly confronted her in a disrespectful way. Most students exerted enough effort in activity and classroom to get A's and B's, while generally keeping levels of noise, informality, and jocularity within limits acceptable to Mrs. Warren. As the following comments illustrate, most students recognized the implicit classroom bargain:

Lauren: "If you just lay back, you would get a C. If you try hard and really do what she asks, you'll get an A.
Andrew: "Even the lowest person—if they don't do really bad—will pass. A lotta teachers don't want to flunk kids, but some teachers are more prone to *do* something about it. If you know something in health, you'll pass—and Mrs. Warren helps you get a better score."

Students' Role

Nevertheless, students were instrumental in setting the classroom tone, especially during the sex education unit. For example, they repeatedly engaged in muted humorous exchanges with each other, usually only marginally related to the topic being covered by Mrs. Warren:

> While Mrs. Warren is showing students photographs of fetal development, Andrew calls out, "Did you see 'V' [a science fiction movie in which the birth of an alien baby to a human is graphically depicted]?" The noise level suddenly soars as students recount the scene to each other and exclaim, "Gross!" "Yuck!"

On that same day, similar conversational eruptions occur and subside around the topics of multiple births, what babies look like at birth, Mrs. Warren's children, and bizarre food cravings during pregnancy.

Similarly, humorous one-liners (especially from Carrie) were common:

> Mrs. Warren is reading from the birth control worksheet on abstinence. She says that it is 100 percent effective in preventing pregnancy and that she can't think of any risks associated with its use.
>
> Carrie: "Herpes by mouth." (Big laugh from other students, but not Mrs. Warren) "Or you could turn out to be a cranky librarian." (Huge laugh from everyone, including Mrs. Warren)

These ebullient outbursts generally seemed to subside spontaneously. For the most part, Mrs. Warren regarded such interruptions as "release" and problematic only when they interfered with "getting things done." Thus, she good-naturedly accepted them, sometimes getting involved herself, and resumed the lesson as the noise level diminished. If it continued beyond a few minutes, a low-keyed reminder to the group that she needed to get through more material was usually enough to quiet the classroom. When specific individuals persisted in talking among themselves, Mrs. Warren most frequently gained compliance by walking over to those students and making a good-natured request such as:

> Toni, think you could turn this way please? It's hard talking to your back.

> (To a group of young men in the back): Can I interrupt your little coffee klatsch? If you don't want to share what you're saying with the rest of us, keep your mouth shut.

On some occasions, however, she made a more stern response. For example, I heard her threaten a detention three times (twice to Paula and once to Carrie), although she never assigned one. Mrs. Warren's most frequently utilized threat and sanction was moving students to another seat, a procedure with which they always complied without resistance. The following incident, during which Mrs. Warren stood near the two offending students and did not raise her voice, occurred near the beginning of the semester:

> Mrs. Warren is passing out a handout and pauses near Paula and Carrie, who are chatting with each other, although Mrs. Warren has already asked them to stop. She looks at them silently until they are quiet.

> Carrie: "It's Paula's fault."

> Mrs. Warren (to Carrie): "You tend to say too much too often."

> She points to a front row seat, and Carrie moves to it.

Mrs. Warren established a seating chart on the second session of the semester, but students soon rearranged themselves. The same students usually sat together (boys in a cluster, female dirts and black students on either side toward the back, and more quiet young women in the front), with minor variations—some initiated by students and some by Mrs. Warren, who reassigned Toni, Paula, and Carrie to different seats several times during the semester. Nevertheless, because alternate-day activities and absences also made it difficult for her to remember who had been moved where, Mrs. Warren's reassignment would simply be ignored by students the next session, a fact not usually recognized by Mrs. Warren. For example, on September 30 Paula was told to sit in front next time, but during the next classroom session (October 4) she was back in the last row with Toni. In mid October, Mrs. Warren moved Toni to the front row ("This is not temporary; it's *permanent*"). Two classroom sessions later (in another effort to separate the two, who had again moved to the back), Mrs. Warren moved Paula to the front row "forever and ever," although Paula sneaked back one seat by midperiod. On October 21, Toni moved back up next to Paula; on October 28, Mrs. Warren said good-naturedly, "So now you're going to talk up front. The idea was to separate you. If you can be quiet here, Toni can stay." Later, she told me she just wanted to let them know that day she had noticed the move. One day, after being separated by Mrs. Warren, these two came the closest of any students in the class to being openly disrespectful to her. As Toni was moving to the front row where Mrs. Warren had sternly told her to go perma-nently, she muttered "Jesus Christ" under her breath. Later that day, Paula mouthed a "fuck you" at Mrs. Warren from behind her open book; since Mrs. Warren's back was turned, it seems Paula did not choose to openly confront her.

The first day of the sex education unit was another occasion when conversational eruptions and humorous one-liners prompted Mrs. Warren to adopt stricter measures to regain classroom control. After that class Mrs. Warren told me, "I didn't get *anything* done," and the next day she changed the entire seating chart, a harsh measure for her because students had been mostly sitting where they wanted to since the first formal arrangement at the beginning of the semester. Neverthe-less, this stern response was modified somewhat when she allowed Toni and Dawn to remain in nearby seats on the new chart, as long as they were quiet.

Overall, students chose to go along with classroom arrangements. However, as I will further discuss in Chapter 7, student interviews revealed that most were silently but actively calculating their own best interests in doing so. Eighteen of the twenty-five interviewed students said they took the class at least somewhat seriously, mostly for the grade and course requirements. For example:

Kathy: "I took it seriously for the grade, since most infor-mation was a repeat."

Margaret: "[I take it] seriously. I was just trying to get good grades."

Brian: "Just for the need of the credit, I took it seriously."

For the most part, students knew their grade in this required course depended on a combination of test scores and "attitude" (defined variously by them as "paying attention"; "if you try, listen in class and stuff"; "how we did in activity"; "how hard you work"; "if you don't goof around"; and so forth). Thus, they understood and actively participated in the classroom grade bargain by paying attention when Mrs. Warren pointed out exam information and by maintaining an acceptable attitude; the latter was relatively easy since, as previously described, Mrs. Warren allowed a high level of informality and "release," and students seemed to genuinely like her.

For her part, Mrs. Warren saw grades in health class as a form of motivation and encouragement, a way to help students "feel good about themselves" (for example, Paula once received a C$----$ on an exam instead of the D she actually scored. As Mrs. Warren said, "If they worked hard, they deserve a good grade." In addition, because the class was scheduled around both activity and classroom work, Mrs. Warren had the flexibility to justify a high grade; if a test score was low, she could weight participation/effort/attitude more heavily and vice versa. Thus, at the end of the semester, twenty-one of twenty-seven second-period students received A's (thirteen students) and B's (eight students), and no one failed.

However, as the anecdotal evidence already presented suggests, students from marginalized groups (blacks and female dirts) most visibly, collectively, and humorously tested the boundaries of the classroom bargain. It was most frequently their one-liners or anecdotes that initiated conversational eruptions, and these students were most significant in shaping classroom discourse and inducing Mrs. Warren's defensive teaching. These dynamics will be further documented in the next two chapters.

6

School Knowledge about Sexuality:
"Just Stuff You Had to Know"

"You can't get too detailed or you lose them."—Mrs. Warren

"You want to say it just the right way because everyone's going to take it differently. You have to be so careful how you deliver things—especially with this stuff."—Mrs. Warren

"It was just stuff you had to know. I don't know if we'll ever use it."—Sharon

This chapter describes the content and form of knowledge about sexuality and gender relations as selected and presented by Mrs. Warren to her second-period students. It sets forth several verbatim accounts of classroom interaction and begins to document the dynamic process by which such knowledge is jointly constructed by teacher and students. It bears repeating that criticism of Mrs. Warren's teaching strategies is not the major issue or intent. While it may be tempting to regard some of these strategies as evidence of inadequate planning/preparation or of Mrs. Warren's personal bias, I believe they can be more fully understood as emerging from the complex nexus I have just described, which includes organizational arrangements of Van Buren and Woodland District, the demands of Mrs. Warren's multiple and sometimes conflicting roles, and (as I shall elaborate in Chapter 7) unanticipated responses of students. For example, Mrs. Warren consistently presented information in the sex education unit as fragments which could be easily transmitted and graded on exams, thereby reducing the rich and diverse subject matter of sexuality to a narrow range of largely noncontroversial technical knowledge with little relevance to students. This curricular choice is influenced by wider organizational factors, including her fragmented teaching schedule, the large number of students in her classes, pressure to address a multitude of course objectives, students' need to pass this required course, and administrative expectations for classroom control and good community relations. Thus, the content and teaching strategies delineated here can be perceived as active attempts to cope with institutional dilemmas and minimize student resistance.

It also bears repeating that my narrative of this classroom experience can only be a partial telling, since telling stories about lived experience can never be synonymous with the experience itself (Brodkey, 1987). Other observers might have noticed other events and interpreted them differently. This narrative, bound by my perspectives and the methodological constraints outlined in earlier chapters, portrays school-based knowledge about sexuality as it was visible to me in the classroom.

Overview of Content

Sex education was the last and shortest classroom unit of study in the health course, with less than six hours of time spent on it. The unit began on December 4, encompassed a two-week Christmas break and ended on January 10. Thirteen broad content areas, listed here in order of time spent, were covered during this period: sexually transmitted diseases (42 minutes), dating (40 minutes), teenage pregnancy consequences (30 minutes), contraception (30 minutes), communicating with parents (29 minutes), adolescent body changes (25 minutes), reproductive anatomy and physiology (21 minutes), marriage and family (18 minutes), saying "no" to sexual intercourse (15 minutes), pregnancy and prenatal development (13 minutes), love vs. infatuation (10 minutes), childbirth (9 minutes), sexual assault (9 minutes).[1]

Like respondents in large survey research samples (Alan Guttmacher Institute, 1983; Orr, 1982; Sonenstein & Pittman, 1984), Mrs. Warren spent most time on the least controversial sexuality education topics: sexually transmitted diseases, consequences of teenage pregnancy, adolescent body changes, and reproductive anatomy and physiology. She also spent a comparatively large amount of time on other less controversial topics not mentioned in that research: communicating with parents, dating, and marriage and family. Like 75 percent of teachers in a later study (Donovan, 1989), she spent time on birth control.

Controversial Topics

Like respondents in all these surveys who reported they less frequently covered sexual response/pleasure, masturbation, abortion, and homosexuality, Mrs. Warren barely mentioned these more controversial topics. With regard to sexual response/pleasure, she pointed out the clitoris on the female anatomy diagram and said, "It's the *most* sexually sensitive part of the female body." In addition, one of three paragraphs that Mrs. Warren assigned students to read from the text during the first sex education session included the following reference to sexual pleasure:

> Because of the strong biological urge and its association with pleasure, sexual behavior is not always easy to control. Partially for this reason, many people have tried to hide sexual feelings. Total abstinence or illicit sex may cause feelings of guilt, fear, and anxiety. Sex is beautiful and can be an essential part of the total personality of everyone. No one should be forced into a position of guilt, fear, or anxiety about their own sexuality. Sexual feelings are urges that must be directed and handled in each situation or they may destroy trust, respect and integrity. (Julian, Jackson, & Simon, 1980, p. 78)

She made no verbal reference to masturbation, although it was one of fourteen terms from the text whose definition—"self stimulation of sex organs"—students copied into notebooks.

Abortion

As I shall detail later, abortion was mentioned only briefly during a classroom movie. Afterwards, when Carrie and Dawn expressed their opinion that abortion is an acceptable alternative for dealing with an unplanned pregnancy, Mrs. Warren neither agreed nor disagreed with them but redirected the discussion. At a subsequent session on pregnancy and prenatal development, Mrs. Warren showed several color photographs illustrating fetal development from a *Life* magazine. In response to several students' exclamations of "Gross," "Yuck," and so on, she said, "They're beautiful. There's a miracle going on here." She added that last year a student had asked if these were pictures of abortions and then explained that they were of either miscarriages or live "babies" within the woman's body, taken by special photographic techniques. As she passed around the photographs, she pointed to such details as the umbilical cord ("the lifeline between the baby and the mother") and a fetus with thumb near its mouth, mostly referring to the fetus as "baby."

One multiple choice question on the exam asked students to identify the word defined as "intentionally terminating (stopping) a pregnancy"; word choices were "adoption, abortion, miscarriage, abstinence." Finally, one of four extra-credit short answer questions (answered by seven students) asked them to describe the "options for a sexually active couple and the girl get [*sic*] pregnant."

Homosexuality

References to homosexuality were presented almost entirely in the context of AIDS, although it was first mentioned while Mrs. Warren was reading from a handout on "saying 'no' " to intercourse. One of the "lines" that "guys" use to convince young women to have intercourse stated: "I've heard that you're 'lezzie.' If you aren't, prove it." Mrs. Warren's reading of this statement was greeted by loud laughter and echoes of the word "lezzie" from many students of both sexes. Beyond this reference, the concept of lesbianism was invisible in the classroom.

Several sessions later Mrs. Warren read the following statement from an AIDS handout given to students: "So far in the United States, gay and bi-sexual men have been most at risk of getting AIDS. More than 70 percent of reported cases are in these two groups" (Network Publications, 1985).[2] At a subsequent session, she made the following statement while distributing a worksheet she had prepared on sexually transmitted diseases: "Ninety-three per cent of AIDS victims are male, 73 percent *because* [emphasis added] they are homosexual." That same day, she said, "New York and California have most AIDS. There are more gay people there." Finally she said, "Because it [AIDS] involves gay people, many others say, 'Don't do anything about it.' But they're human too. There hasn't been enough money spent on it." AIDS was absent from the review sheet distributed before the exam, and only two true/false questions about it appeared on the exam itself: (1) "With AIDS, 93 percent are males, and 73 percent are homosexual and/

or bisexuals"; (2) "AIDS is known as acquired immune deficiency syndrome."

It should be noted that these data were collected at a time when fewer HIV/AIDS educational materials were available. Furthermore, the risk of HIV infection was only beginning to be presented in terms of behaviors rather than risk groups, and political critiques were less widely articulated. While two of Mrs. Warren's comments might now be readily recognized as inaccurate and reinforcing of a negative stereotype, her final comment demonstrates her awareness that the stigma attached to being gay was a factor in early public inattention to AIDS and seemed an attempt to deflect homophobic responses from students. While I am not defending Mrs. Warren's coverage of either homosexuality or HIV infection, it is important to be aware that it was set in an earlier context. Unfortunately, however, most classroom teachers are still largely silent on the issue of homosexuality, do not address issues of homophobia, racism, and sexism that underly the AIDS pandemic, or provide specifics of safer sex practices.

Teaching Strategies

Lecture/Teacher Explanation

Nearly all health information, including sexuality, was conveyed by Mrs. Warren's presentation or teacher-selected media and materials. In terms of complexity, information was presented largely as fact or detail, receiving no elaboration beyond a few sentences. In addition, the seemingly random order in which Mrs. Warren presented various classroom topics (for instance, the menstrual cycle explained before reproductive anatomy), absence of transitions between them, and the two-week Christmas vacation all contributed to an overall impression of fragmentation. This is illustrated by the following list of dates and topics:

Date	Topic
December 4	Child/parent relationships
December 6	Marriage and family; physical changes of adolescence
December 10	Teenage pregnancy (film)
December 12	Quiz on family/physical changes of adolescence; menstrual cycle; dating

December 16   Qualities looked for in a date; love vs. infatuation; saying "no" to intercourse

December 18   Advantages/disadvantages of "going with" one person; teenage marriage; female/male reproductive anatomy

December 20   Pregnancy/prenatal development; childbirth; birth control devices

January 6   Birth control; sexually transmitted diseases

January 8   Sexually transmitted diseases; fourth degree sexual assault; exam review

Further, this overall sequence was interrupted on a daily basis by Mrs. Warren's giving directions, answering questions, or presenting material regarding alternate-day physical activities (fitness tests, timed runs, weight training, and so forth).

Presenting Technical Fragments

Mrs. Warren frequently read pieces of information aloud while students recorded them on worksheets to be kept in notebooks as study guides, a strategy she used in six of the nine sex education sessions. For example, she gave students a worksheet on ten sexually transmitted diseases (gonorrhea, chlamydia, syphilis, herpes, AIDS, vaginitis, yeast, venereal warts, crabs/lice, scabies); it was divided into four columns ("symptoms," "complications," "transmission," "cure/ treatment"), and it is worth noting that "prevention" was not included. She had typed information in the "complications" column and then read aloud details for students to write in the others. Such piecemeal information was fragmented even further when she began by listing symptoms of chlamydia, gonorrhea, syphilis, and herpes before discussing these diseases as separate entities. Other worksheets used in this manner included female/male reproductive anatomy, pregnancy/ birth, and contraception.

With regard to contraception, Mrs. Warren presented brief, mostly technical details about various methods and displayed sample devices in a seven-minute presentation just before Christmas break,[3] with timing based partly on availability of a shared contraceptive kit. In seven minutes, students had brief glimpses of the following (in order): oral contraceptive packets; a diaphragm in combination with a contraceptive foam applicator (diaphragms are actually used with contraceptive cream or jelly, which does not require an applicator); an intrauterine device (Lippes Loop); spermicidal cream; contraceptive sponge, suppositories, and foam (with applicator); and condom packet (uno-pened).

Although Mrs. Warren had previously responded with "lack of time" to my questioning why she didn't show the condom itself, she mentioned two other factors during her subsequent reading of this report: lack of familiarity with condoms in her personal life and a classroom incident that had occurred several years earlier. She had been pregnant and, as she took a condom out of the packet to show students, it accidentally made a loud snapping noise. Two male students "just went nuts" with laughter, while she became red-faced and began to laugh as well. Finally, everyone in the room was laughing uncontrollably; in her words, "I lost it completely."

After the two-week break, she gave students a handout listing various contraceptive methods (abstinence, pill, IUD, diaphragm, sponge, condom, foam, rhythm, withdrawal, vasectomy, and tubal ligation) and their effectiveness percentages and selected risks/advantages. Mrs. Warren read the handout to students, adding a few details on how each method works and "other information" for students to write in the appropriate columns.

The meaning of effectiveness (number of women who do not get pregnant out of every one hundred using the method for one year) was not explained, nor the difference between theoretical effectiveness (maximum success rate when a method is used absolutely correctly) and user effectiveness (actual in-use rate that takes human error into account). A range of effectiveness was given for a few methods (diaphragm: 90–98 percent; condom: 80–96 percent), a precise figure for most, and no information on effectiveness for others (withdrawal and sterilization). Proper use of condoms was mentioned but not explained. In summary, students did receive thirty minutes worth of information on birth control and actually saw the devices. However, the information provided was sometimes inaccurate, not complete enough to enable them to make an informed decision about which method to choose, and almost entirely lacking in directions for use.

Teaching Toward Exams

Presenting bits and pieces of information was in part due to Mrs. Warren's expressed teaching philosophy ("You can't get too detailed or you lose them") and her feeling responsible for helping students "do well" on unit exams, particularly since passing the health course is a state and district requirement for graduation. Mrs. Warren told students at the beginning of the semester that she would point out information on which they would be tested. For example, the day she passed out the health textbooks she said:

> You don't have to take notes on reading because I'll give you notes in class. . . . Anything I put on the board is important . . . I'll give you words that are important.

This strategy of pointing out to students the specific details they would need to know for the exam continued throughout the entire semester. Selected examples from the sex education unit include:

> There are three terms from the male reproductive sheet I need you to know (Dec. 20).

> You need to know that the pill, IUD, and diaphragm are prescription methods. You need to be able to list this (Jan. 6).

> A combination of foam and condoms is the best nonprescription method of birth control. You may want to make a note of that (Jan. 6).

> Chlamydia is the number one sexually transmitted disease. I want you to know that for sure (Jan. 8).

Pointing out specific information on which students would be tested reached a peak in the last few classroom sessions before each exam. They received a review sheet, and Mrs. Warren read brief definitions and explanations of each word and concept while students copied them. In contrast to the other units, when students had to fill in the definitions themselves, Mrs. Warren provided a largely completed review sheet for the sex education unit. Furthermore, after covering birth control and sexually transmitted diseases, she read true/false questions from the upcoming exam for students to call out answers.[4] During the semester, students learned they could do well on exams by saving handouts, jotting down details as Mrs. Warren emphasized them, or—more easily—simply filling in the review sheet. Therefore, during the review sessions students were especially quiet and attentive—talking less among themselves, telling fewer personal interest stories, asking fewer questions (digressive or otherwise), and dutifully taking notes.

Mrs. Warren employed other strategies in designing and grading unit exams to help students get good grades. First, she offered easily answered extra-credit questions on all four exams. On the sex education exam, these included five possible points for short answer questions related to sexuality and twenty possible extra-credit points on material covered earlier in the semester. Fourteen students earned at least fifteen extra credit points—enough to raise their grades one letter. Mrs. Warren also calculated the grading curve to maximize student grades, paying particular attention to minimizing the number of F's. Thus, on all four exams taken during the semester by the twenty-seven students in the classroom, only four F's were given, compared to forty-three A's. It should be noted, however, that Mrs. Warren regarded it as her best class that semester.

In terms of exam points, students might logically perceive the most highly valued information about sexuality to be technical and characterized by one "correct" answer. Seventy-nine of the possible ninety-five exam points involved facts about sexually transmitted diseases, reproductive anatomy and physiology, birth control, pregnancy, and prenatal development. Those topics characterized by several "correct" responses (for example, saying "no" to intercourse; marriage and family; communicating with parents; love vs. infatuation) were reduced to one acceptable answer for the exam. The following true/false questions are typical examples:

If you are not ready to think about birth control, you are not ready for intercourse.

Good communication between husband and wife is the basis for building a good family relationship.

Infatuation is the same as love.

Reading Aloud

The more extended descriptions Mrs. Warren occasionally offered most frequently involved reading verbatim from informational handouts provided for students, for example, "Ann Landers' 18,000 Lines Used by Boys on the Make," "Eight Popular Reasons for Having Intercourse . . . That No Smart Teenager Would Use," "How to Say 'No,' "[5] and "What is AIDS?" (Network Publications, 1985) or from other material such as sexual abuse laws and newspaper clippings. Altogether, Mrs. Warren spent over thirty minutes reading aloud in this manner, including ten minutes on AIDS from a brochure (Network Publications, 1985) she received at a districtwide meeting of health teachers. Similarly, as previously described, she read sexual assault information to students from state sexual assault laws, a newspaper

111

clipping about previous incidents in Woodland schools, and a district memo which urged coverage of legal consequences of sexual assault by all ninth-grade health teachers.

Both topics were additions to the Woodland health curriculum that year, and Mrs. Warren felt uncertain about how to deal with them in her own words. In referring to sexual assault, she said:

> You want to say it just the right way because everyone's going to take it differently. You have to be so careful how you deliver things—especially with this stuff.

Similarly, when asked whether there were topics she would have liked to include but did not, Mrs. Warren mentioned homosexuality and masturbation and went on to say:

> I think I'd have to really work on presenting it. Just like the fourth degree sexual assault, you gotta say it just right. You can't joke about it, and you can't laugh it off because it's not funny. . . . I think I've shied away because I don't know how I want to present it because I have to think about how I feel about it first. I'm comfortable with it myself, but I still haven't found a way that I can say it to ninth-grade girls and boys to make it sound like I'm not out in left field.

Thus, Mrs. Warren attempted to solve the dilemma created by a convergence of administrative priority for "smooth running" classes and few parent complaints, district pressure to incorporate additional and controversial topics into an already full syllabus, the unpredictability of student response, e.g., making a joke out of a serious topic, and little time for reflective planning by reading the words to get them "just right."

Students Reading Textbooks in Class

One method of presenting information unique to the sex education unit was requiring students to read the textbook during class time. Mrs. Warren's students spent half an hour reading assigned pages on dating and adolescent development, copying definitions about the latter. Most of this in-class reading was assigned during the second sex education session, following a noisy first session characterized by many student-initiated digressions, humorous one-liners, and other interruptions. Therefore, at the beginning of the next session she rearranged student seating and assigned in-class reading and definition writing to reestablish control. Furthermore, this strategy (along with having students fill in worksheets and reading aloud to them) helped her deal with the pressure she felt to "say it just the right way"—a pressure which seemed most intense with the sex education unit.

The fact that students had to read the textbook in class if at all was related to economic factors largely beyond Mrs. Warren's control and to the potential for parent complaints. The sex education supplement (*Modern Sex Education*, by Julian, Jackson, & Simon, 1980) to the hardcover health text was printed separately in paperback, a common practice among publishers to facilitate health textbook sales to districts and states (particularly those in which all districts purchase the same texts) where sex education is regarded as inappropriate for schools.[6] While enough hardcover health texts had been purchased to provide each student with a copy, this was not the case with the separate sex education paperback. According to both Mrs. Warren and Mr. Austin (chairperson of Van Buren's physical education department), there was not enough money in the school's health education budget to purchase that many copies, so a set for each classroom was purchased instead. The district health coordinator, Mr. Cox, recalled that money *was* available, but that Van Buren health teachers—along with others in the district—were concerned about possible negative parent reaction if students took copies home, so they chose to purchase only classroom copies. Whatever the explanation, the result was that students had access to the text only during class time.

Mrs. Warren explained the situation to students at the first sex education session as follows:

"This book is going to stay in this room. You'll read it in class. It's not because it's supposed to be only read in class, but we couldn't afford enough copies for everyone." She goes on to say the price of the large text is $15.95 and the sex education paperback is $9.95.

About fifteen minutes later, Tammy asks why the sex education part is not with the rest of the book.

Mrs. Warren: "The people in Texas, where this is published, believe that this information should be kept secret." She adds that people in Texas are "kind of conservative and believe that this [sex education] belongs in the home"—a belief she shares, "but unfortunately Moms and Dads don't do it."

Her comment about Texas is erroneous (the book was actually published in New York) but does demonstrate a partial understanding of the dynamics of textbook sales, since Texas has a statewide selection and purchasing arrangement.

Using Personal Asides

As anyone who has spent time in a classroom can attest, asides (digressive narrative, commentary, or personal stories) can be powerful instructional devices. Mrs. Warren most frequently commented in this way on marriage, pregnancy, childbirth, parenting, and sterilization experiences and her own early ignorance about sex. Altogether, she spent slightly more than twenty minutes on asides during the sex education unit. The following excerpt from my field notes typifies the way she incorporated such experiences into the classroom; it also illustrates the generally relaxed, bantering atmosphere (in which substantive student questions were sometimes lost), and how she handled conversational eruptions. (However, it is *not* typical in that most of Mrs. Warren's other descriptions of her childbirth experiences referred to their difficulty, for example, pain and stitches.)

Mrs. Warren defines afterbirth (a term on the handout) as "placenta (previously defined) and everything left over after the baby is born." She says her doctor asked her if she wanted to see it, but she said, "No thanks."

Paula:	"What's it like?"
Carrie:	"Like having a mass period."
Mrs. Warren:	"It's a little worse than that."
Paula:	"How many things are delivered?"

Mrs. Warren says that the placenta is the third stage of delivery and that the amniotic fluid didn't come, so "the doctor went in there with a fish hook thing to break the sac." She goes on to say that the baby comes second and then "everything else."

Paula:	"What else?"
Carrie:	"A Christmas present from your Gramma."

There is loud laughter from the rest of the students, who have been listening intently.

114

Mrs. Warren says that giving birth is a "beautiful experience. Having kids is very special." She says she feels a lot of love for her children.

> Carrie: "We know you beat 'em."
> Mrs. Warren: "Well, Greg [her son] gets more spankings than Judy [her daughter]."

Students begin talking among themselves, and there is a noisy interlude of about twenty seconds while Mrs. Warren talks with young women near the front.

> Mrs. Warren: (to the whole group) "Amniocentesis [next word on the handout] is a test for birth defects."
> Andrew: "You can check for the baby's sex too."
> Paula: "Did you worry before the baby was born?"
> Mrs. Warren: "Only about whether it was a boy or girl."
> Andrew: "What did you want first?"
> Mrs. Warren: "A boy."

Students begin talking with each other again, and Mrs. Warren directs other comments about her children to those near the front. Some students tell her to bring her children to school. After about a minute, Mrs. Warren addresses the large group and defines the next word on the handout.

In contrast to the economics teachers in McNeil's study (1986), who split off personal information from lecture content, Mrs. Warren's frequent interjections of personal experience into other information she presented might have legitimated her individual experience as wider "fact," for instance, the failure of diaphragm and contraceptive sponge to prevent pregnancy for both herself and a friend. It is noteworthy that Mrs. Warren's socially sanctioned status as heterosexual, wife, and mother probably made such disclosure easier for her and more acceptable as fact than if she had been a lesbian or a heterosexually active yet unmarried female teacher. Thus, most of Mrs. Warren's personal asides implicitly conferred status on dominant cultural values, particularly since students liked her and the class. Nevertheless, some aspects of her life which she mentioned (she makes more money than her husband and their children are in day care) did contradict traditional gender arrangements.

School Knowledge about Sexuality

Showing a Film

Another example of fragmentation occurred around a film on teenage pregnancy consequences, partly because coordination with other schools in the district and room schedules were involved.[7] After Woodland teachers saw the film at a district meeting in September, they agreed to schedule it for one week in December, with each school using it for one day. This prearranged schedule meant that the film was shown on the third day of the sex education unit. Furthermore, because students were scheduled for the weight training room at the next activity session, the film directly followed a 25-minute presentation by Mrs. Warren on muscle groups needed for weight training. When asked later about the rationale for preceding the film with information on muscle groups, Mrs. Warren replied, "It just happened; that wasn't planned right . . . the muscle groups were something I had to get done." Students received the following brief introduction from Mrs. Warren:

"We're seeing a movie today. It's called, 'If You Want to Dance.' It's a film on teenage pregnancy." She goes on to describe the beginning, which alternates between a basketball court and delivery room—father in one place, mother in another. "The delivery is nothing drastic, but you will see the baby oming out."

The fourteen-minute movie, produced for the U.S. Department of Health and Human Services by New Dimension Films (1983a), was designed (according to the accompanying teacher's study guide) to: "impress upon males that pregnancy is not just a girl's problem. Despite peer pressure, it is not fashionable to get a girl pregnant" (New Dimension Films, 1983b). About eight minutes of class time remained after the film, which concluded with an open-ended situation—presumably to invite discussion.[8] At this point, Mrs. Warren asked students what they thought of it. Carrie and Dawn pointed out that the girl in the film might have chosen to have an abortion instead of giving birth, but several other students had begun talking among themselves, and a group focus never materialized. Mrs. Warren then attempted to redirect discussion by asking, "What would you do in the girl or guy's place?" This time, Paula and Toni joined Carrie and Dawn in interjecting their lived experience:

116

Toni: "I'd slap him [the teenage father] up."

Carrie: (sarcastically) "I'd be the sweetest girl in the world."

Paula: (defiantly) "My mom was seventeen when she had me."

Toni: "My mom was married when she was eighteen, and she got married because she had my sister."

Carrie: "My sister had a baby when she was fourteen."

Dawn: "My cousin had a baby when she was fourteen."

They more or less call their comments out into the air, while several other students begin to talk with each other. Mrs. Warren speaks with a small group of young women in the front, and the group focus vanishes.

After about a minute, Mrs. Warren reads a question from the study guide to regain the group focus.

Mrs. Warren: "What message was the film trying to give by switching back and forth from the basketball scene to the delivery room at the beginning, although they didn't really show much of the birth."

Male Student: "Yeah, the censored version."

Mrs. Warren: "The guy in the film said girls know about their own bodies, but they have no idea what the pain's like during birth—no idea." She goes on to talk about her own delivery for several seconds, including the comment, "I felt like my back was coming through my skin. I had back labor." She then points out that the guy in the film seemed uncomfortable in the hospital. Apparently giving up on further film discussion, Mrs. Warren then tells students that the film is going to another high school in Woodland and that Bonnie (this researcher) is taking it there.

This launches a series of digressive questions (directed at this researcher) from several students: "Where do you teach?" "When do you teach?" "How can you come here every morning?" "Do you get paid for this (observing in the classroom)?"

School Knowledge about Sexuality

Mrs. Warren says it is fair for Bonnie to answer their questions, since they are answering hers. Thus, this interaction continues for about a minute until the bell rings.

The film itself was not mentioned again in class by either Mrs. Warren or students.

Dealing with Controversy/Current Topics

I heard Mrs. Warren make no reference in her presentations to controversy (mention that the topic was a subject of debate, encompassing opposing points of view or varying value judgments), although students sometimes expressed opinions that differed with one another's. For example, the following exchange, also illustrating Mrs. Warren's presentation by reading aloud, occurred during her coverage of fourth degree sexual assault:

Mrs. Warren reads a memo from the Woodland health coordinator that expresses a concern about sexual assault and the district's intent to deal seriously with such incidents when they occur at school.

Andrew:	(to Carrie) "Their rules are so strict, though. You couldn't even say 'hi' without getting accused."
Carrie:	(to Andrew) "You can't even touch someone on the shoulder anymore."

Mrs. Warren finishes reading the memo and then reads a legal definition of fourth degree sexual assault.

Andrew:	(louder, for all to hear) "You can't even touch someone on the shoulder anymore."
Mrs. Warren:	"If a girl is enticing—going, 'come on, come on'—that's different."
Andrew:	"What if you do it accidentally?"
Mrs. Warren:	"Your body is private." She explains that a person doesn't have to "put up" with being touched in ways they don't want to be. "It's not right if guys get aggressive."
Andrew:	"What if she's wearing a one-piece bikini?"
Dawn:	"It doesn't matter what kind of clothing a girl wears—they say on TV."

118

Mrs. Warren: "Girls can ask for it. Let's get on with this. I'll read you something else." *She reads an article from the Woodland daily paper reporting sexual assault incidents in local schools.*

This reference to incidents of the previous school year was the only time I heard Mrs. Warren use current events for illustration during the sex education unit, although AIDS was at the time widely covered by the media. In fact, I collected nearly 150 articles on AIDS from the Woodland daily newspaper during the period I was observing at Van Buren. Although Mrs. Warren did not mention that AIDS was a current or controversial topic, student comments and questions during her brief presentation on it seemed to reflect some awareness of the current media coverage. The following exchange took place on January 6:

Mrs. Warren reads the first few paragraphs from the AIDS handout she has given students.

Andrew: (interrupts) "Rock Hudson had that."
Mrs. Warren: (looks at him sternly) "No jokes."
Paula: "Can you die from it?"
Andrew: "It's like in a war with nothing to fight with. Your body has no shields."
Mrs. Warren: "That's pretty good. How did you know that?" (Several other students laugh.)

Mrs. Warren finishes reading the first section of the handout—"What is AIDS?—and begins the second section, "How Do People Get AIDS?"

Doug: (interrupts) "How did it start?"
Mrs. Warren: "It has a six-year history." *She reads the next paragraph which states that gay and bisexual men are groups at most risk of getting AIDS.* "I've read everything there is to read about it, but I'm not sure how it started."

Andrew says there are areas of AIDS "all over the world."

Doug: "There are two states with no AIDS."

Mrs. Warren says that New York and California have the most cases and that there are "more gay people there."

School Knowledge about Sexuality

> Tammy: "It started in Haiti."
>
> Mrs. Warren: (to Tammy, in a lower voice) "Haitians are really bad for this."

Other students whisper/talk among themselves for about thirty seconds, while Mrs. Warren speaks to Tammy and others near the front.

> Mrs. Warren: "Can we read?" She continues from paragraph three in the second section.

Facilitating Class Discussion

Like Mrs. Warren's explanations, wider class discussion (issues discussed with teacher in facilitative rather than explanatory/lecturing role) consisted mainly of fragments, with some students calling out brief remarks related to her discussion-starting questions while others made muted comments to those sitting nearby. For example, during one session Mrs. Warren asked students about qualities they would look for in a date, and she listed responses on the board. The resulting list from young women (particularly Carrie, obviously describing the Van Buren basketball star on whom she had a crush) consisted of the following:

> good listener, older, I can trust, same interests, car/license, over 19, money, dresser, healthy, muscular, physical, nice bod', good complexion, good dancer, sweet, intelligent, waterbed, 6'4", dusty black hair, brown eyes, pretty lips.

The list from young men is as follows:

> body, not too tall, blondes/brunettes, butt, bust, cute/pretty face, soft personality, not too shy or quiet, not stuck-up, not a lot of makeup, sense of humor, casual dress, movies/long bus rides.

However, more muted suggestions for the list in my immediate vicinity of the classroom included "someone who knows you inside and out" (note the double meaning, which was not lost on other students), "take what you can get," and "beaver." Furthermore, Mrs. Warren did not respond to the following audible comments:

Toni: "We could get into detail, but I don't think you'd like it."

Dawn: "Good kisser—good smacker."

Carrie: "Not a wham-bam-thank-you-ma'am."

After spending about fifteen minutes recording these responses on the board, Mrs. Warren commented that the lists largely exemplified infatuation and went on to define the term for students to write in their notebooks: "Just understand it's physical." Next she read several brief definitions of love, telling students, "You don't have to write this down" (another way of saying, "This won't be on the test."). Other topics covered by this form of class "discussion" included activities parents did on dates (based on questions students were assigned to ask their parents) and advantages/disadvantages of "going with one person."

Although Mrs. Warren's expressed teaching ideals included student discussions and small group work, I never observed substantive or ongoing class discussion guided by student questions. However, as previous examples suggest, students did ask some questions that Mrs. Warren answered, frequently about her personal and family life. There was no formal small group discussion; nevertheless, as I have already described, students frequently conducted their own informal small group discussions during Mrs. Warren's classroom presentations.

Classroom Points of View about Gender Relations and Sexuality

The curricular content and form just described can also be understood as "reified" knowledge, a term Robert Everhart (1983) uses for the knowledge system that pervades schooling and underlies empirical science. According to dominant curricular models, school knowledge is based on a linear/causal relationship between elements of reality, with abstract and problematic knowledge treated as if it were concrete and factual. Acceptance of "facts" is part of the definition of what is "known," while their problematic nature, assumptions behind them, or criteria for selection are not explored. Instead, according to Everhart, these accepted "facts" are manipulated or "added up" to produce a predefined product. Both ends and means are rationally planned by curricular experts.

Furthermore, since ends are more significant than means in a reified knowledge system, the "right answer" and (in the case of Mrs. Warren's classroom) preparing students to pass the exam and the required course are primary. Thus, "correct" information is simply handed down from the testmaker rather than investigated and explored by students. As happens within the educational system in general, details about sexuality in this case "added up" to a reified version of a fundamentally abstract, value-laden, and controversial issue. There was little room for meaningful student dialogue with presented information, and its manipulation (writing it down and recalling it for exams) was more significant for students than its exploration.

Although students may mediate and reinterpret this reified knowledge, selection and presentation of information does invite them to identify with particular points of view—in the case of Mrs. Warren's class, about sexuality and the nature of gender relations. These points of view may also be understood as "scripts" that invite students to adopt certain roles and ideologies. Many of the scripts I observed in Mrs. Warren's class coincided with wider official "type-scripts"— dominant societal expectations for appropriate sexual behavior and gender relations (Davies, 1983). However, I also observed moments in which a presented point of view conflicted with the wider type-scripts or other classroom scripts.

I do not suggest by delineating classroom scripts about sexuality that Mrs. Warren necessarily planned to transmit them or was aware that they were sometimes contradictory to dominant norms and to each other. Instead, selection of information, the form of its presentation, and the sometimes contradictory points of view these embody are constructed in the context of the classroom from a complex juncture that includes active responses of students, organizational imperatives of district and school, and Mrs. Warren's gendered position in the society and workplace. Mrs. Warren's defensive teaching strategies— covering mostly noncontroversial topics, presenting fragments of technical information geared toward passing exams, and limiting substantive student discussion—emerge from a particular context as active attempts to cope with structural dilemmas and student resistance. I have begun to show that not all students accepted the offered points of view (scripts) or chose to identify with them. As I shall further document in Chapter 7, students had several differing interpretations of the overall points of view presented in the sex education unit and did *not* passively internalize classroom versions of knowledge about sexuality and gender relations.

Before describing classroom scripts more specifically, I shall comment briefly on the role of Mrs. Warren's personal beliefs in her curricular decisions and some themes underlying the structure of the sex education unit as a whole.

Mrs. Warren's Personal Beliefs

Just as values enter into the selection and presentation of curriculum in all subjects areas, Mrs. Warren's personal bias entered into her curricular decisions. Most notably, Mrs. Warren is against abortion (she describes this stance as pro-life), and she purposely showed pictures of fetal development and referred to the fetus as "baby" as a means to convey that perspective, although she never explicitly said in the classroom that abortion was wrong. Moreover, as previously described, characters in the classroom movie only briefly mentioned abortion as a possibility they had rejected, while stressing adoption or keeping the baby as their preferred choices.

In addition, one semester a speaker from an anti-abortion pregnancy counseling group whose function was to dissuade young women from having abortions called Mrs. Warren and said she needed a place to present her slides to see if they were appropriate for high school age-students. After getting approval for one semester from Mr. Gray, Mrs. Warren arranged for the woman to come to three of her classes because:

> it was a good opportunity to show options—even if I didn't show the other side. But I don't know where, really, to find something for the other side as far as abortions go.

Mrs. Warren also said that she would have continued having this speaker if Mr. Gray had not ruled it out for subsequent semesters. On the other hand, Mrs. Warren has stopped inviting teenage speakers from the district's school-age maternity program because of their "pushing one way [to keep the baby]." She says she believes adoption is a better alternative:

> I just can't imagine someone fifteen-years-old hanging onto someone that's two months old, being totally responsible for that person.

In summary, while Mrs. Warren's personal beliefs about abortion did influence the sexuality curriculum-in-use (sometimes in contradictory ways), practical considerations such as availability of resources, time to look for them, and a sense that the community might support these views also weighed into her curricular decisions.

Like most classroom teachers across the country, Mrs. Warren was largely silent on the issue of homosexuality, except for mentioning it in the context of her brief coverage of AIDS. Her personal values may have been a factor in this exclusion, since her own ambiguity about a gay relative ("I'm not afraid of him, but I'm not comfortable with him") surfaced during the interviews. However, as was the case with abortion, other factors related to organizational constraints and potential student response also played a role in this exclusion. For example, Mrs. Warren made the following comments:

> I want to be able to present it in just the right way, and I haven't found that yet.

> I have to find a way to present it without biases.

> I'd have to have the right class chemistry because most of them [students] wouldn't handle it right. I think they're not mature enough.

It is possible that such practical considerations occasionally served as overt rationalizations for coverage more influenced by personal values. For example, Mrs. Warren's brief display of birth control devices might have been prompted by her concern that actually showing them might "promote sexual activity" (a worry she expressed during a later interview and one also expressed by Mr. Gray). However, as previously discussed, the practical reality was that she had many other topics to cover in the course, previously received a parental complaint about a condom passed around in another teacher's class, and lost control of students while showing one in her classroom. Thus, organizational and student response factors entered into this choice as well.

Finally, Mrs. Warren's personal belief is that ninth-graders are too young to be having intercourse, although she is not against premarital sex in general. She believes that not enough is done to help young people learn to say "no." Nevertheless, in the classroom she did not focus exclusively on abstinence but provided information on birth control as well. Taken together, my observations suggest that Mrs. Warren's personal beliefs about sexuality did consciously enter into some of her curricular decisions; however, they had less of an effect on the sexuality curriculum-in-use than factors related to school and district organization. As Michael Apple (1992) has suggested with regard to textbook publishers "mentioning" isolated and unelaborated fragments of the history and culture of less powerful groups, the reasons behind Mrs. Warren's mere mentioning of certain topics are complex.

Underlying Themes

Because every student could not have their own copy of the sexuality text, they experienced the unit differently from other topics in the health course (fitness, nutrition, alcohol and drugs) in that they could only read the sexuality text within the confines of the classroom. Thus, sexuality knowledge was permeated by a greater aura of secrecy and adult ownership than other topics. The theme of adult ownership might be reinforced, as I shall discuss later, by the fact that sexuality was mostly defined in the classroom in the context of adult models of marriage and parenting, and that most information about sexuality was conveyed in a verbal mode by Mrs. Warren, with the expectation that students used "correct" terminology in the classroom. This curricular form may differ greatly from students' various lived cultural experiences, where sex may be "doing" rather than talking and correct classroom terminology contrasts with everyday student language. Nevertheless, the generally relaxed, informal atmosphere and the prevalence of friendly banter in the classroom could readily contradict this impression of sexuality as a mysterious and strictly adult-owned topic.

Furthermore, since classroom information was presented in a form geared toward passing the exam, the potential for students perceiving testable bits of information as the most noteworthy aspects of sexuality is maximized. Partly because Mrs. Warren felt pressure to cover the material in the district syllabus and to help students pass this required course, content that was actually relevant to their everyday life outside the classroom was reduced to material whose major relevance was meeting grade requirements. This perception that course material may be irrelevant to everyday life could have been reinforced by the following specific incident:

> After finishing the sexually transmitted diseases chart the last day before the exam, Mrs. Warren tells students: "There are places to go if you think you have an STD, but I'm more concerned with the test today." She then mentions the names of two local agencies and says she will get students a list of testing and treatment places "later."

School Knowledge about Sexuality

Students never receive the list, nor are they informed that state law provides for minors to be tested and treated for sexually transmitted diseases by a physician without informing their parents.

Thus, in the words of one student, course content was "just stuff you had to know. I don't know if we'll ever use it." The following discussion of classroom scripts will focus on four interrelated content issues: the nature of gender relations, dangers of sexuality, heterosexual assumptions, and "responsible" sexual behavior.

Nature of Gender Relations

Students might reasonably conclude that females and males are more different than similar based on classroom presentations and many of Mrs. Warren's comments during the sex education unit. For example, she referred only to sex differences rather than similarities in her coverage of developmental changes at puberty[9] and implicitly did the same in soliciting two separate lists of qualities looked for in a person of the other sex. Mrs. Warren made the following specific statements to students about female/male differences in athletic interests and skills: "Girls don't get into long-distance running"; they "don't want to get sweaty"; they "don't want to worry about staying in shape." In contrast, she described males as having greater endurance and an interest in staying in shape. Furthermore, her asides about her own children tended to reinforce stereotypic sex differences, for instance, playfully describing her four-year-old son as "already beating up on" and getting more spankings than her eight-year-old daughter.

Nevertheless, Mrs. Warren's daily presence as a physically strong and active woman was a visible contradiction to these stereotypes; she was enthusiastic about running, seemed to enjoy being sweaty and was obviously staying in shape herself. She ran with students and was able to keep up with most of the fastest young men, who sometimes challenged her to pass them; in most cases, she could and did. In addition, she told students that she ran until she was seven months pregnant with her first child and resumed coaching track after the birth. Finally, the fact that she earns more money than her husband runs counter to traditional gender arrangements.

The movie on teenage pregnancy portrayed stereotypical gender differences and a wide communication chasm between the sexes. At the beginning, three teenage males are depicted in locker-room conver-

126

sation; they begin by joking about sexuality, and two of them tell the third (whose girlfriend is at the hospital giving birth) that he should have used condoms. In contrast, the girlfriend is shown after giving birth in a conversation with another unmarried young woman who has just had her second child. The two (not previously acquainted) have a serious and intimate conversation about their pregnancy/birth experiences, their relationship with the baby's father, and the decision to keep the baby. The only female/male communication depicted in the film is a hospital corridor argument between the young man from the locker room who did not use condoms and the first-time teenage mother about her last-minute decision to keep the baby rather than give it up for adoption as planned. He begins to shout at her; a security guard is summoned and ushers the young man firmly down the corridor, while the crying young woman is led gently in the opposite direction by a comforting nurse. Thus, the movie ends with the message of an unbridgeable communication gap between the sexes—a message that was not contradicted by the few minutes of discussion that followed the film.

Furthermore, the structure of alternate-day activity sessions, with different arrangements for the "ladies" and "guys" (as Mrs. Warren often referred to students) reinforced stereotypic notions of gender differences. The most visible examples occurred during the swimming activity. Although menstruation was not described as debilitating in Mrs. Warren's brief classroom summary, young women were excused for two days during the swimming unit while having their periods. This announcement (with no rationale) was made only to the young women, and during nearly every swimming session at least one or two of them sat on bleachers beside the pool, watching others swim or doing school work. Additionally, the young women in Mrs. Warren's class were dismissed from the pool twenty minutes before the end of the period, twelve minutes ahead of the young men. When Mrs. Warren announced this to all students at the start of the unit ("I'm sorry there's a discrepancy, but they [the ladies] need a lot more time to be beautiful"), there was matter-of-fact acceptance and no complaints from anyone. In fact, this policy made Mrs. Warren very popular with her female students, and she told me later that the guys liked having the time for free play in the pool after the others were dismissed.[10]

Mrs. Warren conveyed the message throughout the semester that appearance is important for females. For example, on the first day of activity, she said to students of both sexes that the ladies (whose locker room she supervised) would have "plenty of time to be beautiful" after every activity session. She added that they would be marked

127

absent if they left the locker room early and commented, "You're supposed to be *in* the locker room getting dressed and looking beautiful—or trying to anyway."[11] Another time she reminded the young women that it is important to "smell nice and feel clean." After female students had run a timed mile and after the first few swimming sessions, Mrs. Warren commented on their appearance as they left the locker room, for example, "See? You look beautiful," "You're still beautiful," and so on. She obviously did not have the opportunity to interact with male students in their locker room, but I never heard Mrs. Warren make comments to male students about their appearance at any time. In contrast, she frequently complimented female students in the classroom or hallways on their hair, clothing, and attractive appearance. However, it should be noted that she readily offered compliments and encouragement for physical exertion to female students as well ("You did a super job, ladies," "You did wonderful," "Good job," and so forth), placing particular emphasis on their trying hard.

Dangers of Sexuality

During Mrs. Warren's presentations and the film, students were offered a picture of sexuality as having problematic rather than pleasurable consequences. Acknowledgement of the physical pleasure of sexual behavior was absent; instead, pleasure was presented as an outcome of "responsible" sexual behavior in a traditional family context. Put another way, marriage and parenting—not physical acts of sexuality—were portrayed as generally positive and pleasurable experiences. Furthermore, these pleasures were depicted as best experienced by mature and financially secure adults—not teenagers.

Sexually transmitted diseases were another danger emphasized in the classroom. More time was devoted to symptoms, complications, and treatment than to any other topic; specifics about transmission were glossed over as Mrs. Warren told students to write "direct contact" (no further explanation offered) in the "transmission" column of the STD worksheet. Similarly, prevention was only mentioned briefly—a true/false test question on self-responsibility as the "key to control" of sexually transmitted diseases. Thus, although they received a few more specifics on AIDS, students might perceive other STD's as a danger to be avoided only by refraining from direct contact.

Teenage pregnancy was one of the major "dangers" of sexual behavior conveyed in the sex education unit; thirty minutes, including the movie, was spent on it. A mostly bleak picture of its consequences was presented, including dropping out of school, financial ramifications, desertion of the father, failure of teenage marriages, health risks to the baby, and so on. However, these consequences were largely based on the assumption that giving birth (characterized at different points as both miraculous and painful) and keeping the baby is the option a young woman would choose. The absence of information/discussion of other options might prompt students to contradictory conclusions: (1) that abortion and adoption are unacceptable/irresponsible options, or (2) that less negative consequences might result from choosing them.

Heterosexual Assumptions

Based on the extensive amount of time spent on dating, qualities desired in the other sex, advantages/disadvantages of going with one person, and references to Mrs. Warren's personal life, students were offered a perception of heterosexual intercourse as the most legitimate expression of sexuality—particularly in the context of reproduction, marriage, and parenting among mature and financially secure adults. In fact, just before Mrs. Warren began her explanation of the menstrual cycle, Andrew asked whether it was necessary to go over this material. Mrs. Warren replied, "You're gonna get married or at least have a girlfriend." Other forms of sexual expression such as homosexual activity, masturbation, and oral sex were mentioned only in connection with gay males and the consequences of AIDS.

"Responsible" Sexual Behavior

Sexual assault was portrayed as a form of "irresponsible" sexual behavior with potentially serious legal consequences; students were told they have a right to body privacy and to not be "touched in ways you don't want to be." During her presentation on fourth degree sexual assault, Mrs. Warren said that it is "not right if guys get aggressive"; nevertheless, she also commented twice during the same presentation that girls can "ask for it" or be too "enticing." Thus, students might conclude that sexual exploitation and assault are wrong; however, avoiding it is the primary responsibility of young women rather than men—by not "asking for it" in the first place or (in view of her earlier statements) resisting by saying "no."

Within the limited context of heterosexual intercourse, students might have readily perceived contradictory points of view about "responsible" sexual behavior. First, since love, marriage and parenting provided much of the context for the discussion of sexuality, they were offered encouragement to postpone intercourse until they are "in love" (nebulously defined in opposition to "infatuation," defined as physical attraction) or married (with "love" as a major "ingredient"). Students of both sexes were urged to not "go too far" (a term that was never clarified) and to "say 'no'." Although Mrs. Warren made a point of prefacing the "say 'no' " materials with a remark that young women sometimes use the same "lines" to get young men to have intercourse, most of the content suggested that it is the young woman's role to say "no" and (as Mrs. Warren reiterated twice during the session) not to be a "tease." Along these same lines, Mrs. Warren specifically told students to write down "abstinence" as the best method of birth control. Thus, students might infer that avoiding pregnancy is a very important reason for not having intercourse.

However, students were also told "If you're not ready for birth control, you're not ready for intercourse" and given some information about various forms of contraception. Thus—in contrast to the "saying 'no' " message—they might also conclude that having intercourse constitutes "responsible" sexual behavior *if* birth control is used. However, information about birth control was neither accurate nor complete enough to enable them to make an informed choice about a method or to use it effectively.

Mrs. Warren also pointed out that most of the birth control devices she showed students are used by the female and added, "It shouldn't really be that way." Even so, she spent a total of only thirty seconds describing condoms and—unlike other forms of contraception—did not show students what they looked like, implicitly reinforcing the notion of female responsibility for pregnancy prevention. Furthermore, condoms were never mentioned as a possible form of prevention for sexually transmitted diseases. In contrast, the film did point out male responsibility in preventing pregnancy. However, it seemed to position males in a protective and thus more powerful role than females; that is, a "responsible" male should "take care of" a young woman by using a condom. A related conclusion students might reach, on the basis of both Mrs. Warren's presentations and the film, is that the "responsible" response to a pregnancy is giving birth and keeping the baby (preferably within a committed male/female relationship) rather than giving it up for adoption or having an abortion.

When students were asked during the interviews, "According to the messages you got about sexuality and relationships, how do you think the class would like you to behave sexually at this time?", their responses reflected the contradictory possibilities discussed above. Student perceptions were clustered around four major themes (two young men were not certain what message they got) and are illustrated below:

130

Wait to have intercourse, "Maybe the beginning of ninth grade is a little too young"; "You shouldn't do anything"; "Supposed to wait for a while—until someone really special and you're in love with him"; "Kinda keepin' it casual—not real active and gettin' some girl pregnant." (seven females, six males)

Better to wait but use birth control if you don't, "Intercourse is not really OK, but if you're going to they told us different things to prevent pregnancy"; "If you're going to be involved, take the right precautions." (four females)

OK to not wait but use birth control, "They didn't tell us in the class 'don't' and stuff—they just said use birth control"; "Using birth control and using a safe method—not withdrawal or rhythm." (one female, one male)

Old enough to make the choice yourself. "You're able to make your own choice now"; "It depends on a person's maturity. Girls are usually more mature right now." (three females)

In summary, most class messages about sexuality and gender relations could be characterized as consistent with such dominant societal norms and values as stereotypic gender relations, heterosexist assumptions, sanction of intercourse only within the contexts of marriage and parenting, and emphasis on negative consequences of teenage sexual activity. However, as I have pointed out, there were also aspects of contradiction about these messages. Furthermore, I have begun to document that the mostly dominant values of reified school knowledge about sexuality are not passively accepted by students. In the next chapter I shall detail student reactions and the process by which they interact with this knowledge and actively participate in constructing the school sex education curriculum-in-use.

7

Students Actively Weighing Their Own Interests: "I Can Put on all Kinds of Faces"

"Everybody's putting on this cool act to give the impression you don't really care—you don't need to care because you're 'Jack Cool.' But if you look too interested, that's not good either. People will wonder what you're doing."—Carol

"If you're in a large group, you really don't want to talk because you feel people will laugh at you or something."—Doug

"I don't know 'jack' about this. Well, I do, but I don't know the scientific names. I know what I call 'em."—Paula

"It's kind of an act for me. I can put on all kinds of faces. Sometimes I talk about serious stuff in a humorous way so people get into it."—Carrie

Other ethnographic research suggests that students are active agents in the classroom, although their opposition to classroom knowledge and the organizational boundaries of the school may be private as well as public. McNeil (1986), for example, demonstrates that private resistance may underlie outward acquiescence to classroom control. Students in her study of economics classrooms offered little or no visible resistance to the teachers' information, methods, or evaluation, yet did not believe or internalize school knowledge. They actively, but privately, calculated their own best interests (earning the credential) in acquiescing to classroom arrangements. Other researchers (Everhart, 1983; McRobbie, 1978; Willis, 1977) have described more readily visible student opposition in the classroom such as "having a laff," "playing up the teacher" and "goofing off."

This chapter further documents Mrs. Warren's students as active participants in constructing their own versions of the sexuality curriculum rather than passively internalizing reified school knowledge. For most, this meant outwardly acquiescing to classroom information and procedures in order to get a good grade in the required course and to avoid embarrassment, while inwardly not necessarily accepting classroom messages about appropriate sexual behavior. For others, whose family and peers were less integrated with the school's reified knowledge system (especially female "dirts" and black students), it meant visibly and collectively contesting school knowledge. They infused the classroom with humor and interjected their own language and lived experience into the discourse. Drawing on classroom observation and student interviews, this chapter discusses two prevalent student classroom behaviors (ambiguous acquiescence and contestation) and explores their underlying meaning to students. Overall, it demonstrates how students played a significant role in shaping classroom discourse and inducing Mrs. Warren's defensive teaching.

Ambiguous Acquiescence

Most student behavior, particularly that of Van Buren "good kids," could be characterized as ambiguous acquiescence (neutral conformity to classroom procedures and information). Although the level of informality and jocularity was higher in Mrs. Warren's classroom than in any of the twelve other Van Buren classrooms I visited, Mrs. Warren's students generally conformed to her expectations and procedures— maintaining sufficient quiet to allow her to "get through" the material, taking notes when she pointed out important exam details, filling in assigned worksheets, and so on. Furthermore, as already mentioned, when brief conversational eruptions or humorous quips occurred, Mrs. Warren usually simply waited them out, restored quiet by low-key remarks ("Let's move on," "The next term you need to know is. . . . ") or by separating students who engaged in too much conversation. In fact, Mrs. Warren spoke of second period on several occasions (to me and to the class itself) as her best class, referring to both behavior and grades.

The majority of students perceived themselves as well behaved and attentive. When asked to comment during the individual interviews on the group's behavior during the sex education unit, seventeen of them made comments like the following:

Tammy: "Everyone acted pretty grown-up about it. There wasn't a lot of snickering or immature attitudes."

Jodie: "It was pretty good—not much goofing off. People paid attention."

Margaret: "Everyone was listening—even though some talked, they were still listening."

Glenn: "A lotta people didn't speak out. Most people are quiet."

Brian: "They were pretty good mostly."

On the other hand, eight students pointed out that some class members were not always well behaved ("There are always a few who goof off"), and seven students said that discomfort/embarrassment about the topic was a factor.

In addition to describing the group as generally well-behaved, students (including the most visible resisters) overwhelmingly expressed satisfaction with the course and Mrs. Warren. For example, when asked what they would tell friends about the class, fifteen students (including Carrie, Dawn, and Paula) responded with superlatives such as "the teacher's real cool," "Mrs. Warren is the nicest teacher," "I hope you [the friend] get Mrs. Warren," "It was fun—one of my best classes." With regard to their overall reaction to the sex education unit, the following positive comments were typical of responses by twelve students:

Jay: "I thought it was pretty good."

Linda: "It was good overall because it was open. Mrs. Warren was good because she didn't close things off. A lot of teachers get embarrassed."

Matt: (who had previously attended a Catholic school) "I think they went over it well—talked a lot about it, really discussed it a lot."

As will be detailed later, most other responses to this question referred to the unit as mostly "review." Mike, the quiet and nonathletic "loner" who was sometimes the object of ridicule and homophobic name-calling from other students, was most critical of the sexuality unit. As I shall discuss later in this chapter, he believed that Mrs. Warren did not adequately cover controversial topics.

Although most students expressed satisfaction with the sex education unit, generally conformed to classroom procedures, and expressed little opposition to Mrs. Warren's points of view, interviews revealed a complex array of meanings behind these classroom responses. Students were actively calculating their own interests rather than passively accepting classroom offerings, choosing to go along with simplified, mostly repetitive content and limited discussion for a good grade in this required course. Put another way, they understood and silently weighed their own interests in complying with the classroom bargain. In addition, their acquiescence seemed partly due to an awareness of certain risks, including the potential for embarrassment and loss of "reputation" in connection with asking questions and participating in a classroom sexuality discussion; they chose to minimize such risks by limiting personal disclosure. In the following sections I shall elaborate on these factors and the active choices behind their apparent acquiescence.

Included & Excluded Topics

In general, students expressed satisfaction with the amount of time spent on various topics, although they would have liked to spend a "little more" time on child/parent relationships, seeing birth control devices, teenage marriage, and fourth degree sexual assault. About two-thirds said they would exclude none of the topics covered, frequently because some other students "might not know about it."

When asked about additional topics they would want included, twenty of the twenty-five students interviewed could initially think of none. I then listed five topics that had been omitted or covered very briefly (masturbation, homosexuality, sexual response [defined when students requested clarification as "what happens when a person is sexually aroused"], where to go for health services regarding birth control and sexually transmitted diseases, and pregnancy options [abortion, adoption, keeping the baby]), and asked students whether they thought these topics should have been included. Table 1 reports responses of both sexes with topics listed in order of overall student preference for inclusion.

Table 1

STUDENT VIEWS ON INCLUSION OF CONTROVERSIAL TOPICS

Topic	Include			Exclude			Unsure		
	F	M	Total	F	M	Total	F	M	Total
Health Services	14	9	(23)	1	–	(1)	1	–	(1)
Pregnancy Options	13	8	(22)	2	2	(4)	–	–	
Homosexuality	11	6	(17)	3	4	(7)	–	1	(1)
Masturbation	9	5	(14)	4	5	(9)	–	2	(2)
Sexual Response	8	6	(14)	5	4	(9)	2	–	(2)

Students' views on topic selection suggest that most of them are willing to deal with more controversial issues in the curriculum. Because this is significant for educators, several noteworthy aspects of student response will be discussed here.

Health Services

Both sexes overwhelmingly believe that specific information about where to go for health services related to birth control and sexually transmitted diseases should be included in school sex education (93 percent of females, 90 percent of males), with sixteen students considering it the most important of the five less frequently covered topics listed. The following comments were typical:

Kathy: "You need birth control if you're thinking of sex— same with diseases, because if you get them you need to know where to get help."

Jay: "What's the purpose of teaching them about it [birth control] if they don't know where to get 'em?"

Russ: "So you know where to go if there's a problem. You won't get all scared and not know how to get help."

Furthermore, although I did not mention confidentiality or parents when referring to these reproductive health services, four young women spoke of the difficulty of talking to parents about birth control or sexually transmitted diseases as a major reason for receiving information about the topic in school:

Dawn: "Schools don't really tell everything they [students] want to know. They need a place to go other than parents. They're not comfortable with parents. I know I'm not."

Linda: "If you know you're gonna have intercourse and can't go to your mom or guardian, you'll know there's a place to go to get it. And they [students] won't not get it because they can't go to their parents."

Margaret: "Kids probably are afraid to talk to parents, so they need to know where to go without them knowing."

Carrie: "It's hard to go up to your mom and say, 'Mom, I need birth control.' "

Pregnancy Options

Nearly as large a percentage of interviewed students (87 percent of females; 80 percent of males) believe that information on pregnancy options is important to include in the course. In the words of one young woman, whose response was typical: "If somebody got pregnant or something, they oughta know all the choices that they have— not just assume there's only one thing they can do." Three students commented specifically that abortion is a controversial topic, with one young woman saying it should therefore not be included ("It's so controversial and would've took [sic] just eight days to figure out whose side who was on"). Another young woman felt this information should be provided "somewhere else," possibly by the doctor if a girl was pregnant. The two young men who thought pregnancy options should be excluded cited peoples' "right to make up their own minds" and having had the material in a class the previous year as their reasons. Two students felt that the brief mention of abortion as one unacceptable option in the movie was sufficient coverage. Finally, no student expressed personal opposition to abortion, although Tammy expressed the following viewpoint:

The pros and cons of all these [options] should be brought out, but I don't believe in abortion as a form of birth control. Under some circumstances, like rape, it's OK. But if a person's not responsible to do something [use birth control] in the beginning, they shouldn't use it to get rid of their mistake.

Homosexuality

Seventeen of the interviewed students (68 percent) indicated, for a variety of reasons, that homosexuality ought to be included in the school sex education curriculum. Most suggested that students don't know enough about it; five pointed out that homosexuality is a current real-life issue. For example, Mike, who expressed a preference for more classroom coverage of all the controversial topics, said about homosexuality:

> Kids have to deal with this—maybe not directly, but they have to deal with it. If you don't cover it, you have myths again. . . . There's not a great big percent of this around here, but it's rising.

Another student responded, "It's a thing that's kind of hitting America today. People should be aware of what's going on." One young woman explicitly referred to the homosexuality/AIDS connection made by Mrs. Warren, saying that homosexuality should be included "because that's how you get AIDS." Another young woman expressed her own confusion over causation as a reason for including the topic ("It's just kind of hard to understand whether it's psychological or instinct or— I don't know"), while two others stated explicitly that homosexuality is not necessarily "wrong" and argued for greater tolerance:

> Dawn: "They [teachers] should talk about mostly positive things—not the negative. If the person wants to be that way, it's their problem. People put others down, with name-calling and stuff. If he's [note the assumption of maleness] doing it, ap-parently he wants to be that. It shouldn't bother anybody else."

> Linda: "It's not a real big issue, but you should talk about it a little bit so people will understand about it—know it's not all wrong, that people can't help what sex they like. There's noth-ing they can do about it."

These two quotes also illustrate differing points of view on what causes a person to be homosexual, with the first suggesting that a person can choose this lifestyle and the second that an individual "can't help" her/ his sexual orientation. The latter perspective underlies the comments of two young men who thought homosexuality should not be included in the curriculum because "you usually just know about that" and "I think kids know what they are."

Two of seven students who believe the topic should not be included said it would be too "embarrassing," although one added that "it might be useful"; two said it was "not that important"; one declared the topic "none of their [teacher's] business." Furthermore, males were more reluctant to include this topic than females; 40 percent of males and 20 percent of females expressed disapproval. No student made an overtly homophobic comment to me during the interviews; however, as I shall subsequently describe, I heard such remarks directed at Mike during informal student interactions. Thus, although student responses generally indicated support for the inclusion of homosexuality in the school sex education curriculum, it is difficult to judge the degree to which this preference for more information is permeated with homophobia and/or based on a fear of AIDS.

Masturbation

Slightly more than half (56 percent) of interviewed students thought the topic of masturbation should have a place in the curriculum. Their reasons for its inclusion are difficult to categorize; however, as the following response from a female student suggests, they include correcting the myth that masturbation is necessarily wrong: "A lot of people have the wrong idea about why people do it. People think it's gross and disgusting." One male student pointed out that "last year they said it was normal" and concluded that silence this year might make a student think that masturbation is "bad." One young woman made the following observation about why the topic should be included: "Everyone jokes about it. You hear it in the halls, but most teenagers don't know anything about it really."

Half the interviewed males thought that masturbation should not be included, compared to about one-quarter of females—although two additional young women were not sure. Several students succinctly expressed discomfort with talking about masturbation in a sex education classroom as their reason for not including the topic, for instance, "I wouldn't want to hear about it," "I just wouldn't like it." Finally, two female students expressed their own negative attitudes toward masturbation: "It's kinda sick" and "I don't think it's normal."

Sexual Response

Somewhat more than half the students (56 percent) believed that sexual response ("what happens when a person is sexually aroused") should be included in the curriculum, although about one-third of these students qualified their opinion with a "maybe." Reasons for its inclusion were somewhat general ("Because it's what happens," "Just to learn more about it," "No particular reason") or related to understanding what is normal ("Some people need to know because if it happens to them they might think something's wrong," "So people know if they have intercourse what should happen or not happen—if anything goes wrong.").

The nine students who expressed a negative opinion about including sexual response either did not say why (three students), felt that students did not need to learn it (three) or already knew it (one), or said it was too personal and potentially embarrassing to discuss in a classroom (two). Three of these comments were positive; however, the following exchange with one young woman is noteworthy in its revelation of a dilemma that sex education handouts may create for some students.

Margaret: "Some don't like to take them [handouts] home. They're afraid of showing their parents.
Bonnie: "Did you take yours home?"
Margaret: "Yeah. They're stashed in my desk drawer under some books."

In summary, although students did not openly request inclusion of more controversial topics in the classroom, their private responses to questions about content suggest an interest and need. As I shall discuss in the last chapter, this might encourage educators to broaden curricular offerings.

Learning Activities

During the student interviews, I also obtained their reactions to Mrs. Warren's teaching strategies. I listed the major forms of learning experiences they had encountered in the unit and asked students whether they would like to have spent less, the same, or more time engaged in them (1 = a lot less, 2 = a little less, 3 = same, 4 = a little more, 5 = a lot more). Based on calculating average responses for each form of learning experience, students indicated satisfaction with the amount of time they had been engaged in each, although they would have liked to spend a little more time in small group discussion (average response = 4.0) and watching audiovisuals (4.1). There were no major differences in female/male opinions, although young women would have preferred slightly more time in small group discussion (4.1) than young men (3.8) and slightly less time in listening to teacher explanation (female average = 3, males = 3.4), reading in class (female average = 2.5, males = 2.9), and using handouts (female average = 2.9, males = 3.5). Students felt the amount of time devoted to teacher explanation was satisfactory, and eighteen of them made no additional remarks beyond that.

Two students thought there had been "a lot of teacher explanation," four thought Mrs. Warren had done a good job, and one thought she had been boring. Most expressed a preference for greater use of audiovisual material in the sex education unit. They offered the following reasons for this preference: "[you] get more out of" seeing a movie than simply listening to a teacher (four students); movies are not boring (three); students like movies (three); students pay' more attention to movies than to a teacher (two); students can relate better to movies than to a teacher (two); movies "tell more" than a teacher (two); there is no pressure to talk during movies (two); it is easier to learn from movies (one). All students with the exception of Mike said they would recommend showing the classroom movie "If You Want to Dance," other semesters.

In contrast, Mike described the major message of the film as "bogus," since it "gave no insight into the decisions [leading up to the unplanned pregnancy] already made" or "the *process* of making the decision of what to do about a pregnancy." He then elaborated on a network television situation comedy that he thought provided better coverage of the decisions involved and focused on characters closer in age to the ninth-graders who watched it. He told me he had videotaped the show and offered to let me watch it. After I did, we arranged another meeting after school to discuss it and to complete the interview. As I will discuss later in the chapter, Mike was one of several students who mostly remained silent during class but offered lengthy, thoughtful responses during the one-to-one interviews.

Sources of Sexuality Information

According to their responses on two separate occasions, students had previously obtained and preferred to obtain information about sexuality mostly from school. The first occasion was an informal survey done by Mrs. Warren on the initial day of the sex education unit, in which she asked students to write anonymously where they got their first information about sex, whether it was correct, and where they would have preferred to get such information. Table 2 shows the results of the survey as she summarized it for students.

Table 2

STUDENT RESPONSES TO SURVEY ON
SOURCES OF SEXUALITY
INFORMATION

	# of Students
First Source:	
school	13
friends	9
mother	7
book	1
magazine	1
nurse	1
TV	1
Perceived Correctness of Information:	
correct	19
mostly correct	2
Preferred source:	
school	12
friends	3
parents	2
mother	2
sister	1

During my interviews with students after the sex education unit, I asked about the importance of various sources of sexuality information. Possibilities were (in order of presentation): mother, father, other relatives, same sex friends, other sex friends, school, doctor, church, other (for example, media). Students rated each of these on a scale of 0 to 10, with 0 indicating that no information was received from that source and 10 that the source was most important. Average responses calculated for each information source are reported in Table 3, with school identified as the most important source of sexual information for both females (average = 7.6) and males (average = 7.1); mothers were the next most important source for both sexes.

Furthermore, like the informal survey, Table 4 indicates that about half of the interviewed students (six females, six males) identified school as their *preferred* source of sexuality information.

Eight students who preferred school cited confidence in the accuracy

Table 3

IMPORTANCE OF SEXUALITY
INFORMATION SOURCES TO STUDENTS

Source	Average Importance (0 to 10)	
	Female	Male
School	7.6	7.1
Mother	6.3	4.9
Same sex friends	4.5	1.8
Other	3.5	2.4
Father	2.9	4.4
Other sex friends	2.3	1.9
Doctor	2.0	1.5
Church	1.3	1.3
Other relatives	1.1	0.4

Table 4

STUDENTS' PREFERRED SOURCES OF
SEXUALITY INFORMATION

Source	Number of Students	
	Female	Male
School	6	6
Both parents	3	2
Friends of same sex	2	0
Mother	2	0
School *and* parents	1	1
Doctor	1	0
Church	0	1
Father	0	0

of school information as the reason for their preference. Even Paula (a dirt and one of the more visible resisters) said, "That's where I think you should learn. They [teachers] won't lie to you. Parents might just put it off or say, 'Don't worry about it.' " While seven students (including five females) said they preferred to get such information from both parents or mother, it is noteworthy that no student of either sex expressed a preference for father as a source of sexuality information. However, in spite of viewing school as an important and reliable source of information about sexuality, students did not seem to view this information as having an important influence on their personal attitudes toward sexuality and personal behavior. In other words, while trusting the accuracy of school information, students do not necessarily accept it as the only version of reality or as applicable to their lives. As I shall discuss later, parents and friends seem to play a more significant role than school in students' construction of personal values.

Enduring Repetitive Information

Although most students reported school as an important source of sexuality information and expressed satisfaction with topics covered in the Van Buren sex education unit, interviews revealed that they "already knew" much of the material Mrs. Warren covered. When asked for their overall reaction to the sex education unit, 56 percent said this material was mostly review. The following comments were typical:

Lauren: "It's basically the same as we've ever had. Most teachers take it about the same way."

Tammy: "Things in health came pretty easily because it was mostly review."

Kristi: "Some days it was like a big joke—a giant review."

Andrew: "I've had that stuff for a lot of years . . . I get the stuff over and over, so it's deep down in my head."

Furthermore, five students from two different middle schools commented that they had learned more about sexuality in eighth grade. On the other hand, three students (including one who transferred from a small district and one from a Catholic school) specified they had learned a lot in Mrs. Warren's class.

Comparing the topics most students said they already knew with accuracy of their answers on the exam is interesting, although not necessarily an indicator of what they learned in the course. A vast majority (nine of ten males, eleven of fifteen females) answered all five questions on male anatomy correctly; a minority (three of ten males, six of fifteen females) answered all questions on female anatomy correctly. However, only six students (one male, five females) were awarded the full ten points on a short-answer question about the menstrual cycle. Twenty students (nine males, eleven females) responded to all fifteen questions involving pregnancy and birth accurately, and all students answered the sole question on adolescent development correctly.

Slightly more than one-third (four males, five females) gave correct answers to all fifteen questions on sexually transmitted diseases, although about half identified it as containing new information.

It is possible that students were, at some level, challenging adult ownership of sexual knowledge by saying that most classroom material was review. Alternatively, they may have been declaring their knowledge of peer group cultural meanings rather than classroom details. Finally, they may actually have been familiar with the specifics presented during the unit. Whatever the explanation, all twenty-five interviewed students said they already knew about physical changes of adolescence, female anatomy, pregnancy and birth; twenty-four about male anatomy; twenty-two about birth control. Fourth degree sexual assault and sexually transmitted diseases were the topics cited most frequently by students as new information, with twelve students mentioning each.

Getting a Good Grade

Not surprisingly, given their perception that much of the material was review and Mrs. Warren's pointing out specifics about the exam, students generally regarded the health class as easy. As I overheard Tammy tell Paula, "The only way to get an F is to never show up." Other comments made to me during the interviews include:

Lauren: "You just pick it up. You don't need to study."
Carrie: "It's kind of a blow-off class . . . it's all review practically."
Matt: "It's easy. . . . You just have to do your best, put forth effort."
Ian: "It's pretty easy—not like other classes I'm more worried about."

While most students said they took the class seriously to get a good grade in a required course, two students (Andrew and Carol) specified that they took the unit seriously because of its content rather than the grade—in spite of appearances to the contrary. Andrew (the only black male in the classroom) made frequent quips, contested and expanded on classroom material, and interjected his own version of sexuality information. Carol (who transferred from a rural district and had never experienced classroom sex education before) frequently looked bored and rarely spoke during class; she was described privately to me by Mrs. Warren as someone at risk of failing because of her lack of interest and effort. However, Carol told me that she deliberately masked her classroom interest in sexuality (especially birth control) because she did not want other students to think she was using it.

Avoiding Embarrassment

Embarrassment, or at least the potential for it, seemed to be another factor in the ambiguous acquiescence I observed, with nineteen of the twenty-five interviewed students (80 percent of females, 70 percent of males) specifically commenting on it without solicitation from me. They seemed most concerned about being laughed at by other students. As expressed by Doug, one of the most popular "jocks," "If you're in a large group, you really don't want to talk because you feel people will laugh at you or something." This fear was not unwarranted, given the general level of jocularity, humorous one-liners, and occasional put-downs from other students. An example of the latter is the following:

> On the fourth day of the sex education unit, Mrs. Warren is go-ing over correct answers to a quiz students have just taken. She reads a true/false statement: "All new living things come from seeds or eggs." Various students call out, "Yes," and Andrew calls out, "No."
>
> Mrs. Warren: "We don't come from eggs?" (Carrie begins to laugh, and other students join in.)
> Andrew: (with conviction)   "Are we *hatched* from an egg?"
> Carrie: "From the eggs in ovaries." (She begins to point at Andrew, howling with laughter.)
> Mrs. Warren: (to Carrie)   "He may not know that." (Carrie stops laughing.)

This incident was one of many that confirmed the possibility of embar-rassment, one that Mrs. Warren herself raised on the first day of the unit when she made the following comment in a stern tone at the end of a particularly noisy and jocular session:

> "I have a major request to make. I realize that some of you have never talked about this stuff before, and you might get em-

barrassed. I won't get too embarrassed. If you try to embarrass me, I'll come back and embarrass you."

She goes on to say she wants students to "feel free to ask questions," but she does not want "people laughing at each other's questions."

Discomfort and potential embarrassment were also factors in students' feelings about certain learning strategies. For example, two students (Kristi and Jay) would have preferred greater use of audiovisuals because they could simply watch rather than feel pressured to talk, and three young men (Doug, Ed, and Matt) wanted the textbook available to read at home so that other students would not (in Doug's words) "bug you." Although most felt the amount of time in large group discussion was satisfactory, four of the seven who would have preferred less commented on the discomfort issue:

Julie: "Hardly anyone talks. They may be embarrassed. I know I would."

Brian: "Personally, I don't like discussing it [sex education]—not with a large class. I'd just rather do it on a worksheet or something. It's a lot easier for me."

Most students would have liked a little more time for small group work—especially if they could choose their "own mixture," i.e., people with whom they are comfortable or who don't "goof around." Five (four females, one male) specified that small groups should be composed of a single sex; three (two females, one male) specified both sexes. The following comments are typical:

Linda: "[Expresses preference for 'a lot more' time in small groups] if you could be with whoever you're comfortable with. But it might go the other way—those goofing around would do it even more."

Kristi: "With your friends you wouldn't be so embarrassed. ... You'd know they liked you even if they laughed."

Andrew: "With good friends you don't have to worry about your secrets going anywhere [pause] or people talking behind your back."

The potential for embarrassment may also have been a factor in the kinds of questions asked by students. While it is impossible to be certain, only a few questions appeared to have personal relevance. Of the forty-one questions asked during the sex education unit (sixteen by Andrew, nine by Paula, five by Dawn, two by Carrie, and ten by an assortment of others), most were requests to repeat terminology so it could be copied in notebooks or geared to technical details on the exam. However, as illustrated by anecdotes in Chapter 5, Paula asked several questions about pregnancy and birth. These included: "Does it [the embryo] turn into a baby and just get bigger and bigger?" "What's birth like?" "How many things are delivered?" "Did you [Mrs. Warren] worry before?" Mrs. Warren answered most of the questions briefly (placenta: third stage of delivery, progesterone: "another female hormone" used in the birth control pill, and so on) or with an extended recount of personal experience of birth. Thus, it is difficult to ascertain how much of the technical classroom language used by Mrs. Warren was understood by students, and the absence of more substantive or personal questions may have reinforced her expressed belief that most of them "already knew it all."

Fear of being embarrassed seemed to be a factor in students bracketing personal information, and sometimes simply refusing to participate in class discussion. For example, in soliciting qualities "guys" look for in a date, Mrs. Warren tried to encourage involvement by calling on Matt and three other young men (two of whom later expressed discomfort to me in talking about sexuality issues). All remained silent; in fact, assembling the list of qualities from male students took only a few minutes, and some of these were called out by female students, Carrie in particular. Similarly, when Mrs. Warren called on Michelle (a young woman she knew had been going with a junior for several months) the student simply did not answer. Michelle talked at considerable length during the interview about a long-term relationship with her older boyfriend and her personal attitudes toward sexuality; she told me she was comfortable with these topics but "just didn't talk," even when called on, in the classroom. Even the most vocal students revealed very little of their personal behavior and opinions, making generalized statements or referring to other people, as exemplified by the comments of Carrie, Dawn, Paula, and Toni after the film. Paula (who described herself as one of the "smart alecks") explicitly admitted revealing little of her personal feelings or behavior in class because she "didn't know [the] others too good . . . I didn't say too much because I didn't want to."

Several students specifically expressed concern during the interviews over possible interpretations by others—both students and teacher—of their interest and participation level in sex education discussion. As mentioned, Carol, a new student at Van Buren who had bleached blond hair and wore heavy makeup and tight jeans, was quiet, looked bored, and was perceived by Mrs. Warren as disinterested. Despite this outward appearance, Carol (for whom this was a first class in sex education) later told me that she learned a great deal and offered the following insight on student behavior:

> Everybody's putting on this cool act to give the impression you don't really care—you don't need to care because you're "Jack Cool." But if you look too interested, that's not good either. People will wonder what you're doing.

When I inquired, she specified that this attitude applied to both females and males. After learning that I had worked at Planned Parenthood, she privately asked me several questions about various methods of birth control and how to obtain them and later said, "I'm not gonna stand up in the middle of class and say, 'I wanna know about birth control.' They'd think I was using it." She believed that this would give her a "bad reputation."

Dawn also chose not to ask questions about birth control in class and expressed this concern:

Dawn: "Students might react or have a reaction. I'm not comfortable saying it in front of an adult—unless they don't know who I am. They might think I'm doing something. [pause] The teacher might wonder why you asked and do something."

Bonnie: "Do you mean refer you to a guidance counselor—something like that?"

Dawn: "Yes. Even my mom gets uptight when I ask questions like that. She thinks I'm obscene."

Her suspicions about school personnel were warranted; I had learned earlier from another staff person at Van Buren that this young woman's name (along with four others) had been forwarded by the middle school she attended in response to a request for names of students potentially "at risk for pregnancy." The all-too-common and inaccurate stereotype of minority adolescents as more sexually active and less sexually responsible than their white counterparts (Nettles & Scott-

Jones, 1992) along with Dawn's cultivation of a sexy image may have been factors in this assessment.

It should be made clear that I phrased interview questions in a general way and did not specifically ask students about their own sexual *behavior*. However, nearly three-quarters of the young women and half the young men elaborated in what seemed to be a comfortable way on several interview questions about peer sexual behavior as well as their own and peer attitudes toward sexuality. In general, their one-to-one levels of ease and disclosure with a relatively unfamiliar adult were similar to experiences I have had with adolescents in other school and community settings. Given the general "absence of safe spaces for exploring sexuality that affects all adolescents," particularly those aspects that go beyond technical details and dominant norms (Fine, 1988, p. 36), these young people may have seized on such an opportunity when it presented itself.[1] Students clearly did not feel such comfort in the classroom. In fact, when I asked students "What would have to happen in the classroom for you to be comfortable talking about the issues [teenage pregnancy, responsibility for birth control] raised by the film?", seven (28 percent: three females, four males) said that *nothing* could make them comfortable talking about such issues in a classroom. As Matt succinctly summarized it: "I can't imagine talking about it in a classroom. I'll listen and think but not talk." In response to the same question, Mike (who described the film as bogus) said his own comfort about sexuality was not a factor in his decision not to participate in classroom discussion. Instead, he perceived that Mrs. Warren herself was ill at ease with some topics, especially male birth control—"plus all the things she didn't cover." Although he made no mention of it, the upcoming discussion of this young man's endurance of ridicule and name-calling may account, at least in part, for his silence.

The fact that Mrs. Warren's students considered participation potentially risky and bracketed personal information is similar to classroom observations by Michelle Fine (1988). Fear of being ostracized affected the personal disclosure of many students in the classrooms she observed—young women who were heterosexually active, heterosexual virgins, as well as gays, bisexuals, and lesbians. Because participation in classroom discussions on sexuality and personal disclosure seemed to have more potential risks than benefits in the eyes of most of Mrs. Warren's students, they did not participate openly or seriously in formal large group discussion. Instead, they chose to bracket personal information and conduct muted "discussions" with friends seated nearby. This seemed to represent an active decision to participate in a

Students Actively Weighing Their Own Interests

way that avoided embarrassment but generally acquiesced to classroom arrangements.

Students' fear of embarrassment and choice to bracket personal information may also be related to wider cultural ambiguity about acceptable contexts and ways of talking about sex. In referring to the initial silences of her first-year college students during a discussion of sexual aspects of *The Color Purple* (Walker, 1982), Claire Buck elaborated this dilemma of classroom language:

> The words they had available to them were wholly inadequate to meet their needs. Most of them felt trapped between the ob- scene and the clinical. The former exposed them to parental and teacherly condemnation. But the proper and emotional left them embarrassed by the gap between the emotional quality of their experience and terms like intercourse, penis, vagina, and clitoris. (1987, p. 32)

As will be evident shortly, a few students vocally contested "proper" classroom language about sexuality, while most simply did not risk public discussion. At the same time, humor provided a culturally ac- ceptable way to "discuss" sexuality in the classroom, and humorous fragments were forms of communication about sexuality that had collective rewards, that is, laughter from peers.

Mediating Classroom Points of View

Although most students did not openly challenge classroom versions of appropriate sexual behavior, interviews revealed contradiction and complexity rather than simple acceptance of school knowledge about sexuality. First, the predominant classroom message as interpreted by students was contradicted by their wider cultural setting at Van Buren. More specifically, seventeen students (eleven females, six males) per- ceived the major classroom message as: it is better for ninth-graders to wait to have intercourse. However, only five (three females, two males) thought other Van Buren students would agree, with fifteen (ten females, five males) saying that others believe the choice should be up to the individual, that is, some ninth-graders are ready. Ten (five females, five males) believed that at least 50 percent of ninth-graders of both sexes were having intercourse, while seventeen (nine females, eight males) had a similar belief about twelfth-graders, fifteen of whom estimated at least 70 percent of Van Buren twelfth-graders having intercourse. With regard to their own attitudes, slightly less than half the interviewed students (seven females, four males) agreed with the predominant classroom message to postpone intercourse. Slightly more (eight females, four males) believed that ninth-graders are ready to make their own choices, with two additional young men expressing uncertainty about their opinion.

Influence on Attitudes

Students also said that parents play the most substantial role in the formation of their sexual attitudes—although, as mentioned earlier, they saw school as the most important source of *information*. On a scale of 0 to 10 (0 = no importance, 10 = most importance) students rated the importance of various sources in influencing their attitudes, and Table 5 displays the average responses for each source.

Table 5
AVERAGE STUDENT RESPONSES BY
GENDER TO THE QUESTION: "HOW
IMPORTANT ARE THESE SOURCES IN
INFLUENCING YOUR OWN ATTITUDES
ABOUT SEXUAL BEHAVIOR?"

	Female	Male
Mother	6.7	6.0
Father	5.0	7.5
Same sex friends	4.3	3.4
Other sex friends	4.0	4.4
School	3.8	3.7
Other relatives	2.7	0
Doctor	1.6	.9
Church	.7	1.6
Other (media, etc.)	.7	1.3

Thus, parents (mothers for females and fathers for males) were reported by students to be the most important factor in their personal attitudes toward sexuality. In addition, six of fourteen females and six of ten males said they would *prefer* to talk to one or both parents if they were concerned about sexuality. Nevertheless, a smaller number (four of fourteen females and four of ten males) said they would *actually* talk to parents with such a concern.

Furthermore, in responding to the question "How do you think your parents would like you to behave sexually?", the overwhelming majority of students reported that parental expectations are clear: you are too young to have intercourse. More specifically, twenty of the twenty-five interviewed students (fourteen of fifteen females, six of ten males) perceived one or both parents to have this expectation—one that is congruent with the predominant classroom message. However, students report school as only slightly more than half as influential as parents in the formation of their own attitudes. Female friends were reported as the second greatest influence for both sexes (female = 4.3; male = 4.4), while male friends were a slightly greater factor for females (4.3), than for males (3.4).

Along these lines, eleven of the fifteen females volunteered (in the context of their response to this question) that males exert pressure on females for greater sexual activity. The following comments were typical:

Kathy: "Most guys want to push." She goes on to explain this is particularly the case with "younger girls from older guys."

Kristi: "They [guys] try to like push you and stuff," although she adds that it "depends on the guy," and happens mostly "after you been goin' together awhile."

Julie: "*All* guys push, but some push sooner than others."

Linda: "It seems like they [guys] want"—[she pauses, starts to speak, stops, starts over]—"you to be more aggressive and open and stuff." (I clarify and learn she means they want you to have intercourse.) She says this is mostly true with "junior and senior guys."

Paula: "Many [guys] think you should go for it."

Although I did not question students about the effect of this pressure on their sexual behavior, Dawn said, "A lot of girls are involved before they're ready."

Brian and Jay (both among the more physically mature males and both possible dirts, according to Mrs. Warren's private description) said they felt pressure to "do it" from young women. As Jay put it, "Girls say the same thing [as guys, i.e., "Go for it."], but less directly. They kind of entice you."

Finally, friends were most frequently cited (by fourteen students) in response to the question, "Who would you *actually* talk to if you had a concern about sexuality?" Twelve (nine females, three males) said they would talk to a friend of the same sex, two (one female, one male) to their mother, one male to his father, and one male to "parents." Only one female said she would talk to school personnel—"a teacher."

In summary, most students—particularly the good kids—acquiesced to school knowledge about sexuality and classroom procedures. They took the course seriously enough to get A's and B's, did the prescribed notetaking, conformed to Mrs. Warren's behavioral expectations, and kept their part of the implicit classroom bargain: reasonable effort and behavior for an easy grade. They generally described themselves as well behaved and expressed satisfaction, at first, with course content (although they also expressed a willingness or desire to include more controversial topics), forms of learning, and Mrs. Warren.

However, subsequent interviews revealed that their acquiescence was not passive acceptance but active calculation of their own interests, with students choosing to go along with simplified, mostly repetitive content and limited discussion for a good grade in the required course. In addition, the outwardly acquiescent behavior of most students seemed partly due to their calculation of the potential for embarrassment and loss of "reputation" in asking questions and participating in a classroom sexuality discussion.

Even when Mrs. Warren created space on a few occasions for students to include their own lived experience in classroom discourse (for example, asking them for qualities they looked for in a date), most did not participate. Those who did made few personal disclosures and seemed aware that signs of interest in sexuality might be interpreted as evidence of inappropriate sexual experience (too much for females, too little for males) by others in the classroom. Given the predominant classroom mode of fragmentation and simplification of content, most students participated by simply calling out brief responses that revealed little personal information, protected them from embarrassment, and minimally met Mrs. Warren's behavioral expectations.

Alternatively, although interview questions did not explore this, it seems possible that the minimal level of participation just described may have elements of collective resistance to school knowledge—with students preferring to interject their cultural knowledge of sexuality as interruptions/diversions rather than as voluntary contributions to a teacher-initiated/controlled classroom discussion of sexuality. Whatever the reason, this silence and bracketing of personal information on the part of most students affected the curriculum-in-use by making honest and relevant classroom discussion about sexuality difficult; thus—if only slightly—students themselves inadvertently contributed to the reification of school sexual knowledge.

Finally, although most students did not overtly challenge classroom formulations of appropriate sexual behavior, interviews suggest that they did not passively internalize them but arrived instead at their own conclusions in the context of parental and peer influence. Thus, behind their apparent acquiescence, students were actively reinterpreting classroom knowledge in the context of their own cultural experiences to construct their own version of acceptable sexual behavior rather than accepting unquestioningly school knowledge about sexuality. In the remainder of this chapter I shall document some of the more visible ways students contested reified school knowledge with their own regenerative knowledge.

Classroom Contestation

Critical ethnographers of education (Everhart, 1983; Hudak, 1985; McRobbie, 1978; Willis, 1977) have demonstrated that student contestation of school knowledge and other regularities of organized school life are an important dimension of what goes on in classrooms.[2] Despite potential barriers I have described, students attempt to make school a more livable institution, constructing their own group culture and becoming active participants in the dynamic interaction that makes a particular class what it is on a given day. Moreover, forms of student contestations are shaped by the tensions and contradictions between and within social groups. In Mrs. Warren's second-period health class, members of marginalized groups (particularly black students and female dirts) most visibly, collectively, and humorously contested school knowledge about sexuality and classroom control by creating an informal, bantering atmosphere and interjecting their own language and cultural experiences into the classroom discourse.

Everhart uses the term "regenerative" knowledge to describe a second way of knowing that emerges as students reinterpret "reified" school knowledge in the context of their own cultural experiences. These attempts to make school knowledge more relevant are based on mutuality of communication and have interactive and collective dimensions.

> Because such knowledge grows out of and is based on social interaction, regenerative knowledge is interpretively rather than empirically based. In this frame of reference, then, reality is not "known" or preordained (as in reified knowledge), but rather is socially constructed and reconstructed as definitions, meanings and values are arrived at through collective communication. (1983, p. 125)

Thus, regenerative knowledge is subjective rather than objective, contextual rather than absolutist, and symbolic rather than factual. In contrast to reified knowledge, in which predefined "facts" are manipulated to produce an end product, individuals and groups create their own meanings out of cultural process and social interaction. Furthermore, Everhart identifies differing interpretations and strategies associated with different social groups.

As anyone who has spent time in a classroom can confirm, students utilize a wide array of "privatized" strategies to make the classroom more livable without necessarily altering the classroom agenda. Mrs. Warren's students were no exception as most of them doodled, read library books, did other homework, wrote Christmas cards, combed their hair, applied makeup (even in the dark during movies), sneaked illicit snacks, made trips to the bathroom, and so on. Beyond contributing to an overall lack of seriousness, such individual responses have little potential for altering the curriculum-in-use until they become interactive and collective, until they become regenerative knowledge. It is to these forms of knowledge construction (using humor to create community, struggling over language, and interjecting lived cultural experience) that I will turn next.

Using "Humor" to Create Community

Along with creating diversionary moments, "humor" (not always perceived as humorous by the person to whom the remarks are directed) serves to establish and reinforce social identity, demonstrate social acceptance, and maintain boundaries within and between various groups (Everhart, 1983, p. 161). In Mrs. Warren's classroom, it helped to define membership in various student "communities" and eligibility for participation in regenerative knowledge construction. For example, on the first day of the sex education unit, I overheard Doug (the popular jock, who had, ironically, expressed privately to me his own fears about being laughed at by other students) and Brian (a dirt) make the following crude remarks to an appreciative nearby male audience about Mike, the tall, thin, nonathletic loner.

Doug: "His mom gave him a hand job."
Brian: "Yeah, he can't get it anywhere; he can only get incest."
Doug: "They like to keep AIDS in the family."

The loner status of this soft-spoken and shy student was continually reinforced by others. During an early activity session (and out of Mrs. Warren's earshot) I heard Paula direct a string of obscenities, ending with "you queer," at Mike. Another time, as Mrs. Warren was going over answers to the first unit test, the following incident occurred:

Mike:	(having discovered a possible error on his exam): "Wait! Wait!"
Mrs. Warren:	"Are you having a problem?" She moves to his desk.
Male Student:	"He *is* a problem."
Male Student:	"He's a nurd."
Mike:	(to Mrs. Warren) "Take it easy. You're wrong."
Doug:	"I say we all get in line and back-hand him once."
Male Student:	"No, twice."

Most nearby students laugh heartily. Mike and Mrs. Warren ignore this, as they discuss the item in question.

On at least five other occasions, Mike was the object of name-calling (including "fag" once) and insults in the classroom; these were usually led by Doug, the jock. Most other students, especially males, laughed loudly at these remarks, while Mike (who sat at the front of the room among the quieter young women) always looked straight ahead and remained silent. As was the case in the incident just cited, Mrs. Warren was usually absorbed elsewhere and never commented on or intervened in these situations. Thus, some students' "humorous" remarks (a term applied to these insults only because others laughed), the general laughter that followed, and the fact that no one challenged them collectively reinforced the bonds of male and heterosexual "community" and kept this less stereotypically masculine young man out.

This use of "queer" and "fag" are, unfortunately, examples of a widespread and growing pattern of violence directed at those whose sexual orientation may not fit dominant norms of heterosexuality. Over 90 percent of two thousand lesbians and gay men in a nationwide survey had experienced some form of verbal or physical abuse (Uribe & Harbeck, 1992, p. 17), and personal narratives describe the form and effects of such behavior in the school setting (Fricke, 1981; Heron, 1983; Nickel, 1992; Sears, 1991). In short, research suggests that lesbian, gay, or bisexual students are either treated as objects of hate and bigotry or—at best—as if they do not exist (Uribe & Harbeck, 1992, p. 13). Such treatment conveys a powerful message that being gay is to be avoided at all costs if a young person is to be accepted and loved by family and friends.

This has a powerful silencing and otherwise devastating effect on the estimated 10 percent of the population that is gay, as well as the countless numbers of young people experiencing same sex attraction or questioning their personal sexual orientation. Unlike some other aspects of identity (like race for Carrie, Dawn, and Andrew), sexual orientation can be and—given the attached social stigma—usually is concealed. Thus, educators need to be aware that for every lesbian, gay or bisexual young person they may recognize in school, there are an indeterminate number of invisible others (Uribe & Harbeck, 1992). Although I did not ask Mike—or any student—questions about same sex attractions or personal sexual orientation, any student in Mrs. Warren's classroom might have been struggling with these issues. Although no student openly acknowledged being gay, lesbian, or bisexual with me or the class, anyone might have self-identified along these lines.

Carrie's Joker/Pet Strategies

As previously discussed, the three African-American students often used humor and mutual insults to symbolize their bond of intimacy around race ("nappy-headed reject from Africa," "African boody-scratcher," and so on). Occasionally, however, humor was an expression of within-group tensions between Carrie and Dawn ("between your legs is crusty"). Carrie, in particular, played a major role in using humor to make the classroom more liveable and to contest school knowledge and Mrs. Warren's authority. Her loud voice and humorous, often outrageous, remarks accounted for many of the diversionary moments in the classroom.

This central role seemed due in part to Carrie's attempts to find a place for herself in the classroom by cultivating the status of Mrs. Warren's "pet," another form of regenerative knowledge construction (Everhart, 1983). Using the terminology of Everhart's junior high subjects, Carrie was not a "goody-goody pet" (one who passively accepts the teacher's designation as "good"—being compliant and getting high grades) but a pet who largely engaged in noncompliance while "psyching out" the teacher and actively seeking a privileged relationship. A good-goody pet is not respected by other students, while the other pet is looked up to because this role symbolizes a sense of student control and visibly demonstrates student ability to change the teacher-imposed classroom agenda. The latter form of pet seemed to apply to Carrie's relationship to Mrs. Warren and her regard by other students. Because she was an important factor in classroom contestation, I shall elaborate her activities more fully.

From the beginning of the semester, Carrie used her brashness and humor to cultivate a more personal relationship with Mrs. Warren—asking questions about her family, using familiar terms of address ("buddy," "babe," "teach," "woman"), teasing ("I say we call out the hickey inspector [to investigate a red mark on Mrs. Warren's neck]"), initiating joking exchanges, offering compliments ("You're pretty hip for an old lady"), asking her to wrap and rewrap several times a hand injured in basketball, stopping after class to tell personal anecdotes, and so forth. This use of humor served to reduce social distance between teacher and student, simultaneously enhancing their relationship and undermining teacher control (Davies, 1983). Carrie's humorous digressions and quips ("I'm gonna hang this [male reproductive anatomy diagram] in my bathroom window"; "It [the prostate gland] sounds like a piece of real estate to me") reinforced her membership in the "community" of peers. These nearly always resulted in big laughs and related quips from other students.

Mrs. Warren usually responded in a good-natured way to Carrie's informality and humor, once answering Carrie's "Thank you, babe" with a "You're welcome, babe." Furthermore, there were several occasions when Mrs. Warren (and everyone else in the room, including me) could simply not keep from laughing at Carrie's one-liners. However, Carrie did not usually push Mrs. Warren too far in negotiating her status as pet; she responded to Mrs. Warren's gentle admonitions and reserved her most caustic or obscene comments for muted exchanges with other students, especially Paula. For example, the following incident occurred while Mrs. Warren was returning and going over correct answers to the nutrition test:

Carrie and Dawn are out of their seats and "boogeying" in the aisle.

Mrs. Warren:	"It's Monday, but you should be quiet for me."
Carrie:	"I'm not talking, am I?"
Mrs. Warren:	"No, but you're dancing. Sit down."

The two students return to their seats, and Paula whispers
something to Carrie, who whispers back: "Paula, you such a
rag—a 'ho too." They both grin.

Carrie consciously cultivated her status as pet and central classroom
role as humorist. During the interview, she told me that her participation in class was "kind of an act for me. I can put on all kinds of
faces. Sometimes I talk about serious stuff in a humorous way so
people get into it." Thus, she was a leader in the construction of
regenerative knowledge, using humor as a means of affiliation with
other students (members of her racial and gender-based groups and
the entire class) and Mrs. Warren, as well as a form of resistance to
classroom control. Carrie facilitated student interpretation and recon-
struction of reified knowledge (objective, absolutist, and factual) into
subjective, contextual, and symbolic forms. Mrs. Warren recognized
that Carrie was a key factor in the bantering classroom atmosphere:
shifting the boundaries of discussion from technical details to irreverent
humor, entertaining students plus teacher and guest, initiating barrages
of humorous one-liners from classmates, and genially contesting Mrs.
Warren's authority.

Mrs. Warren expressed ambiguity about how to deal with black
students (recognizing differences but not wanting to provide "special
treatment"), an ambiguity of which Carrie seemed aware. This is
evidenced by the following incident early in the semester, one of the
occasions when Mrs. Warren and Carrie seemed to just barely avoid
a more serious confrontation.

Mrs. Warren is passing out forms on which students will record tomorrow's twelve-minute run. Toni gets permission from
her and leaves the room.

Carrie:	"Where did she go? I want to get an aspirin. I have a headache."
Mrs. Warren:	"You can go when she gets back. Just be quiet for now."
Carrie:	"I'm yellin' at you for discrimination. I should take you to court."
Mrs. Warren:	(continuing to hand out forms) "Get real."
Carrie:	"How come she gets to get aspirin?"
Mrs. Warren:	"Be patient—or maybe you should just leave for good."
Carrie:	"Maybe I should."

160

Mrs. Warren: "Just because you have a bad morning, don't take it out on me."
Carrie: "I didn't have a bad morning until I came in here."

Since other students are talking among themselves, this conversation blends in. About a minute later Toni returns, and Carrie leaves the room.

In spite of Mrs. Warren's ambiguity in dealing with black students, it is important to note that she was cognizant of the difficulties Carrie faced as a racially mixed, fat young woman at Van Buren. Recognizing this problem, she attempted throughout the semester to make school life somewhat easier by showing a special interest in Carrie, offering encouragement at her often unsuccessful attempts at physical activity, and tolerating her classroom quips. It is a testimony to her ability to relate effectively with this student that Carrie considered Mrs. Warren an ally and sought her out to talk about personal concerns, including the previously described racial incident at the end of the semester in which Carrie's "mixed" status became problematic. In fact, Carrie continued to initiate contact with Mrs. Warren when the semester was over. Furthermore, when Mrs. Warren left Van Buren the following year, Carrie regularly kept in touch with her. In this one-to-one context, Carrie had begun to ask such questions as "Does it [intercourse] hurt?" This was a marked contrast to the image she had attempted to convey in the classroom.

Contesting Classroom Language about Sex

Language was an ongoing area of contestation between Mrs. Warren and the all-female social grouping that included Carrie, Dawn, Paula, and Toni. These four were responsible for most of the audible classroom contestation around language; however, as earlier examples have illustrated, their remarks and Mrs. Warren's responses were generally good-natured and humorous rather than openly belligerent.

Mrs. Warren's own use of language and her expectations regarding student usage seem related to the previously mentioned dilemma of maintaining a balance between discipline/control and being enough of a "buddy" to secure students' participation in physical activities in which these four had no particular interest. Thus, she generally kept her own language in the medical technical realm and expected the same from students. For example, during the swimming unit, when young women were allowed two days of nonparticipation while having their periods, students would most frequently make vague announcements to Mrs. Warren ("I'm not swimming today"; "I've got something"; or "My thing came") rather than make explicit reference to their period. Mrs. Warren tried on a few occasions that I observed to get them to verbalize the reasons more explicitly; one student (Margaret) looked totally embarrassed and could not say the words, while another (Paula) responded with, "I'm on the rag."

Mrs. Warren occasionally used relatively inoffensive slang terms herself and usually ignored their use by students, as illustrated by the following interaction with Paula:

> Students are working individually at their desks, using the textbook as a resource to complete mimeographed worksheets on female and male reproductive anatomy.

> Paula: "I don't know 'jack' about this. Well, I do, but I don't know the scientific names. I know what *I* call 'em."

> Mrs. Warren does not comment on Paula's use of an abbreviated version of "jack-shit" and describes her own embarrassment at being asked to list slang terms at a teacher workshop on sexuality. She concludes, "My face was red for twenty minutes."

Later, Mrs. Warren used the word "anus" in labelling a diagram and then added, "I'm sure you have other words." Several students snickered, but no one audibly used the slang terms. However, on another occasion, Mrs. Warren wrote "butt" on the board after a male student had called out "nice derriere" as a characteristic males look for in females. She told the students, with a big grin, that she couldn't spell "derriere." Mrs. Warren could occasionally be heard during activity sessions saying to students (in a good-natured way) such things as, "Get your buns over here" or "Get off your butt."

The only time I heard Mrs. Warren herself use a slang term directly related to sexual behavior occurred early in a session when students were listing advantages and disadvantages of going with only one person:

> Mrs. Warren adds "might get boring" to the list of disadvantages.

> Carrie: "My mom told me to make a list of every guy I like then get to know them all."

Mrs. Warren:	"You might get a reputation."
Toni:	"It's OK for guys to do that, but not for girls."
Mrs. Warren:	"Girls get a reputation. They used to be called 'whores' but now—what are they called— 'slut?' "

Several students murmur, but there are no audible responses from them.

There is also no follow-up on Toni's reference to the double standard.

There were several other occasions when Carrie, Dawn, Paula, and Toni interjected slightly more "acceptable" but clearly their informal version of language into the classroom. In these cases, Mrs. Warren generally offered a low-key response, rephrasing their words into "classroom" language. For example, when Dawn pronounced epididymis as "epi-titty-mis," Mrs. Warren simply said, "Not titty—didy" and moved on to the next item of male reproductive anatomy. Similarly, Mrs. Warren first ignored and then rephrased Toni's responses of "going out and getting drunk" and "slamming down beers" into "partying" for inclusion on the blackboard list of parents' favorite dating activities.

However, Mrs. Warren also demonstrated her willingness to more actively intervene in student language on a few occasions. For example, after an activity session early in the semester, she heard Paula tell another student (within earshot of a Van Buren custodian) that running "sucked." Mrs. Warren responded as follows:

Mrs. Warren:	(sternly) "No talk like that."
Paula:	"I could've said a lot worse." She starts toward the locker room.
Mrs. Warren:	(calling after her) "Not in my class. That'll give you a detention."

For the most part, however, student classroom use of the least acceptable forms of sexual language ("dick, "fuck," "suck," "beaver," and so on) were infrequent and confined to muted interactions with each other. If Mrs. Warren overheard any such remarks between students during the sex education unit, she did not acknowledge it.

Mrs. Warren's dilemma around language and classroom control—allowing sufficient informality to be a "buddy" but not letting students "get out of hand"—is encapsulated in the following incident, during which she first responded matter-of-factly to Dawn's hesitancy to use the term "penis":

> Mrs. Warren has given students a short quiz on family issues
> and adolescent development and is going over correct responses
> to the question: "What are some changes boys and girls go
> through during adolescence?" She mentions chest and under-
> arm hair as one change for guys.
>
> | | |
> |---|---|
> | Dawn: | "Enlargement of. . . ." (pauses) |
> | Mrs. Warren: | "The penis does get bigger—also the testes and scrotum. What about girls?" |

Nevertheless, about five minutes later, Mrs. Warren intervened when Dawn used the word "erection" in the context of escalating conversational eruptions.

> As Mrs. Warren begins to write menstrual cycle terms on the
> blackboard, the noise level in the room increases greatly as stu-
> dents talk with each other. Dawn says "erection" loudly
> enough to be heard over the noise, just as Mrs. Warren finishes
> writing on the board. She turns to address Dawn in a firm man-
> ner: "Is that necessary? To blurt out whatever?" Dawn grins,
> and Mrs. Warren goes on to explain the terms she has written.

On other occasions, these four—Carrie, Dawn, Paula, and Toni—asserted themselves by rephrasing Mrs. Warren's terminology. For example, her original heading for a previously described list was "Going Steady," with advantages and disadvantages in two columns. Paula said the heading should be "Going With," and Mrs. Warren changed it. As she was writing, Carrie called out, "Who are you messin' with?" to a chorus of laughter. Similarly, Paula replaced Mrs. Warren's technical definition of contraception with an everyday one:

> Mrs. Warren defines contraception as "preventing conception
> or the union of the sperm and egg."
>
> | | |
> |---|---|
> | Paula: | "Preventing you from getting pregnant, in other words." |
> | Mrs. Warren: | "Yes." She goes on with the lesson. |

That same day, Mrs. Warren showed fetal development pictures and pointed out the umbilical cord.

Mrs. Warren: "You can see the cord. It's the lifeline between the baby and the mother."

Carrie: "That's the *umbilical* cord, since you defined it and didn't tell us."

Interjecting Lived Cultural Experience

Everhart (1983) discusses a discrepancy between some students' "interpretive setting" in family and peer groups, and classroom behavioral expectations and ideology about family life. In Mrs. Warren's classroom, Paula and Toni most frequently revealed this discrepancy in their classroom remarks. For example:

Mrs. Warren is having students write down questions to ask their parents for a homework assignment early in the sex education unit; these include: "How did they meet? Where? Where did they go? What did they do on dates? How old were they when they got married?"

After the last question, Paula asks: "What if your parents are *not* married?"

Toni: "What if your parents were married more than once?"

They each repeat their question in a louder voice, but Mrs. Warren does not look at them or respond verbally.

The bell rings, and Mrs. Warren adds a final question: "What changes happened when you were born?"

Toni moves toward the door. As she passes Mrs. Warren, she says, "What if your parents were married more than once?" Mrs. Warren pauses for a moment and says, "Think about your real mom and your real dad." Toni leaves.

Similarly, after the movie, these two (plus Carrie and Dawn) mentioned relatives whose life experience included an unplanned pregnancy.

Paula and Toni also engaged in muted discussions of their extracurricular activities (getting home at 4:30 a.m., fights they had witnessed, and so on), parents ("Your mom's more of a bitch than mine"), and other teachers. One Monday (ironically, the first day of the alcohol and drug unit) Toni told Paula that her mother had seen Paula in juvenile detention for drinking the past weekend; Toni's mother had come to pick up her younger sister, after she had been detained for the same offense. In addition to engaging in conversations with each other, both young women interjected their lived cultural experience into the classroom in more a public way. For example, Paula would announce she was "dying for a cigarette," and Toni wore a Budweiser hat on Homecoming Week "Hat Day" and a beer T-shirt during running emblazoned with "I got this body from lifting weights—12 ounces at a time."

This interjection of lived experience related to alcohol and other drugs was similar to the sexy image they maintained in that specific personal information was mostly bracketed, while an aura of "experience" was promoted. As the following incident on the first day of the alcohol and drug unit illustrates, Mrs. Warren sometimes actively intervened in this:

Mrs. Warren: (passing out a worksheet) "We'll be answering some drug questions next."

Paula: "That's cool. Hey Toni, what about L.S.D.?" (to Mrs. Warren) "Do we have to put down if we've done these?"

Mrs. Warren walks over to Paula and says (in a muted voice): "I don't want to hear that kind of talk." She then speaks in a louder voice to the whole group: "I realize some know very little and some know a lot about drugs, but I won't allow any discussion of other class members' behavior." She gives them directions for doing the worksheet.

Five minutes later, Paula calls out, "Toni needs a twelve-pack to get drunk."

Mrs. Warren: "I don't want fingers pointed in class about anyone's behavior. I don't need to know."

However, on other occasions, Mrs. Warren attempted to capitalize on the lived experiences of dirts to make a point with them and other students. For example, she went through a role-play in which she repeatedly offered Paula a beer, which the student was supposed to refuse. Instead, Paula (who never stopped smiling) accepted the can after Mrs. Warren's fourth attempt—which netted a big laugh from other students and prompted Mrs. Warren to say, "Paula, you shouldn't give in so easily."

Students Actively Weighing Their Own Interests

Constructing the Sexuality Curriculum-in-Use

As I have described in this chapter, Mrs. Warren's students were active participants in constructing the daily classroom experience. Defining *power* in a broad sense as "the ability to alter or influence the course of events, to create a happening, *whether or not a particular goal is in view* (Davies, 1983, p. 39), I have shown how students exercised their power in the classroom. While most outwardly acquiesced both to school knowledge about sexuality and to Mrs. Warren's authority, they actively calculated their own best interests—especially getting a good grade in the required course and avoiding embarrassment. Furthermore, although most did not overtly challenge classroom information and messages about appropriate sexual behavior, interviews revealed that—influenced more by peers and parents than school—students arrived at their own meanings of appropriate sexual behavior.

I have also analyzed the classroom as a complex social arena, detailing how the tensions between and within specific social groups generated oppositional strategies for defining various "communities" within the classroom (groupings related to gender, race, class, and sexual orientation) and for testing the boundaries of the classroom bargain. A small group of marginalized students (blacks and female dirts) was most visible in contesting both school knowledge about sexuality and classroom control. These students engaged in a variety of interactive and collective activities, including making humorous quips, initiating conversational eruptions, accentuating female sexuality, and interjecting their own lived experience and language. Thus, they constructed regenerative knowledge forms out of social interaction and cultural process.

Like many teachers who cite student reactions as one of their most important concerns (Forrest & Silverman, 1989), Mrs. Warren acknowledges that potential student classroom response is an element in her curricular selection and presentation and expresses a worry about being perceived as "out in left field" by them. Furthermore, she is aware that students can create alternate meanings out of whatever she says, which leads to a concern with choosing her words carefully:

> If you don't say it right and . . . if they get it wrong too in how
> they understand what you say. I feel that it's real important
> that I get it together.

Mrs. Warren also says it is hard trying out new topics such as sexual assault, AIDS and homosexuality because she has "no idea" how

167

students will respond. Turning a serious topic into a joke is one possibility; thus Mrs. Warren believes that students are "not mature enough" to deal with these and other complex issues. In the final sections of this chapter, I shall briefly highlight the sometimes contradictory effects of student cultural responses on the sexuality curriculum-in-use.

Creating a Bantering Atmosphere

Students clearly played a role in creating the humorous, bantering classroom climate that had the potential to make a joke out of any sexuality topic, however serious. On the other hand, this relaxed and informal atmosphere contradicted the notion of sexuality as a solemn, adult-owned topic, with some humorous interjections acknowledging the pleasurable rather than dangerous aspects of adolescent sexuality. While humorous quips represented brief points when students controlled the classroom discourse, such remarks also added up to an overall atmosphere that tended to trivialize information about sexuality, a topic relevant to students.

Furthermore, the "humorous" insults and potential for embarrassment inherent in this atmosphere seemed to have several effects. First, since humor and insults were a major factor in defining peer boundaries and status, students bracketed personal information, and may therefore have refrained from asking questions (especially those with personal relevance) or expressing points of view for fear of being ridiculed by others. It was safer for most students to keep quiet. Second, even when serious questions were asked, they were frequently lost in quips. Finally, it was difficult for Mrs. Warren to ascertain what information students may have already known; the cavalier attitude and cultivation of a sexy image by some students may have given the impression that they knew more (in terms of both information and experience) than they actually did.

There was a continual threat that this general ebullience would erupt into bedlam against which Mrs. Warren's customary genial authority would be ineffective—as it did on a few occasions, including the first day of the sex education unit. Thus, defensive teaching strategies were called upon by Mrs. Warren partly in response to student-initiated activity. For example, the first day of the sex education unit could be accurately described as chaotic: Carrie was in top quipping form; Paula was sitting near Doug and Toni, chatting merrily with both; several students were beginning to test the boundaries of acceptable classroom sexual language; conversational eruptions were audible everywhere. By the end of the period, Mrs. Warren was exasperated enough to be less than genial and later told me, "I didn't get *anything* done today."

During the second session she regained control by changing the seating arrangement and then adopting defensive teaching strategies to minimize student interaction (a requirement for regenerative knowledge) and resistance—providing a worksheet, assigning in-class textbook reading and vocabulary words to be copied, etc. As discussed in Chapter 5, other such strategies were prevalent in the rest of the unit and were instrumental in constructing reified (objective, non-negotiable, and factual) school knowledge about sexuality. Thus, while student creation of a humorous, bantering environment contributed to their feeling of ownership and control and offered diversionary moments, it had the unintended and contradictory effect of triggering defensive teaching strategies that ultimately made classroom knowledge about sexuality less relevant to their needs. While I do not suggest that students would have received relevant sex education if only they had been better behaved, I maintain that reified school knowledge was—at least in part—an unintended consequence of their regenerative knowledge production. Put more theoretically, resistance that was liberating at one level actually contributed to their subordination at another.

Broadening the Parameters of Classroom Discourse

Despite the potentially constricting overall effects just described, there were several moments when students expanded the parameters of the classroom discourse to accommodate their language and cultural experience. As Hudak (1985) points out, student attempts to become code-finers of this discourse (the quips, interjected lived experiences, and struggle over language I have been describing) temporarily and in a highly truncated way expand the boundaries of school knowledge. However, on a structural level, these brief points of control became part of the social and communicative environment of the classroom. Thus, along with simply creating diversionary moments, some students initiated possibilities for classroom discussion and debate which could have resulted in affirming the pleasures of sexuality, broadening the spectrum of acceptable sexual behavior, and generally making school sex education more relevant to their lives. However, for the most part, Mrs. Warren did not follow up on these possibilities.

It bears reiterating here that students were not a unified, coherent

169

group but smaller, sometimes overlapping groupings with a variety of distinct identities related to gender, race, class, and so on. Thus, students themselves had varying definitions of what counts as a pleasure of sexuality or acceptable sexual behavior. Although none overtly challenged classroom norms of sexual activity as heterosexual intercourse, it is noteworthy that students in general expressed an interest in having more controversial topics (pregnancy options, homosexuality, sexual assault, and so on) covered in the classroom. Since students regard school as a reliable source of sexuality information, the parameters of classroom discussion should be broadened to debunk myths and stereotypes about these topics.

Taken together, these findings suggest opportunities for progressive educators to transform school sex education discourse and make it more relevant to students. Although Mrs. Warren's attempts to maintain classroom control seemed to work against these possibilities, I do not imply that she consciously chose to narrow sexuality information to mostly technical topics with little relevance to students' lives—an approach that is contrary to her expressed teaching philosophy. Instead, the reified knowledge about sexuality in her classroom was an unintended outcome of her defensive teaching strategies, which arose partly in response to student behavior and to organizational imperatives within the school and district.

8

Situation-Specific Constraints and Possibilities: "Much Has Been Said. Now Much Must be Done"

In *Doing Sex Education* I have drawn on extensive naturalistic data to illuminate the active, complex, contradictory, and situation-specific process by which school sexuality knowledge was constructed in one classroom.[1] These everyday dynamics of students and teachers have been largely unexamined in the sex education literature and excluded from the dialogue and debates among policy makers, academics, school personnel, health professionals, and others concerned with such programs. I do not present my analysis of Mrs. Warren and her students at Van Buren as generalizable to all situations or as "capable of identifying and justifying actions guaranteed to be the most effective or the most strategic educational and political interventions" (Ellsworth, 1992). Instead, I hope that my narrative, which uncovers this unique and dynamic juncture, will be useful in future formulation of multiple, situation-specific strategies to make school sex education more relevant to students' lives, broaden the spectrum of acceptable sexual behavior, encourage nonexploitive and mutually responsible sexual relationships, and affirm the pleasures of sexuality. In this final chapter I will briefly summarize major findings and comment on some of their implications for practice and future research.

Doing Sex Education revealed that the classroom teacher, Mrs. Warren, spent most time on noncontroversial topics (sexually transmitted diseases, dating, teenage pregnancy consequences, and so on), while barely mentioning more controversial topics like sexual pleasure, mas-

171

turbation, and homosexuality. Information was presented largely as fragmented details geared toward passing the exams. A film, worksheets, in-class textbook reading, and Mrs. Warren's reading aloud to students were all forms by which information was conveyed. There was no mention of controversy or current topics and no small group discussion. The overall atmosphere was mostly informal and bantering, with large group "discussion" consisting mainly of Mrs. Warren's personal asides, brief student remarks, or clever quips.

Most of Mrs. Warren's classroom strategies were similar to those identified by Linda McNeil (1986) as components of "defensive teaching," in which teachers control students by controlling the knowledge and making the work easy. Defensive teaching transforms controversial, value-laden cultural knowledge about sexuality into "reified" school knowledge (Everhart, 1983), in which the "right answer" is presumed to be known. Learning it for an exam becomes more significant than exploring a variety of possibilities, and personal relevance is lost. As one of Mrs. Warren's students said, "It was just stuff you had to know. I don't know if we'll ever use it."

Most—but not all—of the classroom points of view about sexuality and gender relations with which students were invited to identify were consistent with dominant social norms, including heterosexuality, intercourse as the onlyform of sexual activity and sanctioned mainly in the context of marriage and parenting, and stereotypic gender relations. However, there were also moments when both teacher and students questioned and contradicted these points of view, and student interviews subsequently revealed that they did not passively accept them.

Instead, students reinterpreted reified school knowledge about sexuality through their cultural experiences (which differed by gender, race, and class) to reach different understandings about appropriate sexual behavior. Furthermore, they actively weighed their own interests in acquiescing to or contesting course content and form. Most expressed satisfaction with the class and conformed to classroom procedures; however, interviews revealed that they chose to do so largely for a good grade in the required course and to avoid embarrassment.

Tensions related to gender, race, and class were also lived out in the classroom. Members of most marginalized groups (black students and female "dirts") visibly and collectively used humor and a sexy image to define group membership and interject their own language and lived cultural experience into the classroom. They created alternate cultural meanings or "regenerative" knowledge (Everhart, 1983) and were key factors in initiating the bantering atmosphere and testing the boundaries of Mrs. Warren's genial authority. Keeping this interactive regenerative knowledge under control was instrumental in Mrs. Warren's use of defensive teaching and, therefore, played an important role in constructing the sexuality curriculum-in-use. However, this had the unintended and contradictory outcome for students of making course material even less relevant.

Doing Sex Education documents that school and district organization and the conditions in which teachers work are major elements in their adoption of defensive teaching strategies. First, administrative concern with efficient procedures and good community relations, along with distance from classroom instruction, contributed to a working environment in which conforming to procedural expectations and avoiding problems were more valued than in-depth exploration of controversial issues. Mrs. Warren's offering noncontroversial content and making the required course easy was a way to fulfill administrative expectations; however, it also contradicted her own educative ideals.

The alternate-day classroom/physical activity format and requirement of the course for graduation also presented a structural dilemma for Mrs. Warren. She had to achieve a balance between maintaining classroom control and being personable enough to secure student participation in physical activities; between creating an atmosphere of fun and encouraging students to take the class seriously; between covering material on a long district syllabus and helping students get a good grade in the required course. Thus, informality, genial authority, and making work easy in the classroom were part of her effort to achieve this balance.

Furthermore, defensive teaching was shown to be a partial outcome of labor intensification, including the addition of required certification in health, having to learn classroom skills by "doing," a fragmented and grueling schedule, and a long and ever-expanding syllabus. Thus, Mrs. Warren had little time for reflective thinking and keeping up-to-date, became primarily concerned with "getting through" the material, relied on reading aloud to students and was unable to conform to her own ideals for in-depth discussion and problem solving.

Finally, pressures related to gender (especially the patriarchal authority relations of the school and dual demands of work and family) contributed to Mrs. Warren's defensive teaching and her other strategies as well. She attempted to cope with a largely non-nurturing school environment and make her workload easier by being a nurturing "mom," behaving like "one-of-the-girls," cultivating school spirit, and creating fun. However—as was the case with defensive teaching—these strategies had contradictory outcomes, including increasing her workload and reinforcing gender stereotypes.

Situation-Specific Constraints and Possibilities

More theoretically, this close-up description and analysis of the day-to-day interactions in Mrs. Warren's classroom demonstrates that curriculum is not in fact a static product of rational planning but a dynamic selection and organization process, in which teacher and students actively participate in the context of specific organizational arrangements. It also illustrates that the cultural meanings of sexuality encoded in curricular content and form are not neutral but embody the interests of certain groups. Although most classroom messages about sexuality and gender relations were consistent with dominant norms, *Doing Sex Education* suggests that this was not a matter of simple correspondence to values of dominant groups in the wider society. Nor were such views mechanistically imposed on students and passively accepted by them, as cultural and economic reproduction theories imply. Instead, the data show that both Mrs. Warren and her students actively made decisions on their own behalf, continually fracturing and challenging dominant cultural meanings and organizational constraints. Both actively engaged in cultural accommodation and resistance. Thus, the reinforcement of dominant norms—insofar as it occurred in the classroom—was a tentative process only with no predetermined end. However, while teacher and student resistance may be liberating at one level, it may serve to increase subordination at another and does not, therefore, seriously challenge dominant arrangements.

Implications

The focus in *Doing Sex Education* on the lived experience of teacher and students reveals both the progressive and regressive possibilities for school sexuality education. Such programs can potentially reinforce or challenge dominant social norms of heterosexuality, intercourse restricted to the context of marriage, and inequitable gender relations. Furthermore, no matter how restrictive or progressive, the planned curriculum or teaching materials may acquire alternate cultural meanings as they work their way through teacher and students in a particular setting. For example, although Mrs. Warren took the official district curriculum seriously, she was only able to "touch on" various topics because of organizational limitations and had to consider student lived cultural responses in her presentations. In the context of the school and community described here, these factors functioned mostly to narrow content and reinforce dominant norms. Although Van Buren's

174

bureaucratic arrangements are similar to most U.S. schools (McNeil, 1986), it is located in a largely homogeneous community (middle-class, white, religious, traditional). Administrators in other districts might be similarly concerned with procedure and community relations; however, potential controversies about classroom sex education would likely differ by community.

Room to Maneuver

The study also suggests there is room for skilled and creative educators to maneuver within official curriculum and policy. As most teachers are aware, especially given an administration distanced from instruction, the privacy of the classroom offers considerable autonomy. It has been my observation in working with school sex education programs, one substantiated by Fine (1988), that many progressive teachers subvert the official curriculum to provide information on controversial topics relevant to students' lives and to foster an atmosphere in which critical discussion can take place.

Beck and Marshall (1992) confirm this in their qualitative study of thirty-three educators whose work focused on adolescent sexuality. Their respondents describe several well-developed strategies for operating within and around hierarchical structures, including use of shrewd communication skills when dealing with sensitive issues. For example, one parochial school counselor, who was not Catholic herself, reported on her circumvention of school policy banning discussion of condoms as birth control by talking about them as a method of disease prevention. Capitalizing on ambiguous policy was a frequently cited strategy, as typified by a school official who was responsible for health curricula in junior and senior high schools throughout the city. She spoke with pride of authoring a policy statement that contraception would be covered in the classroom if students asked about it. She knew this would satisfy conservative demands within the community while allowing teachers to discuss contraception, since she also knew "students always ask" (p. 327).

Classroom Constraints

Nevertheless, *Doing Sex Education* also suggests that within the bureaucratic organization that characterizes most schools, even a skilled, creative, progressive, and "sexuality affirming" (Scales, 1987) teacher

175

might be constrained in the classroom. This is particularly true in the context of the current New Right campaign to exclusively promote conservative and fundamentalist Christian values in public school sex education. In fact, administrative and community pressure have been named by sex educators as their "biggest problem," especially in teaching about such topics as homosexuality, abortion, condom use, and safer sex practices (Donovan, 1989).

Yet policy makers, academic researchers, teacher educators, and others outside the classroom who do not encounter such day-to-day working conditions as those experienced by Mrs. Warren may question the reality of these pressures. For example, the research finding that sexuality educators believe administrative and community pressure to be their biggest problem is followed by the statement, "It is unclear whether this pressure is real or perceived, but, whatever the reality, teachers see themselves caught in the middle" (Donovan, 1989, p. 6).

Without acknowledgement of the context in which teachers work, it can be easy to focus narrowly and critically on the individual practitioner as primarily responsible for content and teaching strategies regarded as unsatisfactory. For instance, in her otherwise excellent analysis of the "missing discourse of desire" in school sex education, Michelle Fine argues for more comprehensive, relevant programs yet ignores the organizational setting, accusing teachers of "systematic refusal to name issues" that make them uncomfortable and of projecting their discomfort onto students (1988, p. 38). Similarly, evaluators of elementary school sexual abuse prevention curricula criticize teachers for injecting personal fear and bias into a planned curriculum and organizational arrangements they assume to be satisfactory. Teachers, especially those who may be survivors of sexual abuse, need considerably more school and district support than the nonexistent or brief training sessions they are frequently offered. In light of estimates that one of three women and one of seven men are likely to experience some form of sexual abuse by age eighteen (Bass & Davis, 1988), this focus of criticism on individual teachers seems particularly problematic where predominantly female elementary teachers are increasingly being asked and een mandated, with minimal preparation, to add sexual abuse prevention and other aspects of sexuality education to an already full syllabus (Trudell & Whatley, 1988).

Like others concerned with the inclusivity and relevance of school sex education, I believe that many of Mrs. Warren's curricular decisions are problematic. At the beginning of my observations in her classroom, my criticisms were directed more narrowly and personally at her.

Situation-Specific Constraints and Possibilities

Although I reminded myself that I was not in the classroom to criticize but to understand the factors behind this teacher's choices, I was appalled at the seemingly random order of topics, fragmented technical details, and absence of meaningful student discussion. Yet, as I followed Mrs. Warren through the hectic days described in earlier chapters, grew more aware of her working conditions, and came to understand the demands of her social positioning by gender, marital status and motherhood, I began to adopt a wider perspective and to regard her with less personal criticism and more compassion. I still considered some of Mrs. Warren's teaching strategies unsatisfactory, but I began to see them as active attempts to deal with dilemmas and contradictions created by institutional constraints, student classroom responses, and her social positioning by gender, marital status, and motherhood. As I have described in considerable detail, Mrs. Warren was one participant in the dynamic, complex, and contradictory process of constructing the sexuality curriculum in the context of particular constraints and possibilities.

In spite of my careful earlier attempts to portray these broader constraints experienced by Mrs. Warren during conference presentations and in writing more distilled versions of the research, I have been distressed at how readily listeners/readers focus blame on her. For instance, her avoidance of homosexuality has been described as an individualized decision: "teachers, like Mrs. Warren . . . , take it upon themselves to avoid them [such controversial topics]" (Sears, 1992c, p. 148). I hope that this longer narration of Mrs. Warren's defensive teaching has more fully elaborated the context of her work and will not contribute to placing unwarranted blame on individual educators for the problematic aspects of school sex education.

However, in asserting that external factors such as working conditions within the school are significant factors in defensive teaching, I do not deny the importance of an individual teacher's personal beliefs or comfort with sexual issues as important to good teaching, particularly with regard to inclusion of more controversial topics (Sears, 1992d). Yet positive personal attitudes and feelings about homosexuality or other controversial topics are unlikely to be sufficient for teachers to meaningfully address them in a constraining and even hostile school and community setting (Woods & Harbeck, 1992). In short, while not denying the significance of a teacher's personal beliefs, we also need to remain cognizant of the constraints, such as those revealed in *Doing Sex Education*, that even the most open-minded teacher encounters on a daily basis. Further naturalistic investigation is needed to explore the factors behind other teachers' selection and presentation of sex education material. It may be that ideology and personal values play a more important role for some.

Those of us involved in preservice and inservice for sexuality educators (all educators, for that matter) need to address both personal and contextual issues. We can challenge patriarchal, heterosexual, and antisex norms by first examining our own personal assumptions and attitudes and then assisting other educators in the same process. As James Sears suggests, we must also raise and encourage school personnel to address political questions about the extent to which respect for diversity and critical thinking are fostered in the curriculum (1992c, p. 147). We might better prepare teachers for the day-to-day reality of organizational constraints and possibilities in the school setting by helping them critically examine both. Instead of blaming individual teachers for the narrow content and simplified messages that result from defensive teaching, progressive educators must nourish the idealism that, like Mrs. Warren's, can get lost in less than ideal working conditions. We must work to circumvent and change the constraints and to expand the possibilities.

We must not *avoid* conflict and controversy by narrowing the parameters of what is taught, although a growing number of teachers, worried about getting "in trouble" during the present conservative resurgence, seem inclined to censor themselves (Whatley, 1992). With compassion for these worries, we must courageously and collectively challenge extremist attacks on comprehensive and progressive school sex education. The Sex Information and Education Council of the U.S. Community Advocacy Project, which documents local struggles over sexuality education and offers technical assistance and a "Community Action Kit" as tools to counter New Right efforts, is a promising beginning.[2] We need to perceive controversy as an inherent and positive aspect of democratic process rather than something to be feared, and to challenge patriarchal, heterosexist, and antisex norms wherever they surface within the school and community.

Whatley maintains that if sexuality education programs are "even partially determined by the fear of controversy, then educators are probably ignoring what should be a major determinant of sexuality curricula—the reality of students' lives" (1992, p. 80). The following realities are clearly not addressed by programs that exclusively emphasize abstinence and the dangers of premarital intercourse:

> Students are sexually active in every way possible, with themselves and with others, feel sexual desires, are sexually ex-

ploited, become pregnant, cause pregnancy, have abortions, have babies, catch diseases, explore their own sexuality, explore and exploit others' sexualities, are sexually violent, wrestle with issues of power and control. (1992, p. 80)

Enhancing Relevance to Student's Lives

Doing Sex Education reveals that students themselves can create progressive possibilities within the classroom that educators might pursue. For example, Mrs. Warren's students expressed privately to me a desire expressed consistently by other students (Cranston, 1992)—an interest in learning more about such controversial topics as homosexuality and abortion. There were moments (such as Andrew and Dawn's comments on sexual assault and Carrie's reference to abortion after the movie) when students' interjections might have opened up more pertinent discussion. Relevance of materials to students' lives might be further enhanced by providing opportunities for them to write anonymous questions and comments (everyone writes something on identical sheets of paper) and discuss them in class. This anonymity would also partially address concerns around embarrassment expressed by students in Mrs. Warren's class, as would joint teacher/student established guidelines for respectful classroom discussion (Sapon-Shevin & Goodman, 1992).

Educators might make themselves more aware of current levels of adolescent sexual knowledge and concerns and draw on this awareness to plan classroom content and approaches (Sapon-Shevin & Goodman, 1992). Insight into young peoples' interests and concerns around sexuality might be gained by paying more attention to what adolescents watch and listen to in popular films and music videos. Classroom analysis of these popular media might offer educators a chance to enter into this discussion and begin a critique of the cultural constructions of sexuality and gender (Whatley, 1992).

An example of more relevant classroom discussion generated by students is recorded by health educator Shelley Mains (1992). In contrast to Mrs. Warren, who was teaching a required ninth-grade health class with twenty-eight students in a small Midwestern city, Mains was facilitating a discussion in a sex education course in a Boston GED program. The discussion involved four young women between the ages of seventeen and twenty who described themselves as "Black Hispanic," "Black Indian American," "West Indian," and "Black Hispanic American." All had previously quit school and were returning for their GEDs; they knew one another as classmates and, in some

179

cases, as friends. As the following exchange illustrates, these four were able to "talk openly—and quite raucously—about sex" (p. 16H), ask questions, and use their own language forms:

> Jo: "I have a question. How come when girls come they can come all night and guys can't. . . ."
>
> Stacey: ". . . come right afterwards?"
>
> Lakeisha: "Yeah, that's what I've always wondered. When girls have orgasms they can bust 'em left and right, but boys, they have to wait until it get hard. Why are men like that?"
>
> Mains: "That's just how their bodies are. They have to get hard again, and women don't have to wait to come again."
>
> Kenia: "I like it when a guy busts a nut [comes]. . . ."
>
> Lakeisha: "It's really funny! They're like, '(pant, pant) Here it comes!' "
>
> Stacy: " 'It's coming!' " (Laughter)
>
> (Mains, 1992, pp. 17H–18H)

However, even though these young women seemed comfortable with each other and the teacher in this small group setting, like Mrs. Warren's students, they also restricted personal disclosure by alluding vaguely to their personal past or current relationship problems and referring only to friends—not themselves—as having been sexually assaulted.

Thus, while the relevance of sexuality discussion can be increased beyond what occurred in Mrs. Warren's classroom, the school setting itself may constrain discussion. It may be that small informal community-based programs developed for and with young people, especially those that involve peer leaders, offer the most realistic possibilities for truly open and honest interaction about sexuality. A growing number of such programs have been developed in a variety of settings across the country. One example is Project HOPE's Poder Latino (Latin Power) Youth Group in Jamaica Plains, MA, where all peer leaders are Latino and bilingual. One unique aspect of this program is that peer leaders invite individual friends and small groups to their homes for HIV/AIDS education sessions in addition to doing community outreach in churches, shelters, libraries, and the street (Kanoff, 1992). Not surprisingly, school versions of peer education are likely to operate under many of the same pressures encountered by Mrs. Warren, making them less relevant to students.

Furthermore, the role of student voices in debates and policy decisions about school sex education might be expanded with their inclusion on district and state advisory committees in sufficient numbers so they are not overwhelmed by adults. In the state where I live, committees are mandated at the local district level to review school sexuality curricula every three years, and they are composed overwhelmingly of adults. The advisory committee of my local district, of which I have been a member for the last two reviews, includes a student from each of the high schools. During the first review, they attended meetings infrequently and rarely spoke. This year, however, is a different story. A combination of activist, outspoken students representing different racial groups as well as schools (including one who volunteers for the city's AIDS Support Network), school staff willing to provide transportation to and from meetings and a personal connection with students, and genuine efforts from adult committee members to solicit and listen to student concerns is resulting in the committee's consideration of a student-initiated proposal for condom distribution in the schools. Furthermore, the committee (which consists of school and district staff, clergy, parents, and other community members in addition to students) has supported my suggestion that we make systematic student evaluation of their classroom experience regarding sexuality curricula a priority for this year's review. A subcommittee is currently planning specifics, which may include some combination of surveys, individual interviews, or focus groups conducted by committee members, including students, at the high school and possibly middle school levels. While this does not guarantee a sexuality curriculum more relevant to students, I offer it as one example of a situation-specific strategy that emerged when activist students and adults willing to listen to them used an existing organizational structure in progressive ways.

Future academic research, such as focus groups with immigrant and minority students described by Ward and Taylor (1992), might further explore students themselves—what they already know about sexuality, what they want to know, their lived cultural concerns, and factors behind their classroom responses. As student willingness to speak openly about sexuality during my one-to-one interviews suggests, this type of research would also have potential for increasing participants' self-understanding.

Needs of Multicultural Populations

Because the expectations, norms, and taboos of different cultural groups are largely missing from school sexuality education discourse and curricular materials (Nettles & Scott-Jones, 1992; Ward & Taylor, 1992) and because the Census Bureau estimates that nearly half the U.S. population will be Hispanic, black, or Asian by 2050 (Eskey, 1992), developing culturally sensitive curriculum is crucial to making sexuality education relevant to the lives of these students. In considering differences between groups, we must be aware of linguistic, historical, geographic, and cultural dimensions. With regard to sexuality education, there may be variations in perspectives on the nature of sexuality, theories of reproduction, beliefs about the way sexuality information should be transmitted across generations, and attribution of erotic meaning to stimula (Davenport, 1977).

However, as Carrie and Dawn illustrated in Mrs. Warren's classroom, significant differences also exist *within* groups. These include such standard demographic elements as age, education, and social class plus elements particular to minority populations in the U.S., such as extent of identification with parents or country of origin and generational status (Wong, Kim, Lim, & Morishima, 1983, cited in Nettles & Scott-Jones, 1992). Although attention to this complexity can seem overwhelming, failure to recognize these forms of diversity between and within groups can perpetuate inequity by reinforcing old myths (for example, promiscuous premarital sexual activity as normative behavior in minority communities) and creating new ones (Nettles & Scott-Jones, 1992).

Meeting the needs of a culturally diverse population is important, particularly since rates of unprotected sexual activity, intravenous drug use, and sex with intravenous drug users are high and growing among low-income black and Hispanic adolescents (Flora & Thoresen, 1988). Ward and Taylor's (1992) research with immigrant and minority groups in one school district illustrates another situation-specific strategy for enhancing relevance of sexuality curriculum to students' lives. They worked with the Somerville-Cambridge (MA) Teen Pregnancy Coalition to arrange twenty-one focus groups with adolescents and parents from six populations (Vietnamese, Portuguese, black, white, Haitian, and Hispanic) represented in the district. Each was facilitated by an adult from the same background who spoke the participants' language. Before the groups met, sexuality educators met with social service providers and community leaders working with the groups to gather culturally specific information later synthesized into open-ended questions or scripts for use in the groups. These were revised after being reviewed by service providers. Transcripts of the groups' discussions were analyzed with community representatives.

The most common response of immigrant and minority teens in the focus groups was similar to views expressed by Mrs. Warren's mostly white students. The words of one black male ("it [school sex education] doesn't teach you, like, the things you want to know. . . . You get your own questions and they don't show it in the movies or books or whatever, y'know") (Ward & Taylor, 1992, p. 191) bear striking resemblance to the observation of Sharon, a white female in Mrs. Warren's class ("It was just stuff you had to know. I don't know if we'll ever use it"). Most teens in the focus groups believed school sex education overemphasized reproductive biology, although they held a great many misconceptions mostly about preventing pregnancy and sexually transmitted diseases. They felt their questions—especially about the complexity of social relationships—were mostly ignored or unanswered.

Overall, Ward and Taylor conclude that the needs of multicultural populations are not being addressed. They recommend building upon existing models of multicultural education that involve community collaboration with service providers, parents, teens, and teachers from diverse cultural groups; careful selection of curriculum content and materials for cultural relevance/sensitivity, with bicultural or bilingual paraprofessionals teaching or supplementing certain aspects of material; and peer education networks so that teens may talk about sexuality with knowledgeable older peers of the same ethnic group (1992, pp. 197–98).

Needs of Gay, Lesbian, and Bisexual Students

Students who are questioning their sexual orientation and those who self-identify as gay, lesbian, or bisexual are another group whose experience and needs are not addressed in sex education curricula or anywhere in the school setting. In the words of Virginia Uribe (founder of PROJECT 10, the nation's first school-based program designed specifically to address these needs) and Karen Harbeck (editor of a recent collection of research entitled *Coming Out of the Classroom Closet: Gay and Lesbian Students, Teachers and Curricula*), "the paucity of literature, intervention and understanding in this area is a national disgrace" (1992, pp. 11–12).

Given the social stigma attached to homosexuality, most young people who experience same sex attractions also experience considerable turmoil, isolation, and paranoia. In attempting to distance themselves from negative stereotypes and to avoid being targets of discrimination as well as verbal and physical abuse, most of these students (and teachers) are faced with an appalling choice:

We could keep the truth to ourselves, and become totally isolated from everyone else. Or we could lie to the others, and become alienated from ourselves. Either way we lost. (Nickel,
1992, p. 4)

The toll exacted by systematic discrimination against this largely
invisible sexual minority is high: self-rejection, isolation, and increased
risk of other problems. Most serious is the estimate in the Department
of Health and Human Service Report on the Secretary's Task Force
on Youth Suicide (1989) that gay and lesbian youth (ages 14 to 24)
are five times more likely to attempt suicide than heterosexuals of the
same age. In addition, research has documented higher rates of sexually
transmitted disease, substance abuse, sexual abuse, running away from
home, prostitution, school dropout, and conflict with the law (Remafedi, 1987; Remafedi, Farrow, & Deisher, 1991).

At the level of the informal curriculum, school staff can play an
important role in making school a safer place for this group of oppressed and mostly invisible students by interrupting such sexual slurs
as those described here. Yet, like Mrs. Warren, teachers—even those
who would not tolerate a derogatory remark about a student's race
or disability—may not intervene. Sears' research with prospective
teachers suggests that their personal values may be a factor. He found
their expressed willingness to supportively address homosexuality-re-
lated issues in the school setting (for example, curtailing verbal harassment, encouraging classroom discussions, and integrating the topic
into the curriculum) to be "highly correlated with their attitudes about
homosexuality and their feelings toward lesbians and gay men"
(1992d, p. 69). Nevertheless, it seems too simplistic to suggest that
positive personal attitudes and feelings are sufficient for a teacher to
intervene in the context of a homophobic school setting. Woods and
Harbeck (1992), in their in-depth phenomenological study of twelve
lesbian physical educators, found that all participants expressed positive feelings about their lifestyle outside the school environment. Yet
all twelve believed they would be fired if their sexual orientation was
disclosed there. Thus, they employed a variety of protective strategies
to distance themselves from these issues in the school: pretending not
to hear homophobic name-calling and avoiding AIDS education or
assisting students with questions about sexuality. The fears of these
lesbian teachers that they would lose their jobs is further testimony
to the powerful and silencing social stigma attached to homosexuality.

PROJECT 10 is an example of a low cost, school-based program of counseling, intervention, and education that has had considerable positive impact on most students in the Los Angeles School District. After its implementation the general student population showed greater acceptance of and sensitivity to diversity and sexual orientation. Gay, lesbian, and bisexual participants reported feeling better about themselves as well as greater social acceptance, interpersonal connections, academic success, and safer sexual practices (Uribe & Harbeck, 1992).[3]

Although slight, this increase in safer sexual practices as a result of PROJECT 10 is significant because adolescent gay and bisexual males are at greater risk for HIV infection than other adolescents. In contrast to a downward trend among their adult counterparts, rates of HIV infection and diagnosed cases of AIDS are increasing for these young men. This increased risk is due to their behaviors (unprotected oral and anal intercourse with multiple partners and sharing injection drug needles and paraphernalia (Cranston, 1992; Gelman, 1993). Historically, these young people have experienced the HIV/AIDS pandemic differently from older gay men. From the early 1980s, adult gay men— rather than the medical "experts"—were responsible for developing safer sex practices that effectively reduced their specific risk behaviors within an affirming cultural frame of reference. However, today's gay and bisexual youth have not yet experienced the heavy personal losses known to be a factor in behavioral changes among their older cohorts (Cranston, 1992; Gelman, 1993). Furthermore, they have grown up at a time when AIDS prevention messages have "gone mainstream" in an attempt to convince heterosexuals of their risk of HIV infection. In response to this second wave of HIV infection among young gay men, a variety of community-based prevention education projects are being developed that are run by and for this group and attempt to personalize the issues in a self-affirming context (Gelman, 1993).

Drawing on the work of Paulo Freire, Kevin Cranston (1992) proposes that more relevant and effective HIV/AIDS prevention would emerge if gay, lesbian, and bisexual youth engaged in critical dialogue about the realities of their lives in the context of heterosexism and HIV. This dialogue would also involve adult gay, lesbian, and bisexual communities in "authentic mutuality" with their younger counterparts (1992, pp. 256–257). Cranston suggests three institutional settings that might beneficially utilize this approach. First, school-based programs could educate the entire school population about the concerns of sexual minority youth. Second, multiservice agencies, such as the Gay and Lesbian Community Services Center in Hollywood and the Hetrick-Martin Institute in New York City, could target youth at highest risk with intensive programs and services. Finally, self-help groups controlled by youth could be sites for empowerment and support (1992, p. 258).

In the classroom, however, many educators are emphasizing that AIDS is not a gay disease, and a growing number of schools are requesting that guest speakers on HIV/AIDS avoid discussing homosexuality. While such approaches may increase feelings of susceptibility among heterosexuals and ward off controversy and some homophobic responses to HIV prevention, they also eliminate one of very few educational moments in the classroom in which gay, lesbian, and bisexual issues might be explored (Cranston, 1992).

Doing Sex Education illuminates potential for progressive individuals and community groups to have an impact on the formal and informal sexuality curriculum. Van Buren teachers who collectively organized Women's Week and resisted the "joking" male parody of it or the woman union steward who tried to persuade Mrs. Warren to file a formal grievance were important elements in the struggle for gender equity. Furthermore, district action on Title IX at Van Buren was initiated by women's groups in the community that monitored schools and complained about noncompliance with the law. Similarly, Woodland has an active and visible gay and lesbian community that has begun to agitate at the district level for greater sensitivity to these issues in both the school setting and the curriculum. One local agency has offered teacher inservices, curricular materials, and support groups for gay and lesbian teens.

Involvement of those who challenge the status quo in public school sex education is especially crucial, given the current conservative resurgence, and must be expanded. Unfortunately, opportunities to have an impact on the sexuality curriculum, through prepackaged materials and censorship attacks, have been used frequently by well-organized conservative networks, while those who are supportive of more comprehensive and progressive course offerings have often remained silent and unorganized. Thus, administrators have been mostly concerned with the vocal minority.

Researchers might usefully investigate two related areas. First, using ethnographic methods, they could examine the process by which community group pressure works its way through the district and school. Second, they might focus attention on school administrators (who are mostly male), including the specific ways they influence classroom sex education and the organizational/community pressure factors that affect administrators themselves. Also, since *Doing Sex Education* makes clear that the classroom is not the only place in the school

Situation-Specific Constraints and Possibilities

where learning about sexuality and gender relations occurs, research might be undertaken with administrators along the lines initiated by Shakeshaft (1989), who investigated the ways that hiring practices, team building, and organizational climate are affected by administrators' beliefs, discomforts, and fears about sexuality. Such research may have potential for what Lather (1986b) labels "catalytic validity," i.e., increasing administrators' self-understanding, which might positively carry over into their decisions affecting staff and students.

Multiple Responses to "Ill-Structured" Problems

The close-up look at the constraints, possibilities, and dynamics within one classroom offered in *Doing Sex Education* underscores the need to conceptualize school sexuality curriculum as one of multiple responses to the "ill-structured" problems associated with teen sexuality. As discussed in Chapter 1, such problems involve multiple causes and responses; require consideration of the context in which they occur; and include interpersonal as well as intrapersonal knowledge in their definitions and solutions (Lee & Berman, 1992).

In her important analysis of prevention models that have had a positive impact on such interconnected adolescent problems as unplanned pregnancy, substance abuse, delinquency, and school failure/dropping out, Joy Dryfoos (1990) identifies two approaches that appear to have widest application. These include providing intensive individual attention to children in high-risk situations and developing community-wide interventions in response to particular needs. Schools can play a crucial role in implementing both these approaches, and many of the successful prevention models detailed by Dryfoos are physically located within schools. With regard to teen sexuality, access via school and community clinics to such services as contraception, STD diagnosis and treatment, pregnancy testing, prenatal care, adoption services, and safe abortion are aspects of a solution that go beyond classroom instruction. Churches, youth-serving agencies, police departments, health and social services agencies, and other community-based organizations can play a role in developing situation-specific strategies with and for young people.

Those concerned with increasing the relevance and comprehensiveness of school sex education need to be precise about the kind of programs we advocate. Instead of arguing for sex education in general, we must redouble our efforts toward programs that analyze sexuality in the context of wider power relations, uncovering gender, class, and racial inequalities. More specifically, Mariamne Whatley (1992) has articulated goals for "sex equitable" sexuality education. These include replacing biologically determined sex roles with more flexible, socially constructed gender roles; emphasizing female/male similarities rather than differences; recognizing female sexual pleasure and desire; presenting intercourse as one of many possible forms of sexual expression; eliminating heterosexual assumptions; establishing common standards of sexual behavior/responsibility for both sexes; and education about violence that applies to both potential victims and perpetrators. In light of the proliferation and wide use of audiovisuals in sexuality education, we might promote change through developing situation-specific materials and pedagogies to meet such goals.

Although legislative mandates for HIV/AIDS in sexuality education are a growing trend, we must be aware that such institutionalization of curriculum offers both regressive and progressive possibilities. Although most mandates seem to narrow the parameters of course offerings, Muraskin (1986) demonstrates that monolithic conformity to such curricular initiatives by local districts and teachers is unlikely. Furthermore, like the classroom knowledge construction just described, the process of formulating, passing and implementing legislation and policy at the state and local levels is dynamic, complex and often contradictory. As Earls et al. point out in their analysis of such a process in South Carolina, it offers opportunities for ideological struggle and "opens multiple arenas for dialogue and action" (1992, p. 324). State legislation has been used as a basis for arguing against and legally challenging New Right curricular materials. For example, parents in East Troy, Wisconsin, with assistance from the American Civil Liberties Union, challenged the use of *Sex Respect* for its violation of state laws prohibiting discriminatory stereotyping in curricular materials. The Wisconsin Department of Public Instruction ruled that, while the curriculum did contain such stereotyping and medical misinformation, the agency did not have authority to prohibit it (Wisconsin Department of Public Instruction, 1991). Nevertheless, as local, statewide, and national debates focused on the issue, greater awareness, commitment, and networking possibilities emerged, and the issue of sexuality education was brought to the forefront in elections for State Superintendent. Furthermore, the East Troy school board has begun a process to include other points of view in the curriculum; state legislation is pending to include medical accuracy as a criterion for curriculum selection; and other parents are positioning themselves to bring about a court challenge. Similarly, a lawsuit against *Teen-Aid* brought by six families and Planned Parenthood of Northeast Florida against the Duval County School Board charges that the curriculum violates Florida state law mandating comprehensive sexuality education and cites its inaccurate, biased, and incomplete information as well as its presentation of sectarian philosophy (Hennessy, 1992a). Additional research on the process by which state policy or curriculum guidelines are constructed and their implementation by local districts would provide insight into the dynamics of negotiating competing interests.

As we develop multiple situation-specific responses to the "ill-structured" problems associated with adolescent sexuality, we must not lose sight of the fact that discrimination in education, employment, and material benefits in a capitalistic, patriarchal, heterosexist, and racist society generate more problematic outcomes for members of marginalized groups, i.e., pregnancy among poor teenagers (especially women of color) and HIV infection among young gay men. Sole emphasis on school sex education, a single and individualistic response, can obscure consideration of these wide inequities. Although progressive educators must not abandon the terrain of school sex education to those who advocate saying "no" to sex, we must continue to work in and outside classrooms to change the social and economic conditions that deter all of us from maximizing our potential as fully human, sexual beings.

Methodological Appendix

Several fundamental precepts of ethnographic research guided my process of inquiry. First, I limited my efforts to a case study of one required semester ninth-grade health/physical education course that included a four-week unit of study on sexuality. Becoming immersed in a single classroom in a single school context allowed more in-depth analysis than if I had attempted to become immersed in more than one setting. I tried to become part of the everyday social fabric of this classroom, examining the setting "as it is viewed and constructed by its participants" (Wilcox, 1982, p. 458). At the same time, I endeavored to remain the analytic outsider who continually called into question what I saw and heard, detecting inconsistencies and contradictions of which participants themselves may not have been aware. Finally, I explored the relationships between the classroom I observed and its context—the school as a whole, the community, the cultural experiences of students and teacher outside the school, and the wider political and economic context. Ethnographer Robert Everhart succinctly summarizes these principles:

> As a quasi-member of the groups studied, the fieldworker constantly asks, "what questions does what I am seeing or hearing answer?" as a way of understanding the interpretative process characterizing social groups, as well as the structural factors that influence such a process. (1983, pp. 278–79)

Methodological Appendix

Although my purpose is to illuminate a particular sex education classroom rather than to make generalizations about all sex education courses, the setting I chose was not "markedly dissimilar from other relevant settings. . . ." (Spindler, 1982, p. 8). As discussed earlier, schools in the United States offering some form of sex education are diverse, with no particular type of school or community significantly more likely than another to offer such programs (Orr, 1982); two-thirds of the largest districts require sex education (Kenney, Guardado, & Brown, 1989). Most sexuality instruction occurs as a separate unit in health, home economics, science, or physical education (Sonenstein & Pittman, 1984), usually at the ninth or tenth grade (Forrest & Silverman, 1989). Teachers of high school sex education courses generally have credentials in physical education, home economics, science, or social studies and teach these subjects as well (Orr, 1982). Thus, my choice of a school (one of four large comprehensive public schools in a Midwestern city of about 175,000), classroom (a ninth-grade health/physical education course), and teacher (certified in physical education and health and teaching both) can be considered to represent a more or less typical school sex education setting.

I selected a female teacher largely because of my interest in gender and the labor process of teaching. Since my purpose was not to critique teaching techniques but to analytically describe curriculum-in-use and to explore factors involved in teacher selection of classroom knowledge and pedagogy, I observed a woman with several years of teaching experience who was regarded by the district's central administration and her colleagues as a competent health education teacher. In fact, she was one of the most highly regarded in the district.

Gaining Access for Sex Education Research

Because school sex education is a sensitive and controversial aspect of the curriculum, gaining access to classroom and students for research in this area can be difficult. I was concerned that the open-ended aspect of ethnographic research might make my attempt to attain access even more difficult, particularly getting approval from the district's external research committee and parents of students I hoped to interview. Because my experience in gaining entry (which included fortuitous circumstance as well as carefully planned strategy) may help others, I briefly elaborate it here.

First, I was no stranger to Woodland School District's sex education efforts, having intermittently done classroom presentations, curriculum consultation, and teacher inservices in this curricular area for several years. In so doing, I had acquired credibility as a practicing sex educator and earned the respect of several district personnel, particularly the curriculum/staff development coordinator and health coordinator, Mr. Cox, who recognized that my research questions emerged from actual experience with teachers and students. In short, my experience and reputation as a sex educator, which I also briefly summarized in a cover letter to the external research committee, seemed to facilitate my gaining access in this sensitive area of the curriculum.[1]

Specificity in my prospectus to the research committee was another factor that helped gain their approval. Recognizing sex education as a controversial area, I provided as many specifics as I could, including detailed research questions, categories guiding my observations, and questions I planned to ask school personnel and students; however, I also included the caveat that, given the nature of ethnographic research, these might be revised and other methods generated as a result of my observations. In addition, I submitted the required prototype parent permission letter that asked for signed consent of *all* parents, although I might have chosen an easier option to seek signatures only from parents who did *not* want their ninth-graders to participate. In addition to granting its approval, the committee asked for permission to use my prospectus as a model of specificity for future applicants requesting permission to conduct ethnographic research. The chairperson said that ethnographic proposals frequently lack this specificity, and the committee would have been reluctant to give approval to what might have appeared to be a vague "fishing expedition"—particularly in sex education.

Once approval was granted at the district level, I contacted the classroom teacher, Mrs. Warren. I was acquainted with her, although I had not personally seen her teach or worked closely with her, because she had attended a large teacher inservice I had conducted for several school districts three years earlier.[2] My assumption in conducting inservices is that classroom teachers already have considerable knowledge about their subject matter and the craft of teaching. While recognizing that I may have useful information for them, I function as much as a facilitator for teachers to share their knowledge with each other than as outside expert. Thus, Mrs. Warren seemed to regard me as both experienced in the field of school sex education and a nonthreatening presence, and she readily expressed her willingness to participate in the study. After reading the final manuscript, Mrs. Warren told me she felt "important" and perceived her selection as an honor. The most important factor in her decision to participate was "knowing" that she and the Van Buren health education program would "benefit."

Finally, with regard to parent permission, I met with both the Van Buren principal and Mrs. Warren to get their feedback on the letter requesting permission from parents for their teenagers to participate in the study. I sent these letters the second week of the fall semester, with a stamped, self-addressed envelope, telling parents that I would be available for questions at Go-To-School-Night. I received most permissions by return mail within two weeks. I then checked with students whose permissions were missing and learned that two parents had decided not to give consent. I followed up with phone calls and mailed the planned interview questions to both parents; one changed her mind and granted permission. After they received the letter and had an opportunity to meet me personally at Go-To-School-Night, twenty-seven of twenty-eight parents ultimately gave permission for their ninth-grader's participation.[3]

While prior experience with the district offered some advantages in gaining access, it also set up some potential problems in data collection. I had to work harder at understanding the school setting through the eyes of the participants, instead of my own, than a researcher who was more of an outsider would have. (Actually, no ethnographer who has negotiated the educational system as student or teacher can be truly considered an outsider.) Furthermore, I had to change the nature of my already-established social relationship with both Mr. Cox and Mrs. Warren, moving from the role of consultant to researcher. Since I was perceived by both of them as a resource person with expertise in school sex education, I needed to clearly demonstrate that I was not in the classroom to either critique or assist Mrs. Warren or to report classroom occurrences to Mr. Cox. Developing a trusting and confidential field relationship with both of them simultaneously presented me with a different set of complexities than a stranger might have encountered, although in all ethnographic research gaining entry is an *ongoing* process of initiating and developing social relationships (Schatzman & Strauss, 1973). Finally, having served as a consultant to classroom teachers, I had to stifle my own impulses to be immediately "helpful" in order to assume the role of nonparticipant observer in the classroom.

Collecting the Data

Observations in the Health Education Class

I observed all classroom sessions of Mrs. Warren's second period ninth-grade health class at Van Buren High School during the first semester of the 1985–86 school year (August 26, 1985, through January 17, 1986). The class met daily for about fifty minutes (even-numbered calendar days in classroom activity and odd-numbered calendar days in physical activity). Altogether, the class met for eighty-nine sessions; forty-five were in the classroom, and the last ten of these involved sex education. In addition, I was present at all activity sessions during the first half of the semester and about two-thirds of the activity sessions during the second half.

These observations of both classroom and activity sessions over the entire semester provided a broad context for my observation of the sex education unit. I had originally planned to confine most of my observations to the classroom and to participate only initially in activity sessions, mostly to get acquainted with students. However, I realized from the first fifteen-minute classroom session on Freshman Orientation Day that I needed to consider the course as an organic whole if I hoped to assess its meaning to students and the factors involved in Mrs. Warren's curricular choices. At this session, students naturally arranged themselves with females on the left and males on the right. After Mrs. Warren had explained the structure of the course (lecture on even days, activity on odd days), she told students that they would need gym clothes and a suit for swimming. Then, turning to address the left side of the room, she added, "Ladies, don't wear bikinis. They fall off." To this, a male student replied in a loud voice, "Just what we need." The rest of the group, including Mrs. Warren, began to laugh. With a big smile on her face, she turned to the right side of the room and said (in a way that was playful rather than stern), "What?" Just then the bell rang, and students left the room laughing and talking among themselves.

This brief exchange made me realize that classroom and activity sessions could not be arbitrarily separated if I were to fully explore issues of sexuality and gender relations; such informal interactions between teacher and students would probably abound in activity sessions too. As I shall later describe, my ongoing observations in these very different settings were also crucial to an understanding of the factors behind many of Mrs. Warren's classroom decisions. Such an understanding would not have emerged had I observed only in the

195

classroom or only during the sex education unit. In addition, my ongoing presence at both types of sessions throughout the semester enabled me to become a taken-for-granted presence for both students and Mrs. Warren well before the classroom subject matter I was most interested in observing was presented.

I believe that two factors contributed particularly to this acceptance and unobtrusiveness with students, in spite of our obvious appearance and age differences. First, Mrs. Warren (complying with my request) introduced me to students in an informal matter-of-fact way at the first full-length classroom session as someone "from the University who is interested in experiencing this health class as a student might." She said I would be doing pretty much what they did and that I wanted to be able to ask them some questions later in the semester. At the ninth session, after having more than a week of informal interactions with students, I described my project more fully to them along the same lines, explaining that I needed their permission as well as their parents' permission before I interviewed them. When I passed around a sign-up sheet after my presentation, all but one student (who later changed his mind) gave their consent.

A second factor in my gaining acceptance by students was my presence (in T-shirt and sweat pants) and active participation in seventeen running activity sessions during the first months of the semester. First, my adult status with regard to students was diminished somewhat because I was no better at running than most of the young women, and I had to work as hard as they did to keep up. On the other hand, although I do not run regularly, I am reasonably physically active, so I was not subjected to ridicule or rejection by students as totally physically inept. As I had anticipated, this informal contact with students was an excellent vehicle for getting acquainted and engaging in casual conversation before the more formal interviews; this process was fairly comfortable for me because of my prior experience, as professional and parent, with this age group.

With regard to Mrs. Warren, who is a seasoned runner and could outdo most young men in the class, my mediocre skill level and willingness to put myself in the role of sweating subordinate during activity sessions helped to reinforce her expertise—for herself and for students. In addition, since my knowledge level and experience in teaching the earlier course topics (particularly physical fitness and alcohol/drugs) was much less than that of Mrs. Warren's, any perceptions she might have of me as all-knowing expert were diminished before the sex education unit.

Whatever the reasons, my presence seemed to be largely taken for granted. I sat in various parts of the classroom during the semester and, although she made more frequent eye contact with me in the beginning, Mrs. Warren soon seemed to carry on as if I were not present. She told me after the study that she generally did not feel stress at my presence because I "blended in so well," but said there were occasions when my presence was not comfortable for her, when she felt uncertain about specific information and believed I knew the correct answers. As far as students were concerned, my presence did not seem to deter those sitting near me from engaging in their customary level of muted conversation, humorous quips, and occasional obscenities.

In the classroom, I recorded both the content and form of Mrs. Warren's presentations, attempting to discern what points of view about sexuality and gender relations students were being offered. I took notes in longhand, transcribing key statements verbatim, fleshing out sketchy notes the same day as the observation and, for the most part, typing my notes before the next period of observation. Such verbatim note taking would probably have been more difficult—even impossible—in a class where students had frequent opportunities to engage in small group discussion or to work independently in the library. However, since the class primarily involved the teacher presenting material to the entire group (mostly in an informal lecture format), verbatim note taking proved to be a workable strategy for summarizing curricular content and form.

In general, I maintained silence during the class period unless addressed by Mrs. Warren or students (which happened infrequently), although I often engaged in informal conversations before and after the bell; taking longhand notes during the class left little time to comment had I been so inclined. Partly because my observation and note taking skills had been progressively sharpened during a pilot study and during the units of study that preceded the sex education sessions, I feel confident that my notes are a reasonably accurate reflection of what I actually saw and heard in the sex education unit.

In terms of curricular content, I was cognizant of which sex education topics were included and excluded. I focused on the information and underlying values embedded in four interrelated content issues that appear consistently in the sex education literature: definitions of responsible vs. irresponsible sexual behavior, pleasures vs. dangers of sexuality, teenage pregnancy, and the nature of gender relations. My focus on issues rather than one side of a topic helped me avoid looking primarily for positions with which I agreed and provided sufficiently open categories to encompass a broad spectrum of specific events (McNeil, 1977).

In terms of curricular form, I used several categories to denote level of complexity in presentation of sexuality information. These categories were more than a counting device; they served as a reminder that no inherent match exists between topics and levels of complexity at which they are presented (McNeil, 1977) and enabled me to distinguish between mere mention of a topic and in-depth coverage. Categories included:

1. *Lecture/teacher explanation*: (*a*) Fact or detail: An item of information on a particular topic that receives no elaboration beyond a few sentences, such as "Masturbation is a normal means of sexual expression." (*b*) Extended description: Elaboration beyond a few sentences, filling in with explanation, several details, or illustration. (*c*) Controversy: A mention that the topic under consideration is the subject of debate, is constituted by two or more opposing points of view, or represents varying value judgments. (*d*) Slogan: Use of abstract terminology or phrases assumed to be understood by all students without elaboration. These may have strong value implications, e.g., "responsible sexual decisions." (*e*) Aside: Digressive narrative, commentary, or personal interest stories. (*f*) Current topic: Mention of current event for illustration or comparison.
2. *Class discussion*. Issues discussed by class with teacher in a facilitative rather than lecturing role (categories a–f may apply to teacher).
3. *Small group discussion*. Students divided into groups to discuss material.
4. *Question-answer*. Student responses guide discussion (categories a–f may apply to teacher response).
5. *Media*. Films, slides, or tape recordings, used to present a topic.

While noting curricular content and form, I was especially attentive to language and circumstances under which Mrs. Warren used either medically correct or everyday language.

I similarly recorded student classroom response to teacher-presented information, using general categories of behavior discerned by other ethnographers of education (Everhart, 1983; McNeil, 1977; Willis,

1977). These include acceptance, ambiguous acquiescence, contestation, and rejection. However, it is important to point out that student interviews were essential to understanding the *meaning* of these observed behaviors to students themselves. The observational categories can be broadly characterized as follows:

1. *Acceptance.* Expressions of agreement, both verbal and nonverbal (affirmative nods), with teacher-presented knowledge.
2. *Ambiguous acquiescence.* Silence or neutral conformity to classroom procedures and information.
3. *Contestation.* Attempts to counteract or oppose school knowledge or control, including such behaviors as writing notes, tapping pencils, being late, using humor, talking back, etc. These may be interaction with friends or aimed at "bugging the teacher" (Everhart, 1983). The latter may include both individually or socially-initiated responses done in concert with two or more people.
4. *Rejection.* Direct verbal or nonverbal disagreement with teacher-presented knowledge.

I tried to be equally aware of all four categories of student response; nevertheless, it is readily apparent that describing a particular classroom event may have meant ignoring others that occurred simultaneously. Furthermore, I tend to describe in more detail student behaviors that overtly challenged Mrs. Warren's agenda rather than those that did not, for example when students were listening quietly. It bears repeating that the *meaning* of these observed behaviors to students themselves is also pursued in interviews.

In addition to taking notes in the classroom, I recorded events during the activity sessions that preceded and followed running: physical fitness testing, swimming, weight training, and Fun Days. I paid particular attention to Mrs. Warren's statements regarding the nature of gender relations and similarities/differences between males and females and noted student responses and participation along these lines.

Observations in the Context of the School

In an attempt to situate the health education class and Mrs. Warren in the broader school context, I attended and took notes during faculty orientation at the beginning of the school year, Go-To-School-Night for parents, several faculty meetings, an all-day teacher in-service, and a meeting of district health education teachers. Similarly, I observed Mrs. Warren through two complete days of her teaching activities.

I also attempted to gain insight into the informal structure of gender relations in the school as they were revealed in student rituals and extracurricular activities, seeking to discern through my observation the "symbolic orders of male/female that permeate everyday life" of students (Mechling, 1981, p. 138). Thus, I was present for ninth-grade orientation, several pep rallies, a student dance (at which Mrs. Warren was a chaperone), the Homecoming variety show and parade, and the all-school talent show. I also spent time in the Commons area and hallways during periods between classes and, as the semester progressed and I got better acquainted with students, I asked two of the young women if I could spend a day going to their classes and activities with them. Finally, I ate lunch or had informal conversations with several students during the course of the semester.

Interviews

I formally interviewed several significant subjects during the course of my research. These included students in the health education class, Mrs. Warren, and other relevant district and school staff (Woodland School District's health coordinator, Van Buren's school principals and psychologist, social workers, nurse, biology teacher, and other health education teachers). I attempted to maintain a "delicate balance between probing the motivations, intents, investments, and practices of persons, and respecting their boundaries of privacy and vulnerability" (Britzman, 1990, p. 16).

Students. I interviewed students after the nutrition unit and again after the sex education unit. Formally interviewing students earlier in the semester was useful in several significant ways. First, since I was interested in the context of the wider health education class in which sexuality is presented, I gained insight into students' perceptions and reactions to school knowledge on an additional aspect of the health curriculum. Thus, I was better able to discern whether student reactions to the sex education unit were related to the specific subject or were part of a more general response to school-presented information on health. I also utilized the earlier interview as a source of questions I might include in the later. Furthermore, asking many of the same questions about both topics made the sexuality questions seem less invasive for both students and their parents. Finally, the nutrition interviews enabled me to establish one-to-one rapport with each of the students on relatively safe ground before talking with them about sexuality.

Of the twenty-seven students whose parents gave permission to participate, I interviewed seventeen females and nine males on nutrition and sixteen females and ten males on sex education.[4] The nutrition interviews with students were carried out in the three weeks of November immediately following that unit and ranged from twenty minutes to thirty-five minutes in length, averaging about twenty-five minutes.[5] They could be generally characterized as routine and noncontroversial. Because sex education was the last classroom topic covered during the first semester, the second set of student interviews had to be carried out during the second semester of the school year. Most were completed within the first six weeks of the second semester, and all were completed within eight weeks.[6] Sex education interviews ranged from thirty-five minutes to sixty-five minutes in length, with most taking about forty-five minutes.

Since I wanted students to feel as comfortable as possible during the sex education interview, I gave them choices about its location. I had access to several areas of the school where students routinely congregated, including the cafeteria, the Commons area, library, and a small private room off the counseling area. These locations offered differing degrees of privacy at different periods of the day, so students could choose the level of privacy they wanted for the interview. Most students selected the cafeteria, which was used for studying/visiting by a relatively small numbers of students at periods other than lunch, and they usually led the way to a table close enough to other groups of students not to be too conspicuous but sufficiently distant not to be overheard.

This same concern with student comfort prompted my decision not to tape record the interviews. Although a tape recorder would have allowed me to capture the richness of the students' language more precisely, I felt that it would jeopardize their ease and spontaneity. Thus, for both sets of interviews, I dittoed questions on sheets of paper, leaving space for me to record their responses in longhand. Before beginning the interviews, I assured students of confidentiality; I explained that I was asking everyone basically the same questions and that they could see what I was writing as they answered. I subsequently recorded responses in full view of the students and never attempted to cover up what I was writing. I recorded their responses in the same way as classroom presentations—transcribing key statements verbatim, fleshing out sketchy notes the same day, and typing each interview within a day or two after its occurrence. I began both interviews with concrete questions about student response to the unit and proceeded to more personal questions. In general, the questions for both interviews attempted to assess students' perceptions of school-presented information and the degree to which this school knowledge reinforced or contradicted other sources of information and student cultural experiences on these two topics.

In the case of sex education, I went into more detail with students about topics covered within the unit. For example, I prepared a summary of topics and time spent on each and asked students to tell me whether they would have liked to spend more or less time on them. When I sensed that a student was willing, I pursued certain questions relating to her/his perception of peer attitudes toward sexuality in more depth. For example, "How do classroom messages about sexuality compare with what you see as the attitudes of most students in the school about how a person your age should behave sexually?" "How do you think your same sex/other sex friends would like you to behave sexually?" "How important are they in influencing your own attitudes?" If a student appeared hesitant, I did not press further. I never asked a student specifically about her/his sexual behavior—only about attitudes; for instance, "How are class messages you got about sexuality similar or different from your own ideas about how you should behave sexually?" In general, students seemed interested in talking about the issues raised in the sex education interviews, with most giving longer and more personal responses than they had during the nutrition interviews.

I believe that my past experience and empathy in talking with adolescents about sexuality was significant in the level of their personal response; however, in one instance, student trust created an ethical dilemma for me. One of the young women who had seemed most comfortable in describing the social/sexual attitudes of her peers asked if she could talk with me again; I agreed, hoping to collect further data. During our subsequent talk, she disclosed that she had been sexually abused as a young child and that she had not felt until now that she could tell an adult. Fortunately, because of my work experience, I was able to respond in an appropriate and supportive way, ultimately facilitating a series of sessions between this student and the school psychologist. Nevertheless, her emotional disclosure took me beyond the relatively neutral role of researcher; instead of providing me with data for objective use, she was asking for help with a painful issue. As a result, I experienced an intense personal struggle over my degree of involvement with this "subject"—not in terms of possible over-rapport that might interfere with valid data collection but in terms of moral obligation to a human being in pain. I invested additional time and energy talking with her and introducing her to the school psychologist, which moved me beyond the realm of uninvolved observer. Had she been unwilling or unable to seek professional help, my struggle would have been even more intense. Ethnography obligates the researcher, if invited, to "sympathetically participate in the lives of those she studies" (Britzman, 1990), and adults who undertake this kind of research with adolescents need to be aware of the possibility of such disclosure and to consider in advance the ethical dilemmas it can create.

Classroom Teacher. Throughout the semester, I conducted both formal and informal interviews with Mrs. Warren, the health education teacher. She was generous with her time and seemed to welcome the opportunity to talk about herself and her work, frequently volunteering information she perceived to be of interest and which I would have otherwise not requested. Mrs. Warren originally agreed to be interviewed during her free period, however, I quickly discovered that this fifty-minute period preceding the health education class I observed—contrary to its name—was never "free." Although we scheduled formal interviews during this period early in the semester, I found myself asking questions in the context of numerous distractions, including a steady stream of students, comments from Mrs. Warren's office mate, and other work projects such as recording test scores, locating gym equipment, and so on, in which Mrs. Warren was engaged. After three early and frustrating attempts at interviews, during which Mrs. Warren was willing to answer my questions but apologetic about interruptions and other work she had to complete, I decided not to add to this pressure. Thus, I chose to ask questions as opportunities arose during periods of observation rather than try to schedule formal interviews during the school day. I hoped that there would be other opportunities for formal interviews later in the semester, and several did in fact occur.

In October, Mrs. Warren initiated an invitation for me to spend time with her during a state teachers' convention she had chosen not to attend. This interview was the first of four that I would classify as formal, meaning that I had Mrs. Warren's undivided attention to my questions. On this occasion I recorded the interview in longhand. The other three formal interviews occurred after the sex education unit, two during exam week when regular classes were not held and one on a school in-service day. Since Mrs. Warren seemed very comfortable with me by this time, I asked for and got her permission to tape record these last three interviews. Each of the four formal interviews lasted about ninety minutes and were generally focused on factors that influenced the content and methods she selected in the sex education unit and her philosophy of teaching such a class. I had not planned for the interviews to be this long; however, their length and the range of information Mrs. Warren offered verify my assertion that she welcomed the opportunity to talk about herself and her work—particularly with someone who had observed the incredible amount of energy her job required. Furthermore, Mrs. Warren said that at this period in her life, given the demands of her work and her role as a wife and mother of two young children, she had few chances to be heard in this way.

Significant Other School Personnel. As a means of gaining insight into Van Buren's ninth-grade health education program, I interviewed the other two health education teachers: Mr. Austin (also chairperson of the physical department) and Mrs. Crocker (Mrs. Warren's office mate). After learning that some reproductive information is also provided in ninth-grade biology, I interviewed one of the biology teachers. Furthermore, I interviewed Van Buren's principal, Mr. Gray; the assistant principal who supervises health and physical education teachers, Mr. Brunswick; and Woodland District's coordinator of health education, Mr. Cox.

I also interviewed several support staff at Van Buren who dealt with student sexuality issues in a variety of ways. These included two social workers, the school psychologist, the school nurse, and two special education teachers. I was primarily interested in exploring their perceptions of the ninth-grade sex education unit, the role of the school in sex education, what information regarding sexuality they considered essential for ninth-graders, what sexual issues arise for Van Buren students, and what strategies the school had implemented to help students deal with these issues. For most interviews, I recorded the subjects' responses to my questions in longhand. In general, as I interacted informally with these individuals throughout the semester, it became easier to propose using a tape recorder during the interviews. Thus, the later interviews (with social workers, special education teachers, and principal) were taped.

Reporting the Data

I have attempted throughout the final narration to follow several basic methodological conventions to enable readers to assess for themselves whether or not my conclusions are warranted. First, I have supported my contentions with detail from observations or quotations from interviews, accounting as well for instances that may not coincide with the overall pattern. I have offered as many specific examples as is practical, selecting those that represent the dynamics I observed over the entire semester and pointing out those unique to the sex education unit. Where I did not provide specific examples, the description summarizes my dominant impressions as they emerged from an accumulation of numerous small examples.

Furthermore, I contextualized my observations, exploring the significance of events or ideas in the framework of the immediate setting but pursuing them as necessary into broader contexts (Spindler, 1982). I also tried to specify my own role as researcher in data collection and interpretation. For example, if a direct question from me seemed significant in evoking a specific response, I tried to report that as part of the data. If my interpretation of events differed from another's account, I provided both interpretations and speculated on possible reasons for the difference and tried to reflect on competing explanations for a given happening (Becker & Geer, 1960).

I periodically compared my interpretations of events with Mrs. Warren's by discussing them with her during the semester. She also read an initial draft of the study as a check on accuracy and adequate inclusion of her interpretations in the reporting, seeing drafts of the first and second chapters as they were completed and later chapters together. I made the decision to show Mrs. Warren these last chapters at one sitting because she left Van Buren for personal reasons the following school year, and I was afraid that the third and fourth chapters in the original versions (which describe the classroom curriculum-in-use) without the accompanying analysis of factors involved in her classroom selection and presentation (documented in later chapters in the original version) would sound too disparaging. Thus, I sacrificed to some extent her ongoing involvement in checking the reporting for what I judged at the time to be more important issues of self-esteem.

After Mrs. Warren had read all of the original study, she made a few minor corrections (for instance, she graduated from college in 1972 rather than 1971). She also suggested a few additional perspectives which were incorporated and noted as subsequent additions to the text, and told me she was "amazed" at the accuracy and thoroughness of the report. I then asked for her reaction to the decision to show her the final chapters as a group rather than individually and separated by time. Mrs. Warren responded that she was glad I made this decision. She felt that the fourth chapter alone would have worried her by seeming too critical, since it did not reveal why she spent so little time on various topics. Drawing on this experience, in the present manuscript I describe factors influencing Mrs. Warren's curricular choices (contradictory gender role expectations, her working conditions and student cultural responses) *before* describing what actually occurs in the classroom. Thus, her curricular choices are more firmly embedded here in the factors that affected them. She also indicated that reading the whole study enhanced her understanding of the difficulty of her overall situation while teaching at Van Buren.

In addition to methodological conventions, certain ethical considerations influenced my reporting of the data. Like other ethnographers (and all social researchers for that matter), I had to balance intellectual honesty with ethical responsibility and "sympathetic participation" in the lives of those I studied (Britzman, 1990, p. 15). Writing the final report was an ongoing process of balancing these considerations, and I tried to adhere to principles set forth by Howard Becker in my deliberations:

> One should refrain from publishing items of fact or conclusions that are not necessary to one's argument or that would cause suffering out of proportion to the scientific gain of making them public. This judgment is of course ambiguous. In particular, it suggests on the one hand that the scientist must be able to give himself good reasons for including potentially harmful material, rather than including it simply because it is "interesting." On the other hand, it guards him against either an overly formal or an overly sentimental view of the harm those he studies may suffer, requiring that it be serious and substantial enough to warrant calling it "suffering." Finally, it insists that he know enough about the situation he has studied to know whether the suffering will in any sense be proportional to gains science may expect from publication of his finding. (1969, p. 275)

Thus, I occasionally deviated from the rule of reporting specific detail for ethical reasons of preserving the anonymity and personal privacy of research participants. For example, I have demonstrated that Mrs. Warren's personal beliefs about sexuality did consciously enter into some curricular decisions; however, they had less of an effect than factors related to district and school organization and student classroom response. Thus, although Mrs. Warren volunteered a great deal of information about her personal life during the course of the fieldwork, I reported less of this specific personal detail and more about organizational factors within the school and district as these relate to her classroom decisions.

Notes

Series Editor's Introduction

Apple, Michael W. (1988). *Teachers and texts: A political economy of the class and gender relations in education.* New York: Routledge.

———. (1993). *Official knowledge: Democratic education in a conservative age.* New York: Routledge.

Apple, Michael W., and Christian-Smith, Linda (eds.). (1991). *The politics of the textbook.* New York: Routledge.

Delfattore, Joan. (1992). *What johnny can't read.* New Haven: Yale University Press.

Hunter, Allen. (1988). *Children in the service of conservatism.* Madison: Institute for Legal Studies, University of Wisconsin Law School.

1 The Politics of School Sex Education

1. Among professionals concerned with the issue, "sex education" generally refers to a narrow focus on the anatomical and reproductive aspects of a broader lifelong process of "sexuality education." The latter also encompasses a wide range of other sexual knowledge, sexual development, reproductive health, gender roles, and interpersonal relationships as well as sexual attitudes, feelings, and behaviors. "Sexuality education" is most

Notes

commonly used by professionals to reinforce the preferred comprehensive nature of this education. I use "sex education" in the title because of the narrow focus I observed in the classroom; however, because both terms are used interchangeably in public discourse, I use them interchangeably in the text to refer to the more comprehensive definition.

2. See Kantor (1993) for a list and brief description of national Far Right organizations most actively involved in school sex education issues and the eleven "fear-based" curricula they promote.

3. Most statistics in these initial pages are drawn from a series of one-page fact sheets on issues related to adolescent sexuality published by the Center for Population Options, 1025 Vermont Avenue, NW, Suite 210, Washington, D.C. 20005. They are an inexpensive and up-to-date source of statistics, trends, and resources that may be helpful to educators and curriculum decision makers.

4. The 1991 figure was obtained by calculating 15 percent (the estimated percentage of sexual abuse) of the total number of reported cases of all types of child abuse (total = 2,694,000).

5. The following organizations are included: Alan Guttmacher Institute; American Association for Marriage and Family Therapy; American Association of School Administrators; American Association of Sex Educators, Counselors and Therapists; American Medical Association; American Nurses Association; American School Health Association; American Social Health Association; Association for the Advancement of Health Education; Association of Reproductive Health Professionals; Association of State and Territorial Directors of Public Health Education; B'nai B'rith Women; Center for Population Options; The Coalition on Sexuality and Disability; The Children's Defense Fund; ETR Associates; Girls Incorporated; The Hetrick-Martin Institute; National Coalition of Advocates for Students; National Council on Family Relations; National Education Association Health Information Network; National Family Planning and Reproductive Health Association; National Network of Runaway and Youth Services; National Organization on Adolescent Pregnancy and Parenting; National Resource Center for Youth Services; National Urban League; Planned Parenthood Federation of America, Inc.; Sex Information and Education Council of the U.S.; Society for Adolescent Medicine; Society for the Scientific Study of Sex; United Church Board for Homeland Ministries; United States Conference of Local Health Officers; University of Pennsylvania; YWCA of the U.S.A.

6. See Trudell and Whatley (1992) for a comparison of two prepackaged sexuality curricula that utilize abstinence-only and abstinence-based approaches, that reveals beliefs these curricula have in common.

7. See Michael Imber (1982, 1984) for further analysis of the early school

210

sex education campaign and Trudell (1985) for examination of parallels between this and the current movement to promote school sex education.

8. See Allen Hunter (1984) for a more thorough discussion of the emergence of the New Right.

9. The so-called "Miracle of San Marcos" has been used extensively (including a cassette tape promoted by Citizens for Excellence in Education, network news shows and CNN) as proof of the effectiveness of *Teen-Aid*. In a letter to one of the curriculum's authors, the principal of San Marcos (CA) Junior High reported a drop in teen pregnancy from 147 in 1984–85 to twenty in 1986–87, after inclusion of *Teen-Aid* in the curriculum. Reynolds' investigation found the "miracle" to be totally unsubstantiated. No one in the district knew the source of the "after" figure of twenty pregnancies; there was no proof that pregnancies had declined and evidence they had not. The writer of the original letter was quoted as saying, "I agree that those figures are misleading and people use them for their own reasons" (Reynolds, 1991, p. B-10). In short, Reynolds' investigation makes clear that there is little reason to call it anything other than the "Myth of San Marcos."

10. The National Association for Abstinence Education ("Just say NAAE") is one example. NAAE offers public education (a newsletter, speakers, catalogs of resources), teacher inservices, as well as research and advocacy services. Its steering committee includes LeAnna Benn (Co-founder and International Director of Teen-Aid, Inc.), Kathleen Sullivan (a thirty-year member of the Eagle Forum and Executive Director of the Committee on the Status of Women) and Onalee McGraw (Educational Guidance Institute).

11. A current example illustrates this well-financed national network in operation. In Florida a lawsuit involving *Teen-Aid* is being brought by six families and Planned Parenthood of Northeast Florida against the Duval County School Board. It charges that *Teen-Aid* is in violation of state law that mandates comprehensive sexuality education, citing its inaccurate, biased and incomplete information and presentation of sectarian philosophy (Hennessy, 1992a). Jay Sekulow, a nationally prominent attorney on conservative religious issues who has been involved in eight Supreme Court cases, will assist the Duval County School Board in its defense. Sekulow is also founder of a religious organization (Christian Advocates Serving Evangelism: CASE) concerned with defending Christian free speech rights. His expertise is costing the district nothing, since he will be retained through the American Center for Law and Justice, an anti-abortion and pro-family law firm established by CASE and Pat Robertson, television evangelist, former presidential candidate, and now president and chairman of the board of this firm (Hennessy, 1992b).

Notes

12. See Apple (1982) for a historical analysis of this complex process, which examines class as well as gender dynamics.

2 The Informal Sexuality Curriculum

1. Across the district, this increased enrollment of black students has continued; they currently comprise over 12 percent of the district's total high school population.
2. Socioeconomic status and race seem to be related to differential suspension rates in Woodland. The school with the second highest suspension rate is also located on the less affluent side of the city. Furthermore, black students account for 30 percent of Woodland District suspensions, although they comprise about 10 percent of total enrollment.
3. See E. Genovese (1972) for an analysis of these racial dynamics and J. Anyon (1984) for a discussion of these dynamics around gender.
4. Teachers take their classes to the two performances scheduled during the school day; students from a nearby junior high school come for a special performance; and an evening public performance is given. The auditorium is packed for each of these performances. In contrast, the talent show (in which traditional gender relations also predominate) is a much less prestigious and polished event. Performances are given one evening and during the final period of two school days, when only those students with a study period can attend. Fewer than one hundred students, many staying only to watch an act or two, watched the performance I attended during the school day. The show consisted of ten acts (vocal and instrumental music as well as dance) performed by twenty-one students—three males and eighteen females. Four of the ten acts were performed by black students. An illustration of the degree to which black students are seen as a separate segment of the student body occurred after the show when a white staff member made the following comment to the Minority Services Coordinator: "*Your* [emphasis mine] kids are really involved. That's good." Although she smiled politely, the coordinator later told me that she did not necessarily regard the participation of black students in this event as a "good" thing. In her words, "They do this [music/dance] all the time. They need to do academics."
5. English Department meetings, as conducted by the female chairperson, were satirized in a skit written by one of the assistant principals for faculty orientation. The tape-recorded lyrics of a song from "The Music Man" said, "Pick a little, talk a little. Pick a little, talk a little. Pick, pick, pick. Pick a lot. Talk a little bit." Essentially, the song—both in

lyrics and style of presentation—equates female discussion with the noises made by a flock of chickens. Most staff laughed heartily, but the teacher sitting next to me whispered, "That was a *real* cut."

3   Mrs. Warren's Working Conditions

1. These goals are expressed as follows in the program intent document: Health education in the Woodland School District is planned to provide all students with opportunities to:
    1. develop the knowledge, attitudes, skills and behaviors essential to maintaining physical well-being;
    2. understand how their attitudes and feelings toward self and others and their personal values influence mental and emotional health;
    3. understand the basic characteristics of human growth and development from conception to death and learn to make informed and responsible sexual decisions;
    4. develop positive attitudes toward personal safety, accepting self-responsibility for accident prevention and emergency care; and
    5. to understand the effects of chemical substances on the body and learn how to make responsible and informed decisions about their use. (Woodland K–12 Health Education Program Intent Document, 1985, p. 4)
2. Based on a widely used behavioral model of curricular planning, the process attempts to evaluate how closely the district is meeting its predetermined goals in each curricular area. Every seventh year, a given component of the curriculum is involved in a four-year evaluation process that includes: Year 1: development of program intent documents (goals and student behavioral objectives); Year 2: data collection (parent, staff, and student surveys related to goals); Year 3: self study and school site visits (whether/how the goals are being addressed); Year 4: implementation of evaluation recommendations (further curriculum development and staff in-service as needed). Both the health and physical education programs were engaged in the first of these phases during the school year I observed at Van Buren.
3. Mr. Cox, the district health and physical education coordinator, acknowledges that Woodland District may have been somewhat remiss ("backsliding") in its monitoring of compliance with Title IX. However, he tells physical education teachers that has changed as "the community

is addressing an unusual amount of attention to sex equity issues," particularly the League of Women Voters and "a small group of parents with the law, expertise, and commitment on their side," so the district must be in total compliance or risk being taken to court by these advocacy groups.

4. In a subsequent interview, Mr. Cox told me that most of the district resistance to Title IX comes from middle-aged and older teachers of both sexes. As one woman said, "I don't want those guys teaching my girls"; they feel strongly that girls need to be with a female gym teacher because "guys only play games; we [women teachers] teach skills." Mr. Cox perceives the women's resistance as more silent than the men's, however, and sees them as easier to intimidate into conformity via the legal mandate of Title IX. Finally, across the district, Mr. Cox says there is "only a handful of female physical education teachers willing to publicly stand up for Title IX."

5. The following fall (1986), all ninth-grade physical education classes were offered on a coed basis, although gymnastics was eliminated from the curriculum. Thus, students received instruction in football, soccer, badminton, racquetball, and basketball.

5 The Classroom as Social Arena

1. Carrie was open with me (as well as Mrs. Warren and other students) about this crush, providing almost daily reports of sightings and encounters. For part of the semester, the possibility of interaction with him provided the basis for Carrie's movements around the school. She knew his class schedule and would arrange to be nearby. In fact, on two occasions, Carrie arranged the location of our interviews around the likelihood of his presence.

2. I use the word *fat* deliberately, rather than a euphemism, because I believe *fat* needs to be reclaimed as a descriptive rather than perjorative term.

6 School Knowledge about Sexuality

1. It is important to note that labelling and placement of topics within broad categories represents an arbitrary choice based on my synthesis of information actually presented.

2. Students received a copy of one page of this two-page AIDS brochure, "What Do We Know About AIDS?", which was distributed by a State

Department of Education resource person to Woodland's health teachers at an in-service session.

3. As my field notes for this session illustrate, even the Christmas party was a fragment:

> With three minutes left at the end of the period, Mrs. Warren says, "Just enough time for a quick party." (She points at sugar cookies she has told students she would bake, paper cups, and Pepsi on the front table) "Andrew brought M&M's."
>
> Students noisily converge on the table. A bag of Doritos appears; a student pours the Pepsi. They demolish the treats and begin to move out the door—many still chewing—when the bell rings.

4. In fact, Mrs. Warren decided not to attend a district curriculum meeting because it conflicted with the last classroom session prior to the sex education exam, a time she planned to use for review with the students. As she explained to me, "These kids are more important than a meeting."

5. I feel compelled to acknowledge my role in making these "saying 'no' " materials available to Mrs. Warren and other teachers in a resource packet during a workshop I conducted several years prior to my classroom observations. I had not, at that point, given sufficient consideration to the unintended consequences of such an approach or to the possibility that these materials would be read aloud to students.

6. For further discussion of the political economy of textbook publication see Michael Apple (1988).

7. For a more thorough analysis of the film's use in Mrs. Warren's class see Bonnie Trudell (1990).

8. In her 1990 analysis of open-ended "trigger" films, Marilyn Orner suggests their hidden agenda: students are to be "triggered" into accepting dominant notions of what constitutes proper behavior and attitudes. Nevertheless, she also questions whether students actually accept these notions.

9. For a critique of this approach see Mariamne Whatley (1985). Also see Carolyn Cooperman and Chuck Rhoades (1983) for learning activities that focus on female/male commonalities during puberty.

10. Mr. Austin allowed no extra time for female beautification after swimming—a fact about which some of his female students complained to Mrs. Warren. At one point, a student asked why Mr. Austin had this policy, and Mrs. Warren responded, "Equal opportunity."

11. Not surprisingly, the girls' locker room was the scene of bustling activity during the beautification time after activity, especially during the twenty-

minute period following swimming. After students quickly showered off the pool chlorine (still wearing swimsuits and the T-shirts that most wore over them) and put on their street clothes, they spent the remaining time in front of the long mirrors lining two walls of the locker room. Hair driers and curling irons (the latter plugged in to warm up before swimming) were used by nearly everyone, and the room smelled of makeup, perfume, deodorant, and hair spray. No one showered for other physical activities; they dampened towels and wiped faces and underarms before lining up at the mirrors, and most of them looked completely dry and "arranged" by the time they left the locker room.

7 Students Actively Weighing Their Own Interests

1. Student disclosure in one instance created a dilemma for me that might be problematic for teachers as well. Specifically, teachers and various school support staff are mandated in all states to report child sexual abuse to authorities; in the state where I conducted research, anyone under age sixteen is legally incapable of consenting to sexual activity. Thus, if a teacher became aware of such activity between two fifteen-year-olds (perhaps by being sought out for contraceptive advice) s/he is legally mandated to report. Although Mrs. Warren did not express this dilemma to me, it has been my experience in working with teachers that concerns over mandatory reporting are widespread and behind a great deal of reluctance to get involved with sexual abuse prevention and sexuality education programs. See Trudell and Whatley (1988).

2. I am aware that the terms *contestation* and *resistance* have been used in a variety of ways in the educational literature. I use contestation throughout, mostly in reference to students, to refer to their attempts to counteract or oppose school knowledge and control. Such attempts cover a wide range of behaviors, including being late, whispering, passing notes, making humorous quips, using "street" as opposed to scientific language about sexuality, etc. I use resistance, mostly in reference to the classroom teacher, to refer to active—but not necessarily politically purposeful or wholly successful—attempts to negotiate organizational constraints and contradictory social expectations. The problem of conceptual rigor around use of these terms in the resistance literature in education has been addressed by J. V. Fernandes (1988). For conceptual clarity, he suggests that contestation be understood as distinct from resistance. The former would be used to refer to actions directed against

principles of school control, while the latter be reserved for actions more purposefully directed at challenging wider power relations.

8 Situation-Specific Constraints and Possibilities

1. Peter Gourfain, artist, (1982). New York: One World Artist Cooperative.
2. For further information contact Leslie Kantor, Director, SIECUS Advocacy Project, 130 West 42nd Street, Suite 2500, New York, NY 10036, (212) 819-9770.
3. For further information or the PROJECT 10 Handbook, contact Virginia Uribe, 7850 Melrose Avenue, Los Angeles, CA 90046.

Methodological Appendix

1. I also suspect that my age (mid-forties), graying hair, and status as a mother contributes to my "trustworthiness" among adults involved in school sex education.
2. My familiarity with the district's sex education efforts also gave me confidence that Mrs. Warren was highly regarded by both central administration and her peers as a competent health education teacher.
3. As might be expected, several students lost their signed permission slips, or forgot them in their lockers, so I had to do a considerable amount of persistent and creative follow-up to finally get twenty-seven parent permissions. I made it a practice to patiently cultivate rapport with students during this process, by using good-humored reminders or offering to go with them to their lockers. I never phoned a parent, including the two who did not initially give consent, without first asking students if they minded.
4. The young man who originally decided not to participate was not interviewed on nutrition but was on sex education. One of the young women (a tenth-grader Mr. Austin had failed the year before in health education) did not participate in the sex education interview, although she participated in the nutrition interview. After she failed to show up for four scheduled interviews on sex education (including a final attempt near the end of the school year), I gave up on interviewing her.
5. I had originally hoped to schedule these interviews during students' study halls. However, since most of the students had no regularly scheduled study period during the first semester, I had to conduct the nutrition interviews at several other times as well, including before and after school

and during lunch periods. In addition, I was able to interview many of the young women while they were officially excused from swimming (the four-week activity immediately after nutrition) during their menstrual periods. Each girl was allowed to sit out two of the ten scheduled swimming sessions while she had her period; during this time she sat on the bleachers and watched others in the pool or did homework. When Mrs. Warren asked if I would like to interview students at these times, I took advantage of this unexpected opportunity. While this interviewing prevented me from taking notes on all of the swimming sessions, I was able to finish the nutrition interviews in a relatively short time—a task that proved considerably more difficult with the sex education interviews.

6. Students who had been enrolled in the health class first semester were required to take a physical education class second semester; this physical education class met on alternate days, with students assigned to study hall on nonclass days. Most of the sex education interviews were conducted during this second-period study hall. It was not unusual for me to schedule an interview with a student for an upcoming study hall only to find that, on the appointed day, the student was absent, had an assignment to complete, or had an exam for which s/he needed to study, etc. Since I did not wish to conduct the sexuality interviews under any kind of duress, I simply rescheduled the appointment when these situations arose. Usually I was able to find another health education student from the class in study hall who had nothing else to do, but sometimes I had to leave without having done an interview. In short, the process of scheduling and completing these interviews was an exercise in patience, tenacity, and flexibility.

References

Acker, S. (1983). Women and teaching: A semi-detached sociology of a semi-profession. In S. Walker and L. Barton (eds.), *Gender, class and education* (pp. 123–39). England: The Falmer Press.

Alan Guttmacher Institute. (1976). *Eleven million teenagers: What can be done about the epidemic of adolescent pregnancies in the United States.* New York: Research & Development Division of Planned Parenthood Federation of America.

———. (1981). *Teenage pregnancy: The problem that hasn't gone away.* New York: Research & Development Division of Planned Parenthood Federation of America.

———. (1983). Addressing teen pregnancy: School sex education policy and practice. In *Issues in Brief 3* (3), 1.

Anyon, J. (1984). Intersections of gender and class: Accommodation and resistance by working-class and affluent females to contradictory sex role ideologies. *Journal of Education 166* (1), 25–48.

Apple, M. W. (1979). *Ideology and curriculum.* Boston: Routledge and Kegan Paul.

———. (1982). *Education and power.* Boston: Routledge and Kegan Paul.

———. (1983). Work, gender and teaching. *Teacher's College Record 81* (3), 611–28.

———. (1988). *Teachers and texts: A political economy of class and gender relations in education.* New York: Routledge, Chapman and Hall.

219

References

————. (1992). The text and cultural politics. *Educational Researcher 21* (7), 4–11, 19.

————. (1993). *Official knowledge: Democratic education in a conservative age.* New York: Routledge, Chapman and Hall.

Baldwin, W. (1990, March). *Adolescent pregnancy and child-bearing: Rates, trends, and research findings from the Center for Population Research of the National Institute of Child Health and Human Development.* Washington, D. C.

Balliet, T. (1913). Points of attack in sex education. *Report of the sex education sessions of the 4th international congress on school hygiene at Buffalo, N.Y.,* (pp. 25–34). New York: American Federation for Sex Hygiene.

Bass, E., and Davis, L. (1988). *The courage to heal: A guide for women survivors of child sexual abuse.* New York: Harper and Row.

Beck, L., and Marshall, C. (1992). Policy into practice: A qualitative inquiry into the work of sexuality educators. *Educational Policy 6* (3), 319–34.

Becker, H. S. (1969). Problems in the publication of field studies. In G. McCall and J. Simmons (eds.), *Issues in participant observation* (pp. 260–75). Reading, MS: Addison-Wesley Publishing Co.

Becker, H. S., and Geer, B. (1960). Participant observation: The analysis of qualitative field data. In R. Adams and J. Preis (eds.), *Human organization research* (pp. 267–89). Homewood, IL: Dorsey Press.

Bernstein, B. (1977). *Class, codes, and control: Towards a theory of educational transmissions* (Vol. 3). London: Routledge and Kegan Paul.

Bigelow, M., Balliet, T., and Morrow, P. (1912). *Report of the special committee on the matter and methods of sex education.* New York: American Federation for Sex Hygiene.

Bogart, K., Simmons, S., Stein, N., and Tomaszewski, E. (1992). Breaking the silence: Sexual and gender-based harassment in elementary, secondary, and postsecondary education. In S. Klein (ed.), *Sex equity and sexuality in education* (pp. 191–222). Albany, NY: State University of New York Press.

Bourdieu, D., and Passeron, J. (1977). *Reproduction in education, society, and culture.* London: Sage Publications.

Bowles, S., and Gintis, H. (1976). *Schooling in capitalist America.* New York: Basic Books.

Britzman, D. (1990). *Practice makes practice: A critical study of learning to teach.* Albany, NY: State University of New York Press.

Brodkey, L. (1987). *Academic writing as social practice.* Philadelphia: Temple University Press.

Buck, C. (1987). "You better not never tell nobody but God. It'd kill your mammy": Obstacles to talking about sex with our students. *Feminist Teacher 2* (3), 31–34.

References

Cabot, H. (1913a). Education v. punishment as a remedy for social evils. *Report on the sex education sessions of the 4th international congress on school hygiene at Buffalo, N.Y.* (pp. 35–44). New York: American Federation for Sex Hygiene.

———. (1913b). General discussion. *Report on the sex education sessions of the 4th international congress on school hygiene at Buffalo, N.Y.* (p. 101). New York: American Federation for Sex Hygiene.

Centers for Disease Control, Division of STD/HIV Prevention. (1989). *Annual Report.*

Centers for Disease Control. (1990, July and 1991, July). *HIV/AIDS Surveillance.*

———. (1991a, January 4). Premarital sexual experience among adolescent women, United States, 1970–1988. *Morbidity and Mortality Weekly Report,* 39 (51/52), 929.

———. (1991b, June). *HIV/AIDS Surveillance.*

Children's Defense Fund. (1986). *Preventing adolescent pregnancy: What schools can do.* Washington, D. C.

Cooperman, C., and Rhoades, C. (1983). *New methods for puberty education: Grades 4–9.* Santa Cruz, CA: Network Publications.

Cranston, K. (1992). HIV education for gay, lesbian, and bisexual youth: Personal risk, personal power, and the community of conscience. In K. Harbeck (ed.), *Coming out of the classroom closet: Gay and lesbian students, teachers and curricula* (pp. 247–59). Binghamton, NY: Harrington Park Press.

Daro, D., and McCurdy, K. (1992, April). *Current Trends in child abuse reporting and fatalities: The results of the 1991 annual 50 state survey.* Chicago: National Committee for Prevention of Child Abuse.

Davenport, W. H. (1977). Sex in cross-cultural perspective. In F. A. Beach (ed.), *Human sexuality in four perspectives* (pp. 115–62). Baltimore: Johns Hopkins University Press.

Davies, L. (1983). Gender, resistance and power. In S. Walker and L. Barton (eds.), *Gender, class, and education* (pp. 39–52). England: The Falmer Press.

de Mauro, D. (1990). Sexuality education 1990: A review of state sexuality and AIDS curricula. *SIECUS Report 18* (2), 1–9.

D'Emilio, J., and Freedman, E. (1988). *Intimate matters: A history of sexuality in America.* New York: Harper & Row.

Donovan, P. (1989). *Risk and responsibility: Teaching sex education in America's schools today.* New York: The Alan Guttmacher Institute.

Dryfoos, J. G. (1990). *Adolescents at risk: Prevalence and prevention.* New York: Oxford University Press.

221

References

Earls, R., Fraser, J., and Sumpter, B. (1992). Sexuality education—in whose interest? An analysis of legislative, state agency, and local change arenas. In J. Sears (ed.), *Sexuality and the curriculum: The politics and practices of sexuality education* (pp. 300–327). New York: Teachers College Press.

Edelman, Marian W. (1987). *Families in peril: An agenda for social change.* Cambridge, MA: Harvard University Press.

Eliot, C. (1913). Public opinion and sex education. *Report of the sex education sessions of the 4th international congress on school hygiene at Buffalo, N.Y.* (pp. 13–24). New York: American Federation for Sex Hygiene.

Ellsworth, E. (1992). A review of AIDS: Cultural analysis/cultural activism (unpublished manuscript) University of Wisconsin-Madison, Dept. of Curriculum & Instruction.

Epstein, B. (1983). Family, sexual morality, and popular movements in turn-of-the-century America. In A. Snitow, C. Stavsell, and S. Thompson (eds.), *Powers of desire: The politics of sexuality* (pp. 117–30). New York: Monthly Review Press.

Eskey, K. (1992, Dec. 4). Minorities to be nearly half of U.S. by 2050. *The Capital Times*, Madison, WI, p. 1C.

Everhart, R. (1983). *Reading, writing, and resistance.* Boston: Routledge and Kegan Paul.

Fernandes, J.V. (1988). From the theories of social and cultural reproduction to the theory of resistance. *British Journal of Sociology of Education 9* (2).

Fine, M. (1988). Sexuality, schooling, and adolescent females: The missing discourse of desire. *Harvard Educational Review 58* (1), 29–53.

Finkelhor, D. (1984). *Child sexual abuse: New theory and research.* New York: Free Press.

Flora, J., and Thoresen, C. (1988). Reducing the risk of AIDS in adolescents. *American Psychologist 43*:965–71.

Forrest, J., and Silverman, J. (1989). What public school teachers teach about preventing pregnancy, AIDS and sexually transmitted diseases. *Family Planning Perspectives 21* (2), 65–72.

Fricke, A. (1981). *Reflections of a rock lobster.* Boston: Alyson Publications.

Gallup, A. M., and Clark, D. L. (1987, September). The 19th annual Gallup Poll of the public's attitudes toward the public schools. *Gallup Polls 69* (1).

Garrett, L. (1913). Some methods of teaching sex hygiene. *Report of the sex education sessions of the 4th international congress on school hygiene at Buffalo, N.Y.* (pp. 55–63). New York: American Federation for Sex Hygiene.

Gelman, D. (1993, Jan. 11). The young and the reckless. *Newsweek*, 60–61.

Genovese, E. (1972). *Roll, Jordan, roll: The world the slaves made.* New York: Vintage.

References

Gitlin, A. (1980). Understanding the work of teachers. Ph.D. diss., Curriculum & Instruction, School of Education, University of Wisconsin-Madison.

Gould, S. (1981). *The mismeasure of man*. New York: Norton.

Greenberg, D. (1992, Feb. 27). State probes Teen-Aid's use of sex-ed funds. *The Gainesville Sun*, p. 1.

Haffner, D. W. (1990). *Sex education 2000: A call to action*. New York: Sex Information and Education Council of the U. S.

———. (1992). 1992 report card on the states: Sexual rights in America. *SIECUS Report 20* (3), 1–7.

Haffner, D. W., and de Mauro, D. (1991). *Winning the battle: Developing support for sexuality and HIV/AIDS education*. New York: Sex Information and Education Council of the U.S.

Hall, W. S. (1914). The relation of education in sex to race betterment. *Journal of Social Hygiene 1* (1), 67–80.

Harbeck, K. (1992). Introduction. In K. Harbeck (ed.), *Coming out of the classroom closet: Gay and lesbian students, teachers and curricula* (pp. 1–7). Binghamton, NY: Harrington Park Press.

Harris, L., and Associates. (1985). *Public attitudes about sex education, family planning, and abortion in the United States*. New York: Louis Harris and Associates, Inc.

Hayes, C. D. (1987). *Risking the future: Adolescent sexuality, pregnancy, and childbearing*. Washington, D. C.: National Academy Press.

Hennessy, J. (1992a, April 29). Teen-Aid suit cites inaccuracies bias in sex-ed curriculum. *The Florida Times-Union*, Jacksonville, FL, p. 8-A.

———. (1992b, May 14). Religion expert to aid schools in Teen-Aid lawsuit. *The Florida Times-Union*, Jacksonville, FL, pp. 1, A–4.

Henshaw, S. K., and Van Vort, J. (1989). Teenage abortion, birth and pregnancy statistics: An update. *Family Planning Perspectives 20* (2), 85–88.

Heron, A. (1983). *One teenager in ten*. Boston: Alyson Publications.

Hudak, G. (1985). Communicating learning and discourse production in the classroom: A case study of a mass media curriculum. Ph.D. diss., Curriculum and Instruction, School of Education, University of Wisconsin-Madison.

Hunter, A. (1984). Virtue with a vengeance: The pro-family politics of the New Right. Ph.D. diss., Dept. of Sociology, Brandeis University.

Imber, M. (1982). Toward a theory of curriculum reform: An analysis of the first campaign for sex education. *Curriculum Inquiry 12* (4), 339–62.

———. (1984). Toward a theory of educational origins: The genesis of sex education. *Educational Theory 34* (3), 275–86.

Jones, E. F., Forrest, J. D., Goldman, N., Henshaw, S. K., Lincoln, R., Rosoff, J. I., Westoff, C. F., and Wulf, D. (1985). Teenage pregnancy in developed

References

countries: Determinants and policy implications. *Family Planning Perspectives 17* (2), 53–63.

Julian, C., Jackson, E., and Simon, N. (1980). *Modern sex education.* New York: Holt, Rinehart, and Winston.

Kahn, J. (1990, Sept. 7). Sex education: U.S. gets an F. *Boston Globe,* p. 37.

Kanoff, I. (1992, March). Teens talking to teens: Prescription for success. *Sojourner,* Boston, MS, pp. 16H–17H.

Kantor, L. M. (1992, Dec./1993, Jan.). Scared Chaste? Fear-based educational curricula. *SIECUS Report 21* (2), 1–18.

Karier, C., Violas, P., and Spring, J. (1973). *Roots of Crisis.* Chicago: Rand McNally.

Kenney, A., Guardado, S., and Brown, L. (1989). Sex education and AIDS education in the schools: What states and large school districts are doing. *Family Planning Perspectives 21* (2), 56–64.

Kerr, J. (1992a, March 4). A is for abstinence. *City Pages,* Minneapolis, MI, pp. 6–8.

———. (1992b, May 8–14). Just don't do it. *Isthmus,* Madison, WI, pp. 1, 8–9.

Kirby, D. (1984). *Sexuality education: An evaluation of programs.* Santa Cruz, CA: Network Publications.

Kliebard, H. (1987). *The struggle for the American curriculum: 1893–1958.* New York: Routledge, Chapman and Hall.

Koss, M. P., Gidycz, C. A., and Wisnewski, N. (1987). The scope of rape: Incidence and prevalence of sexual aggression and victimization in a national sample of higher education students. *Journal of Consulting Clinical Psychology 55* (2), 162–70.

Lather, P. (1986a). Research as praxis. *Harvard Educational Review 56* (3), 257–77.

———. (1986b). Issues of validity in openly ideological research: Between a rock and a soft place. *Interchange 17* (4), 63–84.

Lee, D., and Berman, L. M. (1992). Ill-structured problems: Reconsidering teenage sexuality. In J. Sears (ed.), *Sexuality and the curriculum: The politics and practices of sexuality education* (pp. 284–99). New York: Teachers College Press.

Leming, J. S. (1992). The influence of contemporary issues curricula on school-aged youth. In G. Grant (ed.), *Review of research in education* (Vol. 18, pp. 111–61). Washington, D. C.: American Educational Research Association.

Levy, B. (1991). *Dating violence: Young women in danger.* Seattle, WA: The Seal Press.

Linn, E., Stein, N., and Young, J., with Davis, S. (1992). Bitter lessons for all: Sexual harassment in schools. In J. Sears (ed.), *Sexuality and the curricu-*

lum: The politics and practices of sexuality education (pp. 106–23). New York: Teachers College Press.

Mains, S. (1992, March). Teens talk sex. *Sojourner*, Boston, MS, pp. 16H–18H.

Mast, C. (1986; 1990). *Sex respect: The option of true sexual freedom.* Bradley, IL: Respect Incorporated.

McNeil, L. (1977). Economic dimensions of social studies curricula: Curriculum as institutionalized knowledge. Ph.D. diss., Curriculum and Instruction, School of Education, University of Wisconsin-Madison.

———. (1981). Negotiating classroom knowledge: Beyond achievement and socialization. *Journal of Curriculum Studies, 13* (4), 313–28.

———. (1986). *Contradictions of control: School structure and school knowledge.* New York: Routledge and Kegan Paul.

McRobbie, A. (1978). Working-class girls and the culture of femininity. In Women's Studies Group (eds.), *Women take issue.* London: Hutchinson.

Mechling, J. (1981). Male gender display at a Boy Scout camp. In T. Sieber and A. Gordon (eds.), *Children and their organizations* (pp. 138–160). Boston: G. K. Hall and Co.

Muraskin, L. (1986). Sex education mandates: Are they the answer? *Family Planning Perspectives 18* (4), 171–74.

National Center for Health Statistics (1982 and 1988). *National survey of family growth* (Special tabulations for the National Institute of Child Health and Human Development). Washington, D. C.

National Guidelines Task Force. (1991). *Guidelines for comprehensive sexuality education.* New York: Sex Information and Education Council of the U. S.

National Opinion Research Center. (1982). *General social surveys, 1972–1978: Cumulative code book.* Chicago: National Opinion Research Center.

Nettles, S. M., and Scott-Jones, D. (1992). The role of sexuality and sex equity in the education of minority adolescents. In S. Klein (ed.), *Sex equity and sexuality in education* (pp. 257–72). Albany, NY: State University of New York Press.

Network Publications. (1985). What do we know about AIDS? Santa Cruz, CA.

New Dimension Films (Producer). (1983a). *If you want to dance* (Film). Eugene, OR.

———. (1983b). *If you want to dance* (Discussion guide). Eugene, OR.

Newman, A., and Richard, D. (1990). *Healthy sex education in your schools: A parents handbook.* Colorado Springs, CO: Focus on the Family Publishing.

Nickel, J. (1992, Sept. 21). Growing up gay in America. *Christopher Street*, New York, NY. pp. 3–7.

References

Orner, M. (1990). Trigger films and the construction of knowledge. In E. Ellsworth and M. Whatley (eds.), *The ideology of images in educational media: Hidden curriculums in the classroom*. New York: Teachers College Press.

Orr, M. T. (1982). Sex education and contraceptive education in U.S. public high schools. *Family Planning Perspectives 14* (6), 305–13.

Otto, J.H., Julian, C.J., Tether, J.E., and Nassif, J.Z. (1980). *Modern health*. New York: Holt, Rinehart and Winston.

People for the American Way. (1991). *Attacks on the freedom to learn: 1990–91 report*. Washington, D. C.

Phillips, L., and Fine, M. (1992). Commentary: What's "Left" in sexuality education. In J. Sears (ed.), *Sexuality and the curriculum: The politics and practices of sexuality education* (pp. 242–49). New York: Teachers College Press.

Potter, S., and Roach, N. (1990). *Sexuality, commitment and family* (Senior High Text). Spokane, WA: Teen-Aid, Inc.

Randall, M. (1987). Una Concienia de Mujer. *The Women's Review of Books 5* (3), pp. 1, 3.

Reissman, C. K., and Nathanson, C. (1986). The management of reproduction: Social construction of risk and responsibility. In L. Arken, and D. Mechanic (eds.), *Applications of social science to clinical medicine and health policy* (pp. 251–81). New Brunswick, NJ: Rutgers University Press.

Remafedi, G. (1987). Adolescent homosexuality: Psychosocial and medical implications. *Pediatrics 79*, 331–37.

Remafedi, G., Farrow, J., and Deisher, R. (1991). Risk factors for attempted suicide in gay and bisexual youth. *Pediatrics 87* (6), 869–76.

Reynolds, M. (1991, Dec. 19). So-called San Marcas 'miracle' actually may be merely a myth. *The San Diego Union*, pp. B-1, B-10.

Roach, N., and Benn, L. (1987). *Me, my world, my future* (Junior High Text). Spokane, WA: Teen-Aid, Inc.

Russell, D. (1986). *The secret trauma: Incest in the lives of girls and women*. New York: Basic Books, Inc.

Sapon-Shevin, M., and Goodman, J. (1992). Learning to be the opposite sex: Sexuality education and sexual scripting in early adolescence. In J. Sears (ed.), *Sexuality and the curriculum: The politics and practices of sexuality education* (pp. 89–105). New York: Teachers College Press.

Sapp, A. D. and Carter, D. L. (1978). *Child abuse in Texas: A descriptive study of Texas residents' attitudes*. Huntsville, TX: University Graphic Arts Dept.

Scales, P. (1987). How we can prevent teen pregnancy (and why it's not the real problem). *Journal of Sex Education and Therapy 13* (1), 12–15.

References

Schatzman, L., and Strauss, A. L. (1973). *Field research: Strategies for a natural sociology*. Englewood Cliffs, N.J.: Prentice-Hall, Inc.

Sears, J. (1991). *Growing up gay in the South: Race, gender & journeys of the spirit*. Binghamton, NY: Harrington Park Press.

———. (1992a). Introduction. In J. Sears (ed.), *Sexuality and the curriculum: The politics and practices of sexuality education* (pp. 1–3). New York: Teachers College Press.

———. (1992b). Dilemmas and possibilities of sexuality education: Reproducing the body politic. In J. Sears (ed.), *Sexuality and the curriculum: The politics and practices of sexuality education* (pp. 7–33). New York: Teachers College Press.

———. (1992c). The impact of culture and ideology on the construction of gender and sexual identities: Developing a critically based sexuality curriculum. In J. Sears (ed.), *Sexuality and the curriculum* (pp. 139–56). New York: Teachers College Press.

———. (1992d). Educators, homosexuality, and homosexual students: Are personal feelings related to professional beliefs? In K. Harbeck (ed.), *Coming out of the classroom closet: Gay and lesbian students, teachers and curricula* (pp. 29–80). New York: Harrington Park Press.

Sears, J., and Marshall, J. (1990). *Teaching and thinking about curriculum: Critical inquiries*. New York: Teachers College Press.

Sedway, M. (1992, Feb./March). Far right takes aim at sexuality education. *SIECUS Report 20* (3), 13–19.

Shakeshaft, C. (1989). The gender gap in research in educational administration. *Educational Administration Quarterly 25* (3), 324–37.

SIECUS Report (1992, Feb./March). NY: Sex Information and Education Council of the U.S.

Sonenstein, F. L., and Pittman, K. J. (1984). The availability of sex education in large city school districts. *Family Planning Perspectives 16* (1), 19–25.

Sonenstein, F. L., Pleck, J. H., and Ku, L. C. (1989). Sexual activity, condom use and AIDS awareness among adolescent males. *Family Planning Perspectives 21* (4), 152–58.

Spindler, G. (1982). General introduction. In G. Spindler (ed.), *Doing the ethnography of schooling* (pp. 1–13). New York: Holt, Rinehart and Winston.

Strong, B. (1972). Ideas of the early sex education movement in America, 1890–1920. *History of Education Quarterly 12* (2), 129–61.

Trudell, B. (1985). The first organized campaign for school sex education: A source of critical questions about current efforts. *Journal of Sex Education and Therapy 11* (1), 10–16.

———. (1990). Selection, presentation and student interpretation of an educa-

References

tional film on teenage pregnancy: A critical ethnographic investigation. In E. Ellsworth and M. Whatley (eds.), *The ideology of images in educational media: Hidden curriculums in the classroom* (pp. 74–106). New York: Teachers College Press.

Trudell, B., and Whatley, M., (1988). School sexual abuse prevention: Unintended consequences and dilemmas. *Child Abuse and Neglect: The International Journal 12* (1), 103–13.

———. (1991). *Sex Respect*: A problematic public school sexuality curriculum. *Journal of Sex Education and Therapy 17* (2), 125–40.

———. (1992). Sex equity principles for evaluating sexuality education materials. In S. Klein (ed.), *Sex equity and sexuality in education* (pp. 305–31). Albany, NY: State University of New York Press.

Uribe, V., and Harbeck, K. (1992). Addressing the needs of lesbian, gay, and bisexual youth: The origins of PROJECT 10 and school-based intervention. In K. Harbeck (ed.), *Coming out ot the classroom closet: Gay and lesbian students, teachers and curricula* (pp. 9–28). New York: Harrington Park Press.

U. S. Dept. of Education. (1987). *AIDS and the education of our children: A guide for parents and teachers.*

U.S. Dept. of Health and Human Services. (1989). *Report of the Secretary's task force on youth suicide. Vol. 3: Prevention and intervention in youth suicide.* Rockville, MD.

Valli, L. (1986). *Becoming clerical workers.* Boston: Routledge and Kegan Paul.

Walker, A. (1982). *The color purple.* New York: Pocket Books.

Walker, S., and Barton, L. (1983). In S. Walker and L. Barton (eds.), *Gender, class, and education* (pp. 1–17). England: The Falmer Press.

Ward, J. V., and Taylor, J. M. (1992). Sexuality education for immigrant and minority students: Developing a culturally appropriate curriculum. In J. Sears (ed.), *Sexuality and the curriculum: The politics and practices of sexuality education* (pp. 183–202). New York: Teachers College Press.

Wattleton, F. (1990). Teenage pregnancy: A case for national action. In E. White (ed.), *The black women's health book: Speaking for ourselves* (pp. 107–11). Seattle: The Seal Press.

Whatley, M. (1985). Male and female hormones: Misinterpretations of biology in school health and sex education. In V. Shapiro (ed.), *Women, biology, and public policy.* Sage Publications.

———. (1989). Goals for sex equitable sexuality education. *Peabody Journal of Education 64* (4), 59–70.

———. (1992). Commentary: Whose sexuality is it anyway? In J. Sears (ed.), *Sexuality and the curriculum: The politics and practices of sexuality education* (pp. 78–84). New York: Teachers College Press.

Whatley, M., and Trudell, B. (In press). *Teen-Aid*: Another problematic sexuality curriculum. *Journal of Sex Education and Therapy*.

Whetstone, M. (1992, January). 'Just say no' program says 'yes' to public funds, *Chicago Reporter*, pp. 3–5.

Wilcox, K. (1982). Ethnography as a methodology and its applications to the study of schooling: A review. In G. Spindler (ed.), *Doing the ethnography of schooling* (pp. 456–88). New York: Holt, Rinehart, and Winston.

Williams, R. (1977). *Marxism and literature*. Oxford: Oxford University Press.

Willis, P. (1977). *Learning to labor*. New York: Columbia University Press.

Wisconsin Department of Public Instruction (1991, Oct. 2). Final decision and order: Carol A. McShane and Mark A. McShane, complainants, vs. East Troy School District, respondent, appeal pursuant to Sec. 118.13 Wisconsin Statute and P.I. 9 Wisconsin Administrative Code. Madison, WI: WI DPI.

Wong, H. A., Kim, L. I. C., Lim, D. T., and Morishima, J. K. (1983). The training of psychologists for Asian and Pacific American communities: Problems, perspectives and practices. In J. C. Chunn, P. J. Dunston, and F. Ross-Sheriff (eds.), *Mental health and people of color* (pp. 23–41). Washington, D. C.: Howard University Press.

Woods, S., and Harbeck, K. (1992). Living in two worlds: The identity management strategies used by lesbian physical educators. In K. Harbeck (ed.), *Coming out ot the classroom closet: Gay and lesbian students, teachers and curricula* (pp. 141–66). New York: Harrington Park Press.

Wyatt, G. E. (1985). The sexual abuse of Afro-American and white women in childhood. *Child Abuse and Neglect: The International Journal, 9,* 507–19.

Index

Abortion
  controversial topics and content of sex
    education unit, 105–106
  personal beliefs of teacher and curricu-
    lum, 123
  student views on course content, 137
  teenage pregnancy and, 4–5
Abstinence
  classroom points of view on responsi-
    ble sexual behavior, 129–30
  current debate on approaches to class-
    room instruction on sexuality, 6
  personal beliefs of teacher and curricu-
    lum, 124
Activity, physical, 85–87
Administration, school
  concern with discipline and procedure,
    36–38
  defensive teaching strategies and poli-
    cies of, 173
  distance from classroom instruction,
    38–40
  educators and room to maneuver
    within official curriculum and pol-
    icy, 175
Adoption, teenage pregnancy and, 123
Adult ownership, theme of, 125

Advisory committees, sex education, 181
Affection, physical displays of, 40–41
AIDS
  controversy and current topics in class-
    room, 119–20
  current status of sex education on, 20
  and classroom discussions of homosex-
    uality, 106–107
  rise in cases among teenagers, 5
  sex education needs of gay, lesbian,
    and bisexual students, 185–86
  state-mandated curricula on, 21–22
Alan Guttmacher Institute, 14
Alcohol abuse, 166
Ambiguous acquiescence, as student be-
    havior, 133–55
American Civil Liberties Union, 188
American Social Hygiene Association
    (ASHA), 11
Anti-abortion groups, 123
Anyon, Jean, 78, 79
Appearance, physical, 127–28
Apple, Michael, 28, 54–55, 60, 124–25
Asides, personal as teaching strategy,
    114–15
Athletics, gender roles and, 45–46, 88
Attacks on the Freedom to Learn:

1990–91 Report (People for the American Way, 1991), 18
Attitudes, student sexual, 152–54
Audiovisual aids, 188. *See also* Films
Authority
  administrative concern with discipline and procedure, 37–38
  faculty gender relations and, 64–69

Balliet, Thomas, 13
Beck, L., 175
Becker, Howard, 206
Beliefs, teachers personal, 123–25, 177. *See also* Values
Berman, L. M., 13, 16
Bernstein, B., 43
Biographical information, teacher in case study, 75–77
Birth control. *See* Contraception
Blacks. *See also* Race
  humor and creation of community, 158–61
  social groupings of students, 92–94
Bogart, K., 52
Bowles, S., 23
Britzman, Deborah, 30
Buck, Claire, 151

Case study, as methodological approach, 191–92. *See also* specific topics
Censorship, school, 18–19
Childbirth, teaching strategy on, 114–15
Class, socioeconomic
  bias and stereotypes in New Right curricular materials, 3–4
  context of case study, 33
  and contradictions between femininity and self-esteem, 78
  in early twentieth-century debate on sex education, 12–13
  and race and student social groupings, 94
Classroom
  administrative distance from instruction, 38–40
  constraints on sex education in, 175–79
  dichotomy between teaching philosophy and practice, 73
  informal cultural practices of teacher, 86–87

lack of research on realities of school sexuality education, 7
limitations of survey research on, 22
negotiation of bargain between students and teacher, 97–102
observation and data collection, 195–99
points of view about sexuality, 121–31
students and contestation of knowledge, 155–66
Communication
  omnipresence of sexual harassment in taken-for-granted forms, 42
  stereotypical gender differences in film on teenage pregnancy, 126–27
Community. *See also* Social groupings
  context of case study, 33–35
  humor and creation of by students, 156–61
Community Action Kit (Sex Information and Education Council of U.S. Community Advocacy Project), 178
Condoms, 109, 130
Conservatism. *See* New Right
Content
  current status of sex education, 20–22
  overview of in case study, 104–107
  student opinion on, 135–40
Contraception
  classroom points of view on responsible sexual behavior, 130
  personal beliefs of teacher and curriculum, 124
  student views on course content, 136–37
  teaching strategies on, 108–109
Controversial topics
  content of sex education unit, 105, 171–72
  dealing with in classroom, 118–20
  student opinions on course content, 135–40
Cranston, Kevin, 185–86
Culture
  role of schooling in perpetuating inequitable social relations, 23–31
  sex education needs of multicultural populations, 181–83
  social context of teenage pregnancy, 15

Index

students and informal, 40–48
students and classroom interjection of lived experience, 165–66
students and parameters of classroom discourse, 169–70
Current events, controversial topics and, 118–19
Curriculum. *See also* Curriculum-in-use
criticism of technical model of planning, 8–9
data collection and observational categories, 198
debates about official school, 7
as dynamic selection and organization process, 174
multicultural populations and development of culturally sensitive, 181–83
objectives of sex education, 58–61
Curriculum-in-use
student resistance and, 26–27
students and construction of, 167–70
teachers, bureaucratic arrangements, and, 27–28

Data, methodological issues
collection of, 195–204
reporting of, 204–207
Dating, class discussions of, 120–21
Defensive teaching. *See also* Teaching
as active attempt to cope with structural dilemmas and student resistance, 122
bureaucratic arrangements and curriculum-in-use, 27–28, 173
individual educators and problematic aspects of sex education, 177
student creation of humorous, bantering environment, 169
students and oppositional knowledge forms, 55–56, 170, 172
theoretical framework and interpretation of data, 29–30
Discipline
administrative concern with, 36–38
negotiation of classroom bargain, 97–102
student contestation of classroom language about sex, 161–65
Discourse, students and parameters of classroom, 169–70

Discussion, class
facilitating as teaching strategy, 120–21
students and avoidance of embarrassment, 146–51
Dress, physical education teachers, 62
Drug abuse, 166
Dryfoos, Joy, 187

Earls, R., 188
Economics
construction of teenage pregnancy as "epidemic," 15
role of schooling in perpetuating inequitable social relations, 23–31
student reading of sex education textbook supplements in class, 113–14
11 million Teenagers: What Can Be Done about the Epidemic of Teenage Pregnancies in the United States (Alan Guttmacher Institute, 1976), 14
Eliot, Dr. Charles, 11
Embarrassment, student, 146–51
Ethics, ethnographic research and, 203, 206–207
Ethnographic research. *See* Ethics; Methodology
Eugenics movement, 11
Evaluation committee, curriculum objectives, 60
Everhart, Robert, 30, 155–56, 158, 165, 191
Exams, teaching toward, 109–11, 122, 125, 172
Experience
personal and use of asides as teaching strategy, 114–15
students and interjection of lived cultural, 165–66
Extracurricular activities, students in case study, 90

Family Protection Act (1981), 17
Femininity
accommodation and resistance to feminine ideology, 79–80
and self-esteem in working-class and lower middle-class women, 78

socially acceptable definition of by teacher in case study, 87
Films
  showing of as teaching strategy, 116–18
  stereotypical gender differences portrayed in, 126–27
Fine, Michelle, 6, 150, 175, 176
Florida, New Right curricular materials, 188–89
Focus on the Family (Newman & Richard, 1990), 2
Focus groups, sex education, 181, 182–83
Friends, student sexual attitudes, 153–54

Gender
  bias and stereotypes in New Right curricular materials, 3
  bureaucratic organization of schools and, 28
  classroom points of view about relations, 126–28, 172
  codes in school rituals, 42–48
  contraception and notion of female responsibility, 130
  contradictory role expectations and teacher, 78–88
  defensive teaching and stereotypes, 173
  faculty relations and authority, 48–53, 64–69
  goals for equitable sex education, 188
  social groupings of students, 94–96
Genovese, E., 78
Gintis, H., 23
Grading
  negotiation of classroom bargain and, 101–102
  procedures and philosophy of teacher on, 81–83, 87–88
  and student motivation, 145–46, 154
  teaching toward exams, 110–11
Grafitti, 41–42

Harbeck, Karen, 183, 184
Health education, context of case study, 56–62

Health services, content of sex education unit, 135–37
Hegemony, Williams' concept of, 24
Heterosexuality, classroom assumptions about sexuality, 129
History, of sex education, 10–13
Homophobia
  growing pattern of violence and, 157–58
  sex education needs of gay, lesbian, and bisexual students, 184
  student views on sex education curriculum, 139
Homosexuality
  content of sex education unit, 106–107
  development of curriculum to meet needs of gay, lesbian, and bisexual students, 183–86
  growing pattern of violence against lesbian, gay, and bisexual students, 157–58
  personal beliefs of teacher and curricular decisions, 124
  student views on sex education curriculum, 138–39
Household, duties of teacher in case study, 77
Hudak, G., 169
Humor
  creation of community by students, 156–61
  student construction of sexuality curriculum-in-use, 168–69

Identity, teacher in case study, 75–77
Ideology
  femininity and accommodation and resistance to feminine, 79–80
  official and school rituals, 43
If You Want to Dance (film), 116–18, 126–27, 141
Industrialization, history of sex education, 10–13
Information, sexual
  students and repetitive in curriculum, 144–45
  students on sources of, 141–44
Interviews, data collection, 200–204

Index

The Journal of Social Hygiene, 11

Knowledge
  defensive teaching and creation of op-
    positional forms by students, 55–56
  dominant values and reified about sex-
    uality, 131
  reified system and sex education curric-
    ulum, 121–22
  students and classroom contestation
    of, 155–66

Labor, teaching as process
  concept of, 28, 54–55
  defensive teaching and intensification
    in case study, 72–74, 173
Language, students and sexual
  contestation of classroom terminol-
    ogy, 161–65
  lived cultural experiences and class-
    room terminology, 125
  resistance to adult norms of, 41–42
Lawsuits, challenges to New Right curricular materials, 188–89
Lee, D., 13, 16
Legislation, state
  as basis for challenging New Right
    curricular materials, 188
  curricula for HIV/AIDS education,
    21–22
  mandates for sex education, 5–6
Leming, J. S., 10
Lesbianism, 106, 184

McNeil, Linda, 27–28, 29, 55–56, 115,
  132–33, 172
McRobbie, Angela, 45–46, 94
Mains, Shelley, 179–80
Marshall, C., 175
Masturbation, as controversial topic,
  105, 139
Menstruation, gender stereotypes, 127
Mental measurement movement, 11
Methodology
  case study as approach, 191–92
  data collection, 195–204
  gaining access for sex education re-
    search, 192–94
  reporting of data, 204–207

Modern Sex Education (Julian, Jackson
  & Simon, 1980), 113
Mother, teacher in case study as, 80–83,
  86–87
Multiculturalism, development of cultur-
  ally sensitive curriculum, 181–83
Muraskin, L., 188

National Coalition to Support Sexuality
  Education, 5
New Dimension Films, 116
New Right
  classroom constraints on sex educa-
    tion, 176
  development and marketing of pre-
    packaged curricular materials, 2–3
  emergence of and politics of sex educa-
    tion, 17–19
  legal grounds for challenges to curricu-
    lar materials of, 188–89

Objectives, of sex education, 20–21,
  58–61
Observation, data collection, 195–200
Office of Adolescent Pregnancy Prevention (OAPP), 17–18

Parents
  context of case study, 34
  New Right and sex education, 2, 3
  permission for research on sex educa-
    tion, 193, 194
  potential for complaints and sex edu-
    cation supplements to textbooks,
    113
  students on role in formation of sex-
    ual attitudes, 152–53
Participation, classroom, 146–51
Peer education, 180
Pep rally, as school ritual, 45–46
"Physical displays of affection," 40–41
Physical education, 61–62
Poder Latino (Latin Power) Youth
  Group, 180
Politics, context of sex education, 9–19.
  See also New Right
Power, student, 167
Pregnancy, teenage
  classroom points of view on responsi-
    ble sexual behavior, 130

emphasis on dangers of sexuality in classroom, 128–29
film on, 116–18
political implications of "epidemic," 13–16
portrayal of stereotypical gender differences in film on, 126–27
statistics on, 4–5
student views on course content, 137
Prevention models, 187
Pro-Family Coalition, 17
Project HOPE, 180
PROJECT 10, 184–85
Property, as administrative concern, 36–37

Race. *See also* Blacks
context of case study, 34–35
interracial couples and perceptions of sexual harassment, 52–53
sexual stereotypes of minority adolescents, 149–50
Rape, 5. *See also* Sexual assault
Reading, from informational handouts as teaching strategy, 111–12
Regenerative knowledge, 155–56, 172–73
Reified knowledge, 121–22, 131, 170, 172
Relevancy
course materials on sexually transmitted diseases, 125–26
implications of case study, 179–81
students and parameters of classroom discourse, 169–70
Reproduction theories, of education, 25
Responsibility, sexual, 129–31
Review sessions, teaching toward exams, 110
Rituals, gender codes in school, 42–48

Schafly, Phyllis, 3
School
data collection and observations in context of, 199–200
gender codes in rituals, 42–48
students on as source of sexuality information, 142–44
teacher in case study and "school spirit," 83–85

School-age maternity program, 123
Scripts, classroom about sexuality, 122
Sears, James, 6, 178, 184
Seating arrangements, classroom, 100–101
Sedway, Mark, 18–19
Selective tradition, 23–24, 28–29
Self-esteem, gender roles and, 78
Semen theory, 12
Seniority, teachers and gender hierarchy, 68–69
Sex education. *See also* individual topics related to case study; Methodology
classroom constraints on, 175–79
current status of, 19–22
enhancing of relevance to student's lives, 179–81
multiple responses to problems associated with teen sexuality, 187–89
national public opinion polls on, 5
needs of gay, lesbian, and bisexual students, 183–86
needs of multicultural populations, 181–83
political context of, 9–19
room for educators to maneuver within official curriculum and policy, 175
state-mandated, 5–6, 21–22, 188
Sex Information and Education Council ([SIECUS] U.S. Community Advocacy Project), 20–22, 178
Sex Respect: The Option of True Sexual Freedom (Mast, 1986, 1990), 3–4, 18, 188
Sexual abuse
evaluation of prevention curricula and criticism of teachers, 176
increase in reported cases of, 5
student interview and research ethics, 202–203
Sexual assault
controversy in current topics, 118–19
differentiation from student "horseplay," 51–52
portrayed as form of "irresponsible" sexual behavior, 129
reading aloud from informational handouts as teaching strategy on, 111–12

Index

Sexual behavior, classroom points of view about sexuality, 129–31
Sexual harassment. *See also* Sexual assault
faculty gender relations and, 50–53
omnipresence of in taken-for-granted communication forms, 42
Sexuality
classroom points of view about, 121–31, 172
emphasis on dangers of in classroom, 128–29
gender codes in school rituals and female, 42–48
students and construction of curriculum-in-use, 167–70
student social groupings and female, 94–95
Sexually transmitted diseases (STDs)
emphasis on dangers of sexuality in classroom, 128–29
relevancy of course material, 125–26
teenagers and potential for contracting, 5
Sexual pleasure, 105, 128
Sexual response, 139–40
Social groupings. *See also* Community
marginalized groups and testing of classroom bargain, 102
of students in case study, 90–97
Somerville-Cambridge (MA) Teen Pregnancy Coalition, 182
Stereotypes, gender relations and classroom points of view, 126–28
Students
as active participants in classroom, 29, 97, 132–33
ambiguous acquiescence as prevalent classroom behavior, 133–55
concept of resistance and impact on curriculum-in-use, 26–27
construction of sexuality curriculum-in-use by, 167–70
contestation of knowledge in classroom, 155–66
data collection and interviews with, 200–203
data collection and observational categories, 199
informal culture of, 40–48

negotiation of classroom bargain with teacher, 97–102
perceptions of themes on sexuality and relationships, 130–31
reading of textbooks in class as teaching strategy, 112–14
role of in debates and policy decisions about sex education, 181
social groupings of, 90–97
Suicide, homosexual students and risk of, 184
Sullivan, Kathleen, 4
Syllabus, district in case study, 57–58

Taylor, J. M., 181, 182–83
Teacher, in case study. *See also* Defensive teaching; Teaching
biographical information on, 75–77
contradictory gender role expectations, 78–88
faculty gender relations, 48–53
fragmented and heavy teaching schedule, 62–64
gaining access for sex education research, 193–94
interviews with and data collection, 203–204
labor intensification and, 72–74
negotiation of classroom bargain, 97–102
reporting of data and interpretation of events by, 205–206
Teaching. *See also* Defensive teaching; Teacher
bureaucratic arrangements and curriculum-in-use, 27–28
as labor process, 54–55
room to maneuver within official curriculum and policy, 175
strategies of in case study, 107–21, 140–41
student contestation of classroom language about sex, 161–65
student embarrassment and, 147
teachers as active agents in education process, 29
Technical fragments, presentation of as teaching strategy, 108–109
Teenage Pregnancy: The Problem That

Hasn't Gone Away (Alan Gutt-
macher Institute, 1981), 14–15
Teen-Aid: Me, My World, My Future
(Roach & Benn, 1987), 3, 18, 188
Terminology. *See* Language
Texas, dynamics of textbook sales, 113–
14
Textbooks, student reading in class as
teaching strategy, 112–14
Themes, classroom points of view about
gender relations and sexuality, 125–
26, 130–31
Theory, conceptual perspective of au-
thor, 29–30
Title IX (1972), 65, 66–68, 186

Union, teachers', 68–69
U.S. Community Advocacy Project (Sex
Information and Education Coun-
cil), 20–22, 178
Uribe, Virginia, 183

Values. *See also* Beliefs

dominant and reified school knowledge about sexuality, 131
personal asides and dominant culture,
115
research perspective of author, 30
Variety show, as school ritual, 46–48
Violence, physical. *See also* Rape; Sexual
assault
dating relationships and, 5
growing pattern of against lesbian,
gay, and bisexual students, 157–58

Ward, J. V., 181, 182–83
Wattleton, Faye, 16
Whatley, Marianne, 178, 188
Williams, Raymond, 23–24
Willis, Paul, 25
Wisconsin, New Right curricular materi-
als, 188
Women's Week, faculty gender relations,
49–50, 186
Woods, S., 184